Pror g Positive Outcomes

Arthur J. Reynolds,
Herbert J. Walberg, and
Roger P. Weissberg, Editors

GREAT *Cities*

UIC'S METROPOLITAN COMMITMENT

The University of Illinois at Chicago Series on Children and Youth

Issues in Children's and Families' Lives

CWLA Press • Washington, DC

CWLA Press is an imprint of the Child Welfare League of America. The Child Welfare League of America (CWLA), the nation's oldest and largest membership-based child welfare organization, is committed to engaging all Americans in promoting the well-being of children and protecting every child from harm.

CHILD WELFARE LEAGUE OF AMERICA, INC.
440 First Street, NW, Third Floor, Washington, DC 20001-2085
E-mail: books@cwla.org

CURRENT PRINTING (last digit)
10 9 8 7 6 5 4 3 2 1

Cover design by Luke Johnson

Printed in the United States of America

ISBN # 0–87868-759-9
Library of Congress Cataloging-in-Publication Data
Promoting positive outcomes in children / Arthur J. Reynolds, Herbert J. Walberg & Roger P. Weissberg, editors.
p. cm.
Includes bibliographical references.
ISBN 0-87868-579-9 (alk. paper)
1. Children--Services for--United States. 2. Youth--Services for--United States. 3. Community and school--United States. 4. Home and school--United States. 5. School social work--United States. 6. Child welfare--United States. I. Reynolds, Arthur J. II. Walberg, Herbert J., 1937- . III. Weissberg, Roger P., 1951- .
HV741.P763 1999 99-25170
362.7'0973--dc21 CIP

Issues in Children's and Families' Lives
An Annual Book Series

Drawing upon the resources of the Child and Family Agency of Southeastern Connecticut, one of the nation's leading family service agencies, **Issues in Children's and Families' Lives** is designed to focus attention on the pressing social problems facing children and their families today. Each volume in this series will analyze, integrate, and critique the clinical and research literature on children and their families as it relates to a particular theme. Believing that integrated multidisciplinary approaches offer greater opportunities for program success, volume contributors will reflect the research and clinical knowledge base of the many different disciplines that are committed to enhancing the physical, social, and emotional health of children and their families. Intended for graduate and professional audiences, chapters will be written by scholars and practitioners who will encourage readers to apply their practice skills and intellect to reducing the suffering of children and their families in the society in which they live and work.

Thomas P. Gullotta
Chief Executive Officer
Child and Family Agency of
Southeastern Connecticut

Contents

Tables

Figures

Preface

This book is a volume in The University of Illinois at Chicago Series on Children and Youth. The UIC series began in response to the "Great Cities" initiative taken by our former Chancellor and current President of UIC, James Stukel; David Broski who is the current UIC Chancellor; and other senior administrators, trustees, and civic leaders in Chicago. Its purpose is to marshal scholarly resources to better understand and assist in solving problems of American cities—including Chicago and many other metropolitan areas in the United States and abroad. Senior University administrators have set aside a small allocation of money and expressed their willingness to support this project.

The series is intended to provide an interdisciplinary and "inter-professional" approach to problems facing urban children, with an emphasis on programs and policies that may help solve these problems. Some of the greatest challenges, as well as opportunities, facing young people today can be found in urban areas. Nevertheless, the topics and issues covered in the series affect children and families in suburban and rural areas as well as cities.

The first volume in the series—*Children and Youth: Interdisciplinary Perspectives*— was published by Sage Publications as part of the annual series called Issues in Children's and Families' Lives. The second volume—*Promoting Positive Outcomes*—is published by the CWLA Press, an imprint of the Child Welfare League of America. It is focused on solutions to the problems facing children and youth, with special consideration to education and child development programs, policies, and practices.

The target audiences for the series include policymakers and practitioners, scholars who are specialists or nonspecialists in the topics considered, students and lay citizens, and anyone who seeks greater understanding of ideas for social and educational reform. Given the wide spectrum of intended audiences, the volumes in the series are unlike many other academic volumes written by specialists for their close disciplinary colleagues. As would be expected, the series draws upon nearly all the social, educational, and health sciences for knowledge and guidance. These fields include, among others, psychology, sociology, education, economics, social work, criminal justice, law, public policy, and the allied health fields.

We greatly appreciate the many people who helped make both this volume and the UIC Series on Children and Youth a reality. We thank James Stukel (President of the University of Illinois) and David Broski (Chancellor of the University of Illinois at Chicago) who have provided continuing funding for this series. Their leadership on the Great Cities project has been invaluable in promoting a supportive context for scholars engaged in research with children, youth, and families. We thank Olga Reyes for her help in organizing the Series and this volume. We also thank Lascelles Anderson (Director of the Center for Urban Educational Research and Development) who helped establish a UIC faculty working group that led to the establishment of this series.

We thank the distinguished members of our University of Illinois at Chicago Advisory Board and our National Advisory Board. They provided helpful comments and recommendations on the proposed structure and content of the volume and suggested contributing authors. Thanks also go to Thomas P. Gullotta, who has provided much support for the UIC series and has facilitated a smooth transition to the CWLA Press. Finally, we express our appreciation to the editorial staff of the Child Welfare League of America for their professionalism in bringing this book to publication.

Herbert J. Walberg
Roger P. Weissberg
University of Illinois at Chicago

University Advisory Committee for The University of Illinois at Chicago Series on Children and Youth

Lascelles Anderson, Ph.D.
Director
Center for Urban Educational Research and Development
Professor, College of Education

Boris Astrachan, M.D.
Professor
Department of Psychiatry

David L. Braddock, Ph.D.
Director, Institute on Disability and Human Development

David C. Broski, Ph.D.
Chancellor

Elizabeth A. Burns, M.D.
Head and Professor
Department of Family Practice

Suzann K. Campbell, Ph.D.
Professor
Department of Physical Therapy

Barry R. Chiswick, Ph.D.
Head and Professor
Department of Economics

Victoria Chou, Ph.D.
Dean and Professor
College of Education

Judith A. Cooksey, M.D., M.P.H.
Associate Vice Chancellor for Health Services

Stanley Fish. Ph.D.
Dean
College of Liberal Arts and Sciences

Brian R. Flay, D. Phil.
Professor of Public Health
Director
Health Research and Policy Centers

Creasie Finney Hairston, Ph.D.
Dean and Professor
Jane Addams College of Social Work

Darnell F. Hawkins, Ph.D., J.D.
Professor
African-American Studies

Donald Hellison, Ph.D.
Professor, College of Kinesiology

Elizabeth Hoffman, Ph.D.
Provost and Chancellor for Academic Affairs

John W. C. Johnstone, Ph.D.
Professor
Department of Sociology

Mi Ja Kim, Ph.D.
Vice Chancellor for Research
Professor
Medical Surgical Nursing

Kathleen A. Knafl, Ph.D.
Professor, Department of
Maternal-Child Nursing
Executive Associate Dean
College of Nursing

Patrick McAnany, J.D.
Head and Professor
Department of Criminal Justice

Olga Reyes, Ph.D.
Associate Professor
Department of Psychology

Alexander J. Rosen, Ph.D.
Chair and Professor
Department of Psychology

Susan C. M. Scrimshaw, Ph.D.
Dean
School of Public Health

Gerald S. Strom, Ph.D.
Chair and Professor
Department of Political Science

James J. Stukel, Ph.D.
President
University of Illinois

Patrick H. Tolan, Ph.D.
Professor of Psychology in
Psychiatry
Director of Research
Institute for Juvenile Research

Wim Wiewel, Ph.D.
Dean and Professor
College of Urban Planning and
Public Affairs

National Advisory Committee for The University of Illinois at Chicago Series on Children and Youth

Part I
Introduction and Overview

1 Introduction and Overview

Arthur J. Reynolds, Herbert J. Walberg, and Roger P. Weissberg

In recent years, issues affecting children and youth have received increased attention at the national and local levels. Numerous reports have detailed some of the challenges facing young people and have offered directions for change. These include the Carnegie Corporation's publications on intervention points during the first decade of life [Carnegie Task Force 1994, 1996], the National Research Council's [1996] report on youth development, and the National Science and Technology Council's [1997] report on resource investments in children, youth, and families. Several White House Conferences also have convened to highlight new directions, including the conference on early childhood development and learning in April 1997 and on school safety and violence prevention in October 1998.

This volume of the University of Illinois at Chicago (UIC) Children and Youth Series presents promising solutions—programs, policies, and practices—to the problems facing children and youth in urban and other settings. The contributors summarize and integrate research in their areas of expertise with a wide group of readers in mind and discuss implications of the research for program and policy development. Among the major questions addressed are the following:

- What is the scope of the problem or issue under investigation?
- What practical efforts have been made to address the problem or issue?
- Which programs, policies, and practices have worked?
- How can the ideas reflected in programs and policies be disseminated and used widely to promote positive development in young people?

Following the first book in this series [Walberg et al. 1997], this volume is interdisciplinary. We invited contributions from leading scholars in several academic disciplines to address the period from early childhood through the end of adolescence. We hoped their insights would be useful to policymakers and practitioners, and that the book would be informative to researchers, particularly nonspecialists in the approaches described. The chapters address such topics as child development, early childhood education and care, parent involvement, school-family partnerships, school reform, drug abuse, safety, peer and community influences, literacy, and school-to-work transitions. Consideration of these topics benefits from—indeed requires—knowledge derived from many disciplines and perspectives. Thus, this book is unlike many other academic volumes written by specialists for their close disciplinary colleagues.

This introductory chapter highlights major themes in the main body of the book. The chapters describe conditions and interventions that enhance the prospects of children and youth from early childhood to the beginning of adulthood. For the most part, the chapters focus on the home, school, and community contexts in which children and youth live and which serve as the settings for programs. We can assume that the strengths and limits of programs can be best understood if these contexts are taken into account.

Child and Youth Trends

As indicated in the title of this book, promoting positive outcomes is the key theme. Those responsible for children and youth need to understand the challenges they face and to identify promising solutions. Three contemporary social trends are particularly troubling and, as the chapters highlight, warrant special attention by the public, policymakers, and program designers.

First, the number of poor young children under age 6 reached 6.4 million (or 26% of all young children) in 1993, its highest recorded level. The 1996 rate of 23% remains higher than any other age group, especially for children in urban areas [National Center for Children in Poverty 1998].

This state of affairs is a cause for concern in caring for children and in planning, implementing, and investigating the impact of interventions.

Second, the percentage of the nation's poor who live in central cities with high concentrations of poverty increased by 82% from 1972 to 1991 (or from 33 to 60%; cf. Wilson [1996]). Because both family and neighborhood poverty are associated with increased risk of problematic health, social, and scholastic behaviors, these trends do not bode well for developing children, particularly those in urban settings. In metropolitan areas, for example, homicide remains the leading cause of death for both black and Hispanic youth. It is also estimated that four out of every five children who live in economically distressed census tracks are minorities [O'Hare 1994].

Third, it is estimated that 25% of youth engage in multiple high-risk behaviors with negative consequences [Dryfoos 1990]. These behaviors may include substance use, early sexual behavior, delinquency and antisocial behavior, and school underachievement and failure. Another 25% of young people are at moderate risk, engaging in one or two problem behaviors that can compromise healthy functioning [Dryfoos 1990]. For trends on specific groups, see Dryfoos [1997] and McLoyd [1998].

To counteract these trends and to promote optimal child development, social interventions and policies must not only be effective but widely available to achieve the greatest good for the largest number of people. Given these trends, it could be argued that to be effective, interventions today need to be better than in the past. For this reason, this volume is intended to disseminate knowledge about proven and promising intervention efforts.

Competence Promotion and Problem Prevention

This book highlights competence promotion and the associated concept of problem prevention [Cowen 1994] in serving the needs of young people. Weissberg and Greenberg [1998] make clear that preventive and promotion programs have in common the delivery of services before problems arise or during their earliest stages. The major cross-cutting goal is the promotion of healthy outcomes in the domains of health, education, social, and psychological development. Often this is achieved by building skills (cognitive, socioemotional, and language) and developing relationships with others. Preventing problematic outcomes such as delinquency or school failure also involves competence promotion as instrumental to desirable outcomes. A partial list of such competence-promotion programs includes early childhood education, parenting programs for mothers and fathers of young children, training in life skills and social problemsolving, school-family partnerships, school reforms, developing safe environments, and job training of youth. As illustrated in the subsequent chapters, such programs are mission-based rather than disciplinary in orientation. The chapters also highlight the development, evaluation, and utilization of knowledge for policy and practice.

How much does the nation spend on programs for young people that have as their focus competence promotion and problem prevention? The National Science and Technology Council [1997] estimated that in 1995 government expenditures (at all levels) devoted to children and youth from birth to age 21 totaled $555 billion. Almost all of these, however, went to established sources—K-16 education, social welfare (e.g., AFDC and Medicaid), criminal justice, and health care. Very few expenditures were for programs typically defined as promotion or prevention. Those that are clearly preventive or promotional in focus—including Head Start, Women, Infants and Children, Job Corps, and parts of Title I—are only a small fraction of this total, or about $15 billion. The programs and approaches discussed in the chapters suggest the potential value of greater levels of investment (financial and human resources) in a variety of prevention and promotion programs.

A related indicator of investments in young people is research and development spending. This includes basic research for the potential benefit of children and youth and applied research directed, in part, to identifying the best ways to meet social needs. Like investments in prevention and promotion programs, the United States spends relatively little on research, development, and evaluation for children and youth. In a comprehensive review of investments in children and youth across 23 federal agencies and other sources, the National Science and Technology Council [1997] reported that, of the $71 billion devoted to federal research and development in 1995, only 2.8% ($2 billion) went to research on children and youth (defined from birth to age 21). Yet, this amount was "aimed at understanding the growth and development of 30 percent of the nation's population—over 80 million children and adolescents under age 21" [p. 2]. These investments, along with the contributions by private and nonprofit sectors, are reported in Table 1-1, which shows that investments in research and development on behalf of children and youth are relatively small for all sources, especially from nonprofit and private sectors.

In other words, compared to the 2 to 3% of the Gross Domestic Product devoted to research and development in health (biomedical), energy, and transportation, less than 1/3 of 1% of the total expenditures on children and youth (e.g., K-16 education, social welfare, health care, etc.) goes to research and development [National Science and Technology Council 1997]. This percentage is an upper estimate of spending on research and evaluation for specific programs. The Head Start program, for example, spends about 1/3 of 1% of its total expenditures on research and evaluation [U. S. General Accounting Office 1997]. Other programs fare no different in investments in research [Reynolds 1998]. As illustrated in the chapters, progress in addressing the needs of children and youth could be aided by investments in research and evaluation that approximate those in other areas.

Given these considerations, we now highlight contributions of the chapters in addressing the needs of children and youth. Part II, Child and Youth Development, is the main body of the book. It considers a variety of issues, programs, policies, and services. The chapters are sequenced to roughly follow the stages of development from early childhood and late adolescence. The principles addressed provide insights that span all of childhood during the first two decades of life. Chapters 3, 4, 5, and 10 also highlight the role of families in development. Overall, the authors discuss

Table 1-1. Investments in Research and Development for Children and Youth from Federal and Other Sources (FY 1995)

	Category	Billions of Dollars	% Within Category
A	Federal R & D	71	
	Portion to children and youth	2	2.8
B	Private/nonprofit R & D	100	
	Portion to children and youth	0.4	0.4
	Total R & D	171	
	Portion to children and youth	2.4	1.4

Source: National Science and Technology Council [1997]. Children are youth are defined from birth to age 21. Research from state and local governments are included in category B.

a variety of systematic efforts that have direct implications for investments in research and in programs for young people. Part III of the book provides an integration of research, programs, and policies from a resiliency perspective.

Child and Youth Development

In "Developmental Theory as a Basis for Policy," Olivia N. Saracho discusses how theories of child development organize knowledge about children and inform our programs and policies. The chapter is a good primer in understanding that theories are more than just for academic consumption but give rise to and support a wide variety of programs, policies, and services (see below). As Saracho notes, a theory refers to a "systematic statement of principles that describes and explains observed phenomena." A developmental theory considers and explains the individuals' development, growth, and behavior. Knowledge of developmental theories provides a resource in making assessments of an individuals' level of development. Saracho discusses three influential developmental theories: constructivist theory (developed by Jean Piaget and Lev Vygotsky), maturationist theory (developed by G. Stanley Hall and Arnold Gesell), and ecological theory (developed by Urie Bronfenbrenner).

Ecological theory—a prominent perspective in several chapters—indicates that the environment as experienced often dominates the real environment in guiding behavior and that children's behavior is best understood within the settings in which it occurs. Constructivist theory as developed by Vygotsky, for example, has provided a foundation for literacy programs that highlight the importance of adult modeling and coaching and the need to create learning strategies that advance toward higher levels of understanding. Ecological theory is central to the "whole" child perspective of the Head Start Preschool Program in which health services and family services—not just child educational enrichment—are viewed as crucial to the success of the program. It also is a major perspective for programs that emphasize parent involvement and collaborations among schools, families, and communities. Among the implications for policy discussed are that

- theories are useful guideposts for understanding the principles, effects, and limits of programs;
- theories can help educate policymakers about the nature of learning to enhance communication between researchers and practitioners;
- theories can demystify the research process; and
- theories are important elements in developing effective programs.

The early years of life are a time of promise and possibility. As the foundation of development, the early childhood period from birth to age 8 can initiate a trajectory of positive development or one of challenges and risks that lead to suboptimal functioning. Douglas R. Powell maintains in his chapter, "Early Childhood Development," that investments in early childhood care and education are among the most cost-effective that society can make. As noted, promoting school readiness is a major national educational goal in which all children should have access to high-quality preschool programs, every parent should be his or her child's first teacher, and children should receive adequate nutrition and health care. Toward these ends, an unprecedented number of research-based blueprints for improving federal, state, and local early childhood policies and programs have been issued in the past decade by the federal government, major philanthropic foundations, professional associations, and leading universities and research centers.

As Powell describes, "At no point in history has there been a clearer set of informed recommendations for strengthening early childhood development than now available to policymakers, professionals, and parents." He describes recent research on brain development and early childhood programs indicating that the very early years of life can make a lasting difference in children's lives, that high-quality early childhood programs are effective in the long run, and that the quality of many early childhood programs is low and uneven. Short- and long-term findings of well-known programs such as the Perry Preschool, Abecedarian Project, and Head Start are discussed as building blocks for many ongoing state and local initiatives. Support for full-day kindergarten programs for low-income children, for early childhood programs that extend to the primary grades, and for one-on-one tutoring also are discussed.

Policy actions are recommended in four areas:

- Supports for families through efforts to enhance parent-child interactions and to strengthen the home environment,
- Early childhood program curricula that emphasize developmentally appropriate practices,
- Staff credentials and program standards that encourage advanced and widespread professional practice, and
- Schools that can respond flexibly to a diverse range of child abilities and backgrounds.

Building on the lessons of recent efforts, Powell believes, will require public awareness strategies aimed at changing prevailing myths about the early years, and agreement on and enforcement of standards of quality in environments for young children. The results of such efforts can benefit children greatly.

Powell's chapter calls attention to the important role of parent involvement in early childhood care and education. Indeed, parent involvement appears to be a consistent component of successful early childhood programs. In her chapter "Building Relationships for Learning," Dorothy Rich extends this theme by discussing the importance of strong relationships among children, parents, and others for promoting educational and social success. According to Rich, the success of parent-child programs depends chiefly on "people's motivation to use them and their capacity to learn. Key staff should be able to develop children's habits, behaviors, and attitudes needed to succeed in school and life."

Rich's work, evolved from extensive experience, focuses on meeting the needs of educators as well as children. Therefore, she explains how to develop the personal capacities of educators to create the learning relationships that build and sustain achievement. To these ends, Rich describes the MegaSkills Program, a parent-involvement program to promote children's personal competencies and parents' capacity for nurturing. Rich describes 11 megaskills as critical for optimal learning: confidence, motivation, effort, responsibility, initiative, perseverance, caring, teamwork, common sense, problemsolving, and focus. These skills are described as "The Never-Ending Report Card." Taught through educational workshops and through the aid of popular programs such as "home learning recipes," the MegaSkills Program has been widely distributed to educators and principals. Indeed, the program can be easily integrated within existing parent-child and school-family education programs. While acknowledging the need for more research, Rich makes three recommendations for practice: the importance to educational success of strong relationships among the individual student, family, and school; the need to establish programs that simultaneously build the abilities of adults and children; and the focus on the basics of building capacities and competencies for learning—not just for increasing test scores. Rich's chapter adds to the mounting evidence that parent involvement in children's learning plays a crucial role in children's educational and social development.

In the 1990s, parent involvement has become so highly valued that it has been added as one of the national education goals by the National

Educational Goals Panel sponsored by the U. S. Department of Education and the 50 governors. In their chapter "School-Family Partnerships," Evanthia N. Patrikakou, Roger P. Weissberg, and Michelle I. Rubenstein discuss the significance and implications of the broader concept of school-family relations. The authors prefer the term school-family partnerships to parent involvement because it denotes the reciprocal nature of involvement—both schools and families are responsible for developing and nurturing parent involvement. The authors discuss school-family partnerships as a powerful system of change within the ecology of neighborhoods and communities. The many types of parent involvement are discussed, as are several typologies of involvement. The barriers to greater and higher quality partnerships also are discussed, including the lack of time, schedule conflicts, lack of knowledge, and biases in the school environment associated with cultural differences and attitudes that discourage positive involvement.

To illustrate how parent involvement strategies can be developed, the authors discuss several programs that build positive school-family partnerships. These include James Comer's School Development Program, the School-Family Partnership Project at the University of Illinois at Chicago, and Chicago's Child-Parent Center and Expansion Program. Importantly, each program encourages a variety of ways for parents to get involved—from communicating with and volunteering at school to learning at home and participating in governance. As the authors note, the School Development Program is dedicated to promoting school-family partnerships through implementation of a comprehensive schoolwide parent program under the guidance of a School Management and Planning Team. The goal of the School-Family Partnership Project is to enhance communication between teachers and parents and to promote involvement in children's learning. This usually includes assessing needs, creating a positive school environment, providing ongoing training to educators, and offering specific information to parents about participating in children's education. To develop school-family partnerships that lead to persistent improvements in children's school success, the authors conclude that schools must view parents as valuable allies and must prioritize partnerships as a necessary ingredient of children's school success. Judging from past efforts, effective partnerships require careful attention to implementation and evaluation.

The transition to middle childhood and adolescence at the end of the first decade of life presents new opportunities for children to develop their educational, social, and emotional development. During this period, children's self-concept, motivation, and attitudes undergo substantial alteration. In their chapter, Carol Midgley and Martin L. Maehr discuss how new developments in motivational theory and research can guide institutional reforms. As they note, for example, evidence is growing that the goals for achievement emphasized in schools are related to students' emotional and academic well-being. They describe two goals as particularly important: the goal to develop ability (task goals) and the goal to demonstrate ability or hide the demonstration of lack of ability (performance goals). Midgley and Maehr argue that task goals are associated with adaptive patterns of cognition, affect, and behavior; whereas performance goals tend to be associated with less adaptive patterns of behavior. The authors provide an account of a three-year collaborative project between a team of researchers and the staff of an elementary school to move toward an emphasis on task goals and away from an emphasis on performance goals. They give a year-by-year account of the collaborative process and describe the policies and practices that were changed as a result of this theory-based partnership. They describe the development of the annual "education fair" that was ultimately changed to minimize competition and social comparison and maximize the recognition of students for effort and insight.

Another innovation was the use of Multi-Aged Grouped and Individualized Classrooms (MAGIC) as an alternative to retaining-in-grade low performing students. Documentation of the positive effects on students and teachers of instituting these and other school reforms is included, as well as a discussion of the advantages of a task focus for institutions generally. The authors' experiences provide a number of useful suggestions for improving programs and practices. As Midgley and Maehr note, the key implication is that "working daily in schools at the business of school reform is the sine qua non for translating theory into practice." Clearly, this theme may apply to other learning organizations in the social services, business, and in other educational institutions.

As the previous chapter highlights, children's motivation to accomplish tasks and goals is central to their positive development. Indeed, cooperative learning strategies can be used to address the hazards of school violence and unsafe neighborhoods. Given that violence is increasingly random and can have consequences that are life-threatening, calls by the public to increase school and neighborhood safety is becoming a high priority. In Chapter 7, "Promoting Safe Educational and Community Environments," David W. Johnson and Roger T. Johnson discuss the important role of schools in facilitating the positive social relationships necessary for safety and security among youth. As they note, schools are a "cooperative system in which faculty/staff, students, and parents work together to achieve mutual goals concerning quality education."

The Three Cs Program helps create learning environments that promote positive development by emphasizing cooperative communities (the first C), constructive conflict resolution (second C), and civic values (third C). Cooperative learning is the "instructional use of small groups so that students can work together to maximize their own and each other's learning." This can be generalized to the levels of the classroom at large, among classrooms, among teachers and other groups, and among schools, families, and neighborhoods. According to the Johnsons, constructive conflict resolution helps students deal effectively with problems as they arise. The Teaching Students to be Peacemakers Program and the Resolving Conflict Creatively Program provide examples. The final C, civic values, emphasizes the importance of articulating principles of conduct to guide behavior.

Among the 12 recommendations for promoting positive youth outcomes are that schools and communities should structure learning activities cooperatively instead of competitively, encourage the use of class meetings for discussion of issues and their resolution, provide explicit opportunities for students to take each other's perspective into account, use academic subject matter to teach conflict resolution skills and civic values, and structure cooperation among schools, parents, and the neighborhoods.

The second decade of life can bring additional hazards, especially those caused by experimentation with drugs and the onset of drug abuse. As Gilbert J. Botvin and Kenneth W. Griffin discuss in "Preventing Drug Abuse," national survey data indicate that drug abuse among American youth has increased consistently during the 1990s. Fortunately, over the past two decades, our understanding of the etiology and prevention of drug abuse has increased as well.

Botvin and Griffin provide a comprehensive integration of findings from the growing drug abuse prevention literature, highlight some proven approaches to school-based prevention and competence promotion, and recommend some general principles that can help guide program developers and practitioners. Prevention programs have evolved from traditional information-dissemination approaches to more comprehensive contemporary programs that focus on drug-related attitudes and social resistance skills. As an example of this approach, the authors discuss Botvin's Life Skills Training Program, a validated school-based competence-enhancing program that teaches important personal self-management and social skills, in addition to drug-specific content. Three types of management skills are taught: (1) self-appraisal and goal-setting behavior, (2) decision-making and independent thinking, and (3) anxiety management skills.

Pilot and large-scale evaluations suggest short- and long-term program success in preventing tobacco, alcohol, marijuana use, gateway and polydrug use, and illicit drug use. Initial reductions in the rate of drug use of 50% or more relative to controls have been observed. As much as knowledge has advanced on new and more effectiveness drug prevention programs, the authors also make clear that further research is needed in several areas, including better understanding about the pathways that lead to competence enhancement, the effectiveness of programs for low-income and minority youth, the long-term effectiveness of a variety of approaches, and more effective dissemination and communication of research knowledge for widespread program adoption.

American adolescents today have unbridled opportunities to develop their intellectual, social, and vocational skills and interests. Toward the middle of the second decade of life, youth substantially increase involvement with their peers and communities, seek greater independence from their parents, and delve further into educational and vocational pursuits. In an age of rapidly changing technological, economic, and social norms, adolescence can also be a time of peril and uncertainty when wrong choices can significantly impact youths' prospects for the future.

In Chapter 9, "Promoting Excellence in American Adolescents," Toni Falbo and Robert W. Glover, discuss how youth can achieve excellence to provide a strong foundation for the responsibilities of adulthood. For the authors, excellence is "meeting high standards of academic skills ... as well as meeting high standards of social skills and self-discipline." They argue cogently that excellence must be expected of *all* youth—not just a few. Falbo and Glover document that American youth still perform below the international average on a variety of achievement tests. The authors attribute this partly to widespread use of tracking in American schools, youth's frequent avoidance of challenging courses, and the suboptimal structure of high schools that typically fail to foster a sense of belongingness.

Falbo and Glover argue that high schools should be organized so that teachers exhibit high expectations of youth regardless of personal attributes and that students benefit from stimulating and nurturing educational communities within schools. They also make clear that families, communities, and employers must contribute to the achievement of excellence through increased parent involvement in youth's education and the provision of community resources. The authors note, for example, that employers could require school transcripts in job applications to give students a greater incentive to maintain good grades. They note that one insurance company offers a discount to young drivers who stay in school and maintain a B average. Several design principles are offered to improve high schools, such as those by the Coalition for Essential Schools at Brown University and the New Urban High School Project. Among the principles of the latter project are developing community partnerships, creating personalized settings within larger schools, and collaborative teaching that provides project- and work-based learning experiences. The authors conclude that improving the quality of high schools alone will not result in excellence for most youth but that families, communities, and employers must be full partners with schools in establishing a climate of high standards that can reap substantial rewards in adulthood.

Literacy is a vibrant field and is of great importance to many national education and economic goals. Recent national surveys reveal that, while overall rates of literacy have increased since the 1970s, the performance of children in poverty and from minority groups continue to lag behind that of other children. In "Promoting Literacy and the Concept of Possibility," Vivian L. Gadsden, Wanda Brooks, and Jacqueline K. Jackson discuss current directions in the field of literacy research and practice for children, youth, and families. As noted, the concept of literacy has advanced beyond the dualistic notion of literacy/illiteracy to a multidimensional perspective that includes reading, writing, numeracy, and problem-solving skills. For Gadsden and colleagues, literacy is as much a family and intergenerational issue as it is a schooling issue—more than one-third of U. S. adults exhibited a relatively low level of literacy in a recent national survey. The power of literacy in effecting change should not be overestimated, however. As the author notes, "Although literacy, like the goal of justice itself, may not eliminate the personal hardships that children and adults face, it does promote positive outcomes, and it can begin the process of unlocking doors." Case studies of three children make this clear, especially for low-income African American and Latino children.

Gadsden and colleagues describe a variety of promising and proven programs for promoting child and family literacy. These include school-based reading programs such as Reading Recovery, Success for All, and High Intensity Language Training. After-school and summer-literacy programs include the Friendly Place (in Harlem) and the Montgomery Ward-Cabrini Green Tutoring Program. Parent-child and family literacy programs include the Kenan Model (developed by the National Center for Family Literacy) and the federally funded Even Start Family Literacy Program. Although greater understanding is needed about the impact of these and other interventions, some common elements of success are noted (among others): they communicate a clear vision to staff and participants, they involve parents and community members, and they are tailored to the social and cultural needs of families. Among several recommendations for practice include (1) greater and more sustained national investments in literacy for children and between generations, (2) implementation of programs and approaches beginning prior to school entry and continuing throughout children's development, (3) building upon community resources in program development, and (4) greater focus on the literacy needs of low-income families and children.

In "Preparing Youth for the Work Force," Stephen F. Hamilton discusses contemporary trends in the transition from school to work. As he notes, after high school American young people take a variety of paths into the adult work force. These different paths fragment and stratify high school graduates into several subgroups. The consequences for youth can be lasting, either for better or worse. Today, most jobs that pay enough to support an autonomous individual or a new family increasingly require some form of postsecondary education.

The School-to-Work Opportunities Act of 1994 illustrates the potential value of a comprehensive system of youth training. As noted, this initiative was enacted to ease the transition to adulthood for all youth, but especially for those who in the past have ended their education with high school. Inspired in part by German apprenticeships and demonstration programs in this country, this initiative provides $400 million annually in 39 states to foster work-based learning and school-based learning to contribute to improved academic achievement. It attempts to create a system out of what have been disparate elements, including secondary and postsecondary education, vocational and academic programs, and the labor market. Hamilton notes that evaluations of apprenticeships and work-based learning models in Germany and elsewhere indicate that they do enhance achievement and employability. The quality of training, however, matters. Few in the United States expect a comprehensive system for all youth soon.

Although Hamilton notes that the best preparation for high-paying jobs is to improve the quality of high schools (a theme echoed in the chapter by Falbo and Glover) and to make education beyond high school more accessible, two important conditions for the success of any comprehensive approach are strong employer demand for graduates and a long-term commitment to school reform. As with earlier chapters, encouraging greater collaboration—in this case between employers and educators—seems essential to continued progress on successful school to work transitions.

Integration of Research, Programs, and Policies

In the final integrative chapter "Psychological and Educational Resilience," Margaret C. Wang, Geneva D. Haertel, and Herbert J. Walberg discuss findings and implications of research on resilience. As the authors indicate, psychological resilience is the capacity for successful adaptation despite risk and adversity. Educational resilience is "success in school despite personal vulnerabilities and adversities brought about by environmental conditions and early experiences." Based on a synthesis of 91 meta-analyses, 179 review articles, and a survey of 61 educational researchers, the authors provide an ecological framework for understanding learning and the development of resilience within the contexts of home, school, peer group, and community. They also describe individual attributes that promote the capacity to thrive despite adversity. Among the individual factors reviewed are metacognitive processes such as self-monitoring and use of learning strategies, cognitive and social skills, and achievement motivation.

Family attributes that promote learning and resilience include family cohesion and warmth, living in a structured home environment in which parents have high expectations for academic and social behavior, and the presence of an adult role model either within or outside the family. As the authors note, strong school-family connections and parent involvement in children's education have been found to be especially important for children growing up in poverty. Protective factors within the school context include holding high expectations for all students, providing a motivating context for learning, frequent teacher-student interactions, and the presence of small educational units, such as schools within schools. Peer and community factors that can promote resilience include the presence of peers having positive attitudes toward educational activities, mentoring and cooperative learning strategies, and the availability of resources for engaging in extracurricular and community activities. The authors conclude that the knowledge base about the effects of a wide array of alterable factors warrant improved practices and collaborative roles for educators, parents, peer groups, and others in the community. These practices and roles can promote positive development in children, youth, and families.

Conclusion

A central theme of the chapters is that greater resilience and positive development in young people can be achieved if individuals, families, schools, and communities utilize the knowledge gained over the past two decades on effective programs, policies, services, and practices. As detailed by the contributors, program and policy effectiveness are aided by several cross-cutting principles. One is that early interventions—programs put in place prior to or during the earliest stages of problematic behavior—may have the best chance for success. Another principle supported by many chapters is that comprehensive programs are more likely to be successful than less comprehensive programs. Ranging from preschool intervention to school reform and school-to-work assistance, comprehensive programs typically include multiple components (e.g., family and child, community and child), target several outcome domains, seek to impact behavior in more than one setting, and are of sufficient intensity and duration to promote success over time. A third principle of effective services supported by the chapters is the multidisciplinary nature of both the problems facing young people and the solutions. A wide spectrum of knowledge from all social science and health fields is especially needed today to deal effectively with the challenges and opportunities facing children and youth. Finally, more than ever before, collaboration among all interested groups is needed—whether to develop school-family partnerships, effective schools, safe environments, or effective school-to-work training.

Certainly, our overview is no substitute for the ideas, principles, and recommendations in each of the chapters. Indeed, the authors were generous to provide many examples from their own experiences that may help novices, experts, and observers in the topics addressed. We encourage readers to examine carefully the approaches described and to consult the many practical recommendations offered at the end of the chapters. It is our hope that this volume helps researchers, practitioners, and policymakers collaborate productively in developing, implementing, and evaluating promising approaches to positive child and youth development.

References

Carnegie Task Force on Learning in the Primary Grades. (1996). *Years of promise: A comprehensive learning strategy for America's children.* New York: Carnegie Corporation of New York.

Carnegie Task Force on Meeting the Needs of Young Children. (1994). *Starting points: Meeting the needs of our youngest children.* New York: Carnegie Corporation of New York.

Cowen, E. L. (1994). The enhancement of psychological wellness: Challenges and opportunities. *American Journal of Community Psychology, 22*, 149-179.

Dryfoos, J. G. (1990). *Adolescents at risk: Prevalence and prevention.* New York: Oxford University Press.

Dryfoos, J. G. (1997). The prevalence of problem behaviors: Implications for programs. In R. P. Weissberg, T. P. Gullotta, R. L. Hampton, B. A. Ryan, & G. R. Adams (Eds.), *Healthy children 2010: Enhancing children's wellness* (pp. 17-46). Thousand Oaks, CA: Sage.

McLoyd, V. C. (1998). Changing demographics in the American population: Implications for research on minority children and adolescents. In V. C. McLoyd & L. Steinberg (Eds.), *Studying minority adolescents: Conceptual, methodological, and theoretical issues* (pp. 3-28). Mahwah, NJ: Erlbaum.

National Center for Children in Poverty. (1998, March). *Young children in poverty: A statistical update.* New York: Columbia University.

National Research Council. (1996). *Youth development and neighborhood influences: Challenges and opportunities.* Washington, DC: Author.

National Science and Technology Council. (1997, April). *Investing in our future: A national research initiative for America's children for the 21st century.* Washington, DC: Executive Office of the President, Office of Science and Technology Policy, Committee on Fundamental Science, and the Committee on Health, Safety, and Food.

O'Hare, W. (1994). 3.9 million U.S. children in distressed neighborhoods. *Population Today*, 22, 4-5.

Reynolds, A. J. (1998). Developing early childhood programs for children and families at risk: Research-based principles to promote long-term effectiveness. *Children and Youth Services Review, 20*, 503-523.

U. S. General Accounting Office. (1997). *Head Start: Research provides little information on impact of current program.* Washington, DC: Report GAO/HEHS-97-59.

Walberg, H. J., Reyes, O., & Weissberg, R. P. (Eds.). (1997). *Children and youth: Interdisciplinary perspectives.* Thousand Oaks, CA: Sage.

Weissberg, R. P., & Greenberg, M. T. (1998). School and community competence-enhancement and prevention programs. In W. Damon (Ed.) *Handbook of child psychology: Vol. 4. Child psychology in practice* (5th ed.) (pp. 877-954). New York: Wiley.

Wilson, W. J. (1996). *When work disappears: The world of the new urban poor.* New York: Knopf.

Part II
Child and Youth Development

2 Developmental Theory as a Basis for Policy

Olivia N. Saracho

There is a debate among scholars as to whether they should pursue their studies for the sake of seeking truth or whether they should use their scholarship to address the serious questions underlying contemporary social problems and issues. Often scholars in our society attempt to apply what knowledge we have about human development. Their attempts are not always successful in improving practice in our society [James 1991].

Knowledge entails transformation of behavior. The goal is for individuals to modify their behavior in accordance with their needs, goals, and intrinsic and pragmatic understanding of incidents. Individuals react to their environment, although behavior is also influenced by their previous experiences and perceptions of occurrences. To be constructive, mankind needs to satisfy their needs, goals, and security to be able to cope with their environment.

Knowledge reflects a transformation in behavior caused by the interaction of the organism with its environment. The nature of knowledge is determined by the activity or distinctive interaction within the individuals' environment. Individuals organize and translate data into meaningful knowledge. This type of transformed behavior is learned rather than caused by maturation. Learning differs from maturation in that behaviors that are altered in learning are predominately a result of internal and external stimuli, while maturation is mainly caused by internal forces. Scholars and psychologists are focusing their interest on the nature of this knowledge and its relevant lasting behavioral transformation that is caused by experience. Therefore, they are focusing on the developmental theories they hold about knowledge and influence of these theories on the cognitive processes of thinking and reasoning.

Theoretical Genres

A theory is a system of ideas that describes and explains observed phenomena and their connection to each other. A theory helps to organize information in such a way that it is meaningful. A developmental theory considers and explains the individuals' development, growth, and behavior. It denotes those components in the individuals' genetic makeup and/or the environmental situations that affect evolution and behavior and suggests how these components are related.

The theories discussed in this chapter include constructivist theories (such as those developed by Jean Piaget and Lev Semenovich Vygotsky), maturationist theory (developed by G. Stanley Hall and modified by Arnold Gesell), and ecological theory (such as the one developed by Urie Bronfenbrenner). Each theory provides interpretations of the meaning of the individuals' development and behavior. While the theories are grouped together into genres of thought, there are variations within each genre.

Constructivism Theory

Constructivism theory proposes a way to understand the way individuals develop cognition. According to constructivists, individuals generate knowledge through an active process. They act upon (or think about) information they acquire in their experiences. Throughout their life, they interpret and revise the information they acquire based on their understanding.

Although research and theory construction concerning constructivist beliefs about cognitive development dates back to an earlier era, these beliefs initiated their influence on American human development in the 1960s. The accomplishments of theorists, such as Jean Piaget and Lev Semenovich Vygotsky, were critical in the development of constructivist convictions of the individuals' intellectual development. Presently, constructivist theory is a prominent facet of American psychology, even though research persevered and theories are continuously being revised.

Jean Piaget

One of the pioneers in the development of constructivist theories of cognitive development was Jean Piaget (1896-1980). He believed that individuals have to adjust to the environment in appropriate ways. They generate schemas or schemata to understand their world. A scheme refers to an integrated mode of thinking about elements in the world, such as when infants see a rattle and seize it. Such a seizure relates to the infants' understanding and is depicted in a schema. As these infants age, their schema become more abstract. Developing and revising schemes is a process of *assimilation* and *accommodation.*

Assimilation refers to the process children use when they match environmental stimuli to their knowledge, reconsider an incident, and match the pattern to their repertoire of schemes. When children confront a problem, they contemplate their repertoire of schemes to resolve the problem. Piaget assumes that: "To assimilate an object to a schema means conferring to that object one or several meanings" [Piaget et al. 1958, p. 59].

Accommodation is the process children use when the information in the events differs from their repertoire of schemes. In this case, the event is not assimilated at all, but the unfamiliar information generates revised schema.

As children's cognitive patterns evolve and interact with their environment, an instinctual balance follows between the assimilation and accommodation processes. Such balance, or *equilibrium*, continues until fresh information assists the process to start over. Adjusting to the environment is achieved through the processes of assimilation and accommodation. Consequently, within the child's biological-mental self a process of *organization* occurs to properly combine all schemes that are suitably conformed to each other. Piaget [1963] affirms that

> It is sufficiently well known that every intellectual operation is always related to all the others and that its own elements are controlled by the same law. Every schema is thus coordinated with all the other schemata and itself constitutes a totality with differentiated parts. Every act

> of intelligence presupposes a system of mutual implications and interconnected meanings. [p. 7]

According to Piagetian theory, individuals indirectly refine information and generate concepts. They construct knowledge through experiences. Piaget's theory has become prevalent because it reduced the focus from the dominant influence of the behaviorism theory. His theory became an important step in the growing reaction to the dominance of behaviorism. Bringing knowing back into the picture was central to emerging theories of moral judgment and development [Kohlberg 1971].

Lev Semenovich Vygotsky

Another constructivist theorist is Lev Semenovich Vygotsky (1896-1934). His theory posits both natural and cultural development. Maturation caused natural development, whereas language and reasoning ability is related to cultural development. Hence, the individuals' thinking patterns are caused by the activities repeated within their culture. Furthermore, advanced modes of thought (conceptual thinking) are verbally communicated to students. Consequently, language is an indispensable medium in defining an individual's competence in learning to think. Individuals use language as a device explicitly to indicate their conceptual thinking level. Those who have simplistic or primitive thinking may have experienced a language environment (e.g., direct speech, mass communication media) where simplistic or "primitive" language prevails. In comparison, individuals with divergent and intricate language may have experienced a language environment that caters to varied and complex concepts. Vygotsky recommended three stages of cultural development [Thomas 1992]:

- **Stage 1.** Thinking in *unorganized congeries* or heaps. During this period the child puts things in groups (and may assign the group a label) on the basis of what are only chance links in the child's perception.

- **Stage 2.** Thinking in *complexes*. Individual objects are united in the child's mind not only by subjective impressions but also by bonds that actually exist among the objects. This is a step away from egocentric thinking and in the direction of objectivity. In a complex, the bonds between components are *concrete* and *factual* to some degree rather than abstract and logical. Five types of complexes succeed one another during this stage of thought.

- **Stage 3**: Thinking in *concepts*. On the threshold of this final major stage, we will pause and inspect two paths of thought and development—*synthesizing* and *analyzing*—that have converged to make conceptual thinking possible [Thomas 1992, pp. 335-336].

Vygotsky [1978] defines the zone of proximal development (ZPD) as "the distance between the actual developmental level as determined through problem solving under adult guidance or in collaboration with more capable peers" [p. 86]. In accordance with Vygotsky's framework, the child is more than an ordinary passive recipient of the adult's teachings within the ZPD, while the adult is more than merely a model of expert and successful behavior. Rather, the adult-child dyad participates in a joint problem-solving exercise, where both share knowledge and responsibility during the exercise [Díaz et al. 1994]. Children develop their ZPD, which is the point at which the child is able to function independently with the use of supports provided by more mature thinkers. These depict a model of scaffolding that permits children to perform and learn new competencies. Such competencies then become part of the children's repertoires. Hence learning, within this conception, guides development, instead of following it.

Recently, Vygotsky's theories have captivated the attention of many researchers and child development specialists who embrace a constructivist view of cognitive development but criticize Piagetian theory. Vygotsky's theory has been particularly applied to language and literacy development (see, e.g., Mason & Sinha, [1993]).

Maturationist Theory

Maturation theory proposes that the course of human development is basically determined genetically. Changes in the human organism develop as internal mechanisms direct development in an independent organized manner, although environment has an impact on the individuals' development, to a degree. Whereas environmental circumstances can impede natural developmental patterns, maturationist theory indicates that they cannot modify those patterns.

The genetically timed natural maturation of the child's organism develops as an unfolding process. It is considered that extraordinary attempts to obtain desirable behaviors before its natural manifestation are unnecessary, and may even be detrimental to the child. Children who are coerced to achieve their current maturational level may have an unproductive development and decrease their feeling of worth and self-confidence. When anticipated modifications in the children's course of maturation delay their development, an intervention may be essential. Murray Thomas [1992] concludes that intervention to change an attribute is acceptable when (1) the attribute is viewed to be unacceptable, (2) the child's maturational capacity allows the desirable sequence, and (3) components in the child's environment refuse to "naturally" change the unacceptable attribute.

G. Stanley Hall, the father of the child study movement, contributed his own unique ideology to psychology. Arnold Gesell built on Hall's accomplishments in maturationist theory and introduced current research procedures to further its development.

G. Stanley Hall

G. Stanley Hall (1844-1924) received his doctorate from Harvard University where he studied with William James. Later he studied with Wilhelm Wundt, the renowned pioneer of experimental psychology in Germany. When he returned to the United States, Hall used his knowledge of experimental psychology to study children's development.

Hall's contributions in child study suggested that development is founded in heredity. The children's future is grounded on their genetic makeup. He also generated the fundamental approach on observation as a child study technique. Although there were no qualified child psychologists in the United States during that period, Hall recruited individuals who shared an interest in children to conduct his observations. These individuals, predominately parents and teachers, observed children in their natural environment, instead of in laboratories. Hall's work was also inspired by Darwin's theory of evolution. He hypothesized that each individual in the human race progresses through a developmental sequence that is similar to the development of the species. He assumed that children need to be liberated from the primitive facets of evolution to be able to behave as mature modern individuals. The instinctive activities of childhood were thought of as the structure by which children achieved this. Such developmental dominance is often communicated in the expression, "Ontology recapitulates phylogeny."

Hall's abiding contribution was the principle of the scientific study of childhood. He accumulated a sizable quantity of data concerning children in an effort to describe children at separate stages of life. Hall's techniques, gathering survey data about children from unprepared teachers in observation methods, would be considered unscientific in contemporary psychology. Nonetheless, with this work, he (1) opened new grounds, (2) developed an innovative framework in the study of childhood, (3) instituted a cornerstone for a more scientific study of childhood, and (4) applied child development principles to other disciplines. He strongly believed that the nature of childhood should be acknowledged.

Arnold Gesell (1890-1961)

G. Stanley Hall's student, Arnold Gesell (1890-1961), continued Hall's work in a more organized manner. For approximately 40 years, Gesell investigated children's development in the Yale University Clinic for Child Development. He observed and measured a considerable number of children in many developmental domains (e.g., physical, motor, language, intellectual, personal, social). He created detailed accounts of infants and children from birth through 10 years of age. From his sample, he characterized child development by distinguishing the regular attributes of children of a specific age level. From these attributes, he developed age norms for children, which he used as a guide to normal development.

Gesell's developmental theory was a modest one that concentrated on the influence of maturation in a child's development. He rejected the use of Darwin's theory of evolution in the children's natural development that

Hall advocated, but he did conclude that a child's development is genetically determined. Although Gesell recognized that an individual's personality, developmental pace, and capabilities are unique and distinctive, he concentrated less on individual distinctions in his characterization of developmental levels. He did emphasize the significance of each child's individuality by stressing the importance of appreciating each child's basic in-born individuality.

Gesell and his colleagues, Frances L. Ilg and Louise B. Ames, produced a series of instruments, assessment strategies, and observation techniques. Data on the children's school and home behaviors were gathered in the clinic and through parent interviews. The data permitted them to define *maturity traits* and developmental levels, referred to as *growth gradients*, for the normal child in 10 major areas:

- Motor characteristics (bodily activity, eyes and hands),
- Personal hygiene (eating, sleeping, eliminating, bathing, dressing, health, somatic complaints, tensional outlets),
- Emotional expression (affective attitudes, assertion, anger, crying, and related behavior),
- Fears and dreams,
- Self and sex,
- Interpersonal relations (mother-child, father-child, child-child, siblings, family, grandparents, groupings in play, manners),
- Play and pastimes (general interests, reading, music, radio, television, movies),
- School life (adjustment to school, classroom demeanor, reading, writing, arithmetic),
- Ethical sense (blaming and alibiing; response to direction, punishment, and praise; responsiveness to reason; sense of good and bad, truth and property), and
- Philosophic outlook (time, space, language and thought, death, deity).

Gesell affirmed that development was determined by nature from within the organism, whereas the environment assumed a secondary role in modifying behavior. Gesell proclaimed that children need to be allowed to develop at their own rate, both at home and at school. Pressuring or restricting the child would only create negativism and diminish constructiveness [Thomas 1992].

Ecological Theory

Ecological theory in child development concentrates on the environment's vital impact on children's lives and their development. This theory posits that both apparent and subtle environmental elements directly affect children's growth and development. Children's environments differ in many ways. The effects of these differences are integrated into the child's normal developmental patterns, making their influence on children hard to comprehend. Ecological theory uses knowledge from the child's environments to describe, organize, and clarify their effects. This scheme recognizes the situations in the domain of ecological psychology.

Ecological theory considers the whole child as a combined organism that is affected by environmental factors. Growth continues through diminutive, supplementary increments that periodically accumulate to develop the child's personality by merging in the child's repertoire of experiences. A new incentive or experience adds a new element to the child's knowledge. Thus, every important novel experience can modify the relationship of several or all of the existing components that contribute to the child's personality, influencing the development of the child's individuality [Thomas 1992].

The leading proponent of ecological theory in child development is Urie Bronfenbrenner (1917-). He views the ecology of human development as a means to understand the way active, growing individuals relate to their environment. He attempts to understand how the immediate surroundings where children develop relate to the larger contexts where the surroundings are implanted. Bronfenbrenner concentrates on children's perceptions of their environment. It is crucial to recognize those hindering modifications in children's understanding of their surroundings. For example, in a specific setting (e.g., school, home, peer group locations) and its physical and material features, children encounter a set of activities, roles, and interpersonal relationships. The children's interpretation of the activities, roles, and interpersonal relationships contributes to their development. Activities refer to the individuals' actions; roles suggest the actions society requires corresponding to the individuals' position (e.g., parent, infant, sibling, teacher, friend, coach). Interpersonal relationships indicate the individuals' verbal and nonverbal responses to each other. Bronfenbrenner [1979] proposes that:

- The phenomenological (internally interpreted or experienced) environment dominates the real environment in guiding behavior.
- It is folly to try to understand a child's action solely from the objective qualities of an environment without learning what those qualities mean for the child in that setting.
- It is important to discover how the objects, people and events in the situation affect the child's motivations, and
- It is essential to recognize the influence on behavior of "unreal" elements that arise from the child's imagination, fantasy, and idiosyncratic interpretations [1979, pp. 24-25].

One can understand the children's behavior by knowing how they view the activities, roles, and interpersonal relationships found in their surroundings. Hence, when children attempt to create new meaning, one fragment of their surroundings can affect the intact configuration. Thus, the children's understanding of their surroundings relates to their self.

Differences Among Theories

Developmental theorists differ from one another in their thoughts, areas of development, and several other means. Some theories embrace all developmental areas, while others deal with only a narrow range of development (e.g., intellectual development, socioemotional development). They also vary in the degree of importance they consider the individual's genetic makeup (nature) or the experiences of growing up (nurture) in each individual's development. Theorists, like Vygotsky, believe that the individuals' experiences are important in their future in society, particularly pertaining to cultural development. Many consider that both of these influences and environmental influences are significant. The family as an environmental influence and the social context in which the individual is raised are significant influences in the individual's life. It is important to call attention to that developmental theory and research that describe norms for an average development in individuals. However, most individuals vary from the average. Norms serve as guideposts that predict what children will be like as adults; but as children develop, these initial estimates must be revised for each individual child.

Theoretical Issues

Among the different theories of the individuals' knowledge and how they acquire it emerge many theoretical issues. First the general boundaries and interpretation of the theories differ among researchers and scholars. Second, most theories suggest that knowledge proceeds in a developmental sequence, but each theory proposes a different sequence. Other theories have ignored the developmental stage conceptualization and described them independent of one another. Thus, theories have multifaceted thoughts. A third issue suggests that most theories relate to cognitive development. However, the major theoretical issues that need to be addressed are the interpretation of the theories and the issue that theories have multifaceted thoughts.

Interpretation of Theories

Describing the theory based on existing research is problematic, as each research study can be interpreted differently within different theories. According to Wellman [1990], the following three criteria can be used in considering a body of knowledge a theory:

- A theory has some coherence among its constitutive ideas and concepts.
- A theory makes some ontological discriminations between particular entities and processes in the realm.
- A theory provides a causal explanatory framework for the phenomena in the domain.

In addition, the nature of the relationship between acquiring knowledge and general thinking and reasoning differs with each theory.

In the case of the interpretation of theories, each theory has a different name, description, and assumptions about both the nature of the theory and its function. Researchers vary in their interpretation and use of the theory in approaching it as a (a) cognitive developmental structure; (b) set of beliefs, attitudes, or assumptions that affect cognitive processes; or (c) cognitive process itself. Developmental theories suggest that these ideals are a segment of a structurally coherent, logically sequenced developmental process. The theoretical assumptions are organized as cognitive developmental structures. Although these theories identify various elements of thinking in acquiring knowledge, the cognitive structures and the accompanying general levels or stages proposed in the theories indicate that the components are not separable or orthogonal dimensions. Therefore, they should not be segregated in developing a theoretical framework. Theories should be integrated with one another to be able to help individuals create permanent knowledge.

Theoretical thinking is described as a cognitive process or simply as ways of knowing, which involves the ways in which individuals think about the process of knowing. The different theories have included the nature of knowing, which involves assumptions about the source of knowledge, ranging from a reliance on experts (e.g., Piaget, Vygotsky, Bronfenbrenner) to outcomes from different research studies that use the theories as a theoretical framework. A consideration of the nature of acquiring knowledge includes using data to support and validate knowledge. These processes are usually assumed to be cognitive processes of a higher level than simple inductive reasoning or general critical thinking. Examining how knowledge is generated and justified in comparison to more specific inductive reasoning and thinking is important to contemplate in future research.

Multifaceted Thoughts

Theories are made up of multifaceted thoughts that emerge explicitly in the developmental theories, but all the theories have content related to the nature of knowledge and the processes of knowing. The content of these theories is distinctive and varies somewhat across the different theories.

It may be that the more surrounding ideas about learning are developmental precursors to the essence of thoughts about theories. Some theories have late developments, yet children have a fair amount of early experience with learning and teaching situations in home, school, and community settings. However, considering the multifaceted thoughts of the developmental theories imply that the theories (1) are related to each other in coherent and internally consistent ways, (2) make some important distinctions about knowledge, and (3) may provide a causal explanatory framework for thinking about knowledge.

It is important to consider contemporary transformations in these theories that will unquestionably continue to affect research in this area. These evolutions may modify the approach to research but make scholars and researchers aware of how individuals acquire knowledge. For example, Piaget called attention to ontogenesis, or individual development, recapitulated sociogenesis, or collective development. Analogous parallels will probably be found in this period between an individual's level of constructivism and a constructivist, sociocultural approach to knowledge building in the disciplines. Nevertheless, understanding the developmental theories can provide insight about the individual's beliefs about knowledge and their thinking about knowledge.

Conclusions and Implications

Contemporary psychology can foremost be understood in relation to the distinctive manner that theorists and scholars consider human nature. Individuals have preference for certain theories. Although theories vary, the individuals' preference for the different theories gives insight to the assumptions under which different education programs function, and the basic distinctions among the procedures employed to justify the reasoning among programs based on their theoretical framework.

Intervention Programs

Education programs are interventions that are based on theories. Some of these interventions embrace extremely innovative educational concepts, whereas others have varied into existing themes. Frequently, comparable theoretical concepts are intertwined in many educational programs. Practitioners who have use innovative theoretical programs have typically altered them in their implementation. Few programs presently remain that are true models of one specific theory in its authentic form. Most programs have been replaced by newer programs and ideas, some of which may be within a similar theory or may preserve the theoretical realm.

The function of education programs for children vary at different times based on their theoretical framework that is reflected in their distinctive stated purposes. Sometimes these purposes are based on the children's needs for whom programs are formulated. At other times, they reflect social thought that can be regarded as a branch of parental child rearing or as a way of preparing children to assume a social role in society.

Child-rearing practices is a component that all children experience naturally. The children's school experiences should be as natural as their experiences in other contemporary environments. Three decades ago, Macdonald [1969] described all education as a body of premeditated social intervention. The provision of schools for children of all ages is a result of society's requirement to prepare children to qualify to be in an existing uniformity. School experience can either help children to adapt to an existing social uniformity or prepare them for the contemporary social structure.

The notion of education as a model of social intervention implies that children need more than the intrinsic worth of the activities themselves as the provision of educational opportunities for children, inasmuch as the fact that various educators have rationalize the continuance of schools as a "good place for children to be" [Spodek 1973]. The notion of education has instituted within it the idea of remodeling; that children will somehow change due to the experiences in the program. This notion proposes that a premeditated program focuses toward some expected conclusion. This type of educational program can still be composed of intrinsically worthy experiences, but they are integrated in an authentic and entirely achievable apparent rationale.

Policy Implications

The policy implications of the developmental theories reviewed here are primarily related to what we do to enhance development. This is especially important in relation to children with disabilities as well as children who are considered at risk of future educational failure. Within the maturationist approach, there is nothing that can be done to improve the intelligence of children, while the constructivist views suggest that children's intelligence can be enhanced. Some of the theories have been applied to programs based on particular approaches to curriculum. However, it is unclear whether a curriculum based on one developmental theory is more effective that a curriculum based on any other.

Concepts related to Vygotskian theory have been used as a basis for programs of emerging literacy. Among the key concepts used are: the importance of adult modeling and coaching, the need to create instructional situations that allow learners to advance towards higher levels of understanding, and working within the children's "zone of proximal development" [Mason & Sinha 1993]. Such approaches to beginning reading instruction suggest that rather than wait until "readiness for reading" develops in children, children should be provided early in life with programs and experiences that are language related and that build the concepts and learning strategies that are necessary for successfully learning to read. Such education programs and experiences might be provided in preschool, through the use of technology (such as television and computers), and, most important, through language activities provided in the home by adult members of the family [Saracho 1997].

Science programs for young children have been developed that are based on Piaget's theory of cognitive development. Much of the research on these programs have been simplistic, ignoring language, prior knowledge, motivation, and other factors. Nevertheless, there is a feeling that Piagetian theory provides a basis for understanding children's conceptions of natural phenomena [Howe 1993].

Bronfenbrenner's ecological approach to human development suggests that children's development cannot be understood outside of the social context in which they develop. As a result it is suggested that early intervention programs that focus only on children are viewed as inadequate and most early education programs, especially Head Start, include a parent component as a significant part of the total service. Presently, parent intervention programs such as family literacy are advocated, designed, and implemented from early childhood to secondary school levels.

There is significant evidence that early educational programs can have an impact on children's development, especially those who are considered at-risk [Consortium on Longitudinal Development 1983; Schweinhart et al. 1986]. In spite of the great amount of research that has been conducted on such programs, we still lack evidence of whether intervention programs based on one set of theoretical constructs are more effective than programs based on others. We lack empirical evidence on the relative merits of such programs, especially in relation to their curricula. In addition, there are too few studies that look at the transitions made between early intervention programs and children's experience in the public schools [Karwait 1993]. If we are to be comfortable with the policy implications of any theory of development, we need to know more about the impact of programs related to each developmental theory.

Policy Directions

Research strengthens public policy by offering concepts that help policy makers and the public express, implement, and assess progress [McDonnell 1995] in relation to the theories they most value. Frequently, these theories are ambiguous representations of reality. Sometimes it becomes difficult to agree on the meaning of such theories and their standard definitions also are deficient. Thus, there may not be a way to translate purposes into tangible policy and practice based on theory. The interpretation of the purposes of public policy into conventional practice is normally understood as arranging resources and legal standards into a structure for action. However, the political and administrative mechanisms related to policy enactment usually need a previous instrument—a generative concept that secures the normative assumptions embodied in a particular policy goal, synthesizes empirical data to describe a specific strategy to attain the goal, and offers a guide on ways to assess progress in achieving the goal [McDonnell 1995]. As is the case of a number of policy areas, developmental theories have played a central role in policy decisions.

An approach that has potential for defining state policy is the extension of studies that examine the constructivist, maturationist, and ecological theories. The responsibility in these studies should be to perfect the knowledge that has been found in the previous studies in order to commission local initiatives more effectively. An exceptionally expert strand of conscientious guidance must be extended to prominent figures at the state level, especially in the legislative realm, to make them aware of the intensity of the perspective requirement to reach goals at the levels of school leadership and teaching practice. These research studies can make lawmakers more conscious of the need for flexibility in setting policy goals for those who teach and learn in schools. From the point of view of higher levels of governance, the policy literature recommends that communication be improved between levels of government to enhance performance [James 1991].

Another approach to improve policy communication within local school organizations suggests an additional goal that can be designated the self-education of leaders. The resolution to the problem of public sector performance and resolution to defeat needs more than merely enhancing the public's level of understanding of the current policies that are publicized. After all, legislatures, courts, governors, and the federal government will continue to set priorities and communicate new charges through their existing structure. It will also be essential to persist in more depth to educate policy makers and political leaders concerning the nature of teaching and learning as practiced by others and also by themselves [Scheffler 1984], in order to be able to utilize political power most intelligently to improve school structures and education in general.

Conant and Sanford recommended this approach when the Education Commission of the States was established in the 1960s. It is considered the guidepost for other associations including the National Conference of State Legislatures and the National Governors Association. Currently, new research centers on state policy, grounded in the research community and designed after the Policy Analysis for California Education (PACE) project, have emerged [McCarthy & Hall 1989] to familiarize elected officials and the public concerning educational needs. The achievement of these centers has disintegrated the boundaries of policy analysis by [Guthrie et al. 1990]:

- disassociating the construction of information from agency requirements within specific government programs or under the direct sponsorship of government funding,
- withdrawing research production from academic hierarchies and routing it toward the political process with the packaging of concepts and facts for that purpose,
- networking considerably to overthrow institutional restrictions of higher education, and
- disseminating and gathering opportune information to acquire more firsthand entry to policy processes.

The consequences have been the construction of information that is authoritative from the viewpoint of political leaders and the state level education bureaucracy, which frequently are not able to provide the information in the politicized bureaucracy and the politicized environment of state-level politics. Originating from this attempt are extensive descriptions of educational policy trends and necessities in the state [Guthrie et al., 1990] as well as explanations of the disintegrated appearance of reform across state and national [Guthrie & Koppich 1990] levels.

References

Bronfenbrenner, U. (1979). *The ecology of human development.* Cambridge, MA: Harvard University Press.

Consortium on Longitudinal Development (1983). *As the twig is bent. . . . lasting effects of preschool programs.* Hillsdale, NJ: Erlbaum.

Díaz, R. M., Neal, C. J., & Amaya-Williams, M. (1994). The social origins of self-regulation. In L. C. Moll (Ed.) *Instructional implications and applications of sociohistorical psychology* (pp. 127-154). Cambridge, MA: Harvard University Press.

Guthrie, J. W., Kirst, M. W., Hayward, G. C., Odden, A. R., Koppich, J. E., Adams, Jr., J. E., & Webb, F. R. (1990). *Conditions of education in California 1989* (Policy paper No. PP90–1–2). Berkeley: Policy Analysis for California Education, University of California, Berkeley.

Guthrie, J. W., & Koppich, J. E. (1990, June). *Politics & educational change: making sense of port barrels, iron triangles, high politics, and national social reform.* Paper presented at the third annual conference of the United States and United Kingdom Education and Training Policy in Comparative Perspective, Warkwich University, Coventry, England.

Howe, A. C. (1993). Science in early childhood education. In B. Spodek (Ed.), *Handbook of research on the education of young children.* (pp. 225-235). New York: Macmillan.

James, T. (1991). State authority and the politics of educational change. *Review of Research in Education, 17*, 169-224.

Karwait, N. (1993). Effective preschool and kindergarten programs for students at risk. In B. Spodek (Ed.), *Handbook of research on the education of young children.* (pp. 385-411). New York: Macmillan.

Kohlberg, L. (1971). From is to ought: How to commit the naturalistic fallacy and get away with it in the study of moral development. In T. Mischel (Ed.), *Cognitive development and epistemology* (pp. 151-235). NY: Academic Press.

Macdonald, J. B. (1969). A proper curriculum for young children. *Phi Delta Kappan, 50*(7), 406.

Mason, J. M. & Sinha, S. (1993). Emergent literacy in the early childhood years. In B. Spodek (Ed.), *Handbook of research on the education of young children.* (pp. 137-150). New York: Macmillan.

McCarthy, M. M., & Hall, G. C. (1989). The emergence of university-based education policy centers. *Trends and Issues.* Eugene, Oregon: ERIC Clearinghouse on Educational Management.

McDonnell, L. M. (1995). Opportunity to learn as a research concept and a policy instrument. *Educational Evaluation and Policy Analysis, 17*(3), 305-322.

Piaget, J. (1963). *The origins of intelligence in children.* New York: Norton.

Piaget, J., Jonckheere, A., & Mandelbrot, B. (1958). *La lecture de l'experience.* Etudes d'Epistemologie Genetique V. Paris: Presses Universitaires de France.

Saracho, O. N. (1997). Perspectives in family literacy. *Early Child Development and Care, 127-128*, 3-11.

Schweinhart, L. J., Weikart, D. P. & Larner, M. B. (1986). Consequences of the preschool curriculum models through age 15. *Early Childhood Research Quarterly, 1*, 15-45.

Scheffler, I. (1984). On the education of policymakers. *Harvard Educational Review, 54*, 152-165.

Spodek, B. (1973). *Early childhood education.* Englewood Cliffs, New Jersey: Prentice- Hall, Inc.

Thomas, R. M. (1992). *Comparing theories of development.* 3rd Ed. Belmont, CA: Wadsworth.

Vygotsky, L. S. (1978). *Mind in society: The development of higher psychological processes.* Cambridge, MA: Harvard University Press.

Wellman, J. V. (1990). *Voices of the mind: A sociocultural approach to mediated action.* Cambridge, MA: Harvard University Press.

3 Early Childhood Development

Douglas R. Powell

The United States is entering the 21st century with a well-developed agenda for promoting the competence of young children. An unprecedented number of research-based blueprints for federal, state, and local early childhood policies and programs have been issued in the past decade. At no point in history has there been a clearer set of informed recommendations for strengthening early childhood development than now available to policymakers, professionals, and parents.

Recent recommendations for improving young children's outcomes focus on the quality of children's environments, access to good early childhood programs for children living in vulnerable circumstances, support for families, and significantly stronger infrastructures for enabling early childhood programs to achieve high standards and positive results for all children. The mandates come largely from national commissions and task forces comprising representatives from private and public sectors organized by the federal government, prestigious philanthropic foundations, professional associations, leading universities, and prominent research centers. See Table 3-1 for an illustrative list.

While the recommendations vary in emphasis, the commonalities are striking. There is growing consensus that all children are entitled to environments that are developmentally stimulating, nurturing, and challenging. The strongest national statement about the importance of the early years is the first goal of the National Education Goals adopted by the 50 governors and President Bush in 1989 and subsequently incorporated into

Table 3-1. Selected National Policy Reports on Early Childhood Published in the 1990s

Ready to Learn: A Mandate for the Nation, Carnegie Foundation for the Advancement of Teaching [Boyer 1991]

Caring Communities: Supporting Young Children and Families, National Task Force on School Readiness, National Association of State Boards of Education [1991]

Starting Points: Meeting the Needs of Our Youngest Children, Carnegie Task Force on Meeting the Needs of Young Children [1994]

Years of Promise: A Comprehensive Learning Strategy for America's Children, Carnegie Task Force on Learning in the Primary Grades [1996]

Not by Chance: Creating an Early Care and Education System for America's Children, Quality 2000 Initiative [Kagan & Cohen 1997]

Ready Schools, National Education Goals Panel [Shore 1998]

Learning to Read and Write: Developmentally Appropriate Practices for Young Children, International Reading Association and the National Association for the Education of Young Children [1998]

Preventing Reading Difficulties in Young Children, Committee on the Prevention of Reading Difficulties in Young Children, Commission on Behavioral and Social Sciences and Education, National Research Council [Snow et al. 1998]

---

the Goals 2000: Educate America Act signed into law by President Clinton in 1994. The goal states that "by the year 2000, all children in America will start school ready to learn" and, toward this end, calls for

- All children to have access to high-quality and developmentally appropriate preschool programs that help prepare children for school;
- Every parent in the United States to be a child's first teacher and to devote time each day helping the child learn; and

- All children to receive the nutrition, physical activity experiences, and health care needed to arrive at school with healthy minds and bodies and mental alertness necessary for learning.

This chapter describes sources of the growing interest in early childhood, summarizes lessons of recent efforts to improve child outcomes, and identifies necessary conditions for extending best practices to all children.

Why the Press to Improve Early Childhood Outcomes?

A confluence of factors is stimulating widespread interest in the early years and driving current ideas about needed directions for enabling young children to become productive and competent citizens. These factors include concern about child functioning and outcomes, research demonstrating the long-term effects of early childhood environments, growing recognition of glaring inequities in access to high-quality environments, and a belief that an adequate research base now exists for knowing how to improve the life chances of our youngest citizens.

Indicators of Child Well-being Point to Problems

Compared with most other industrialized countries, the United States does not fare well on many indicators of childhood well-being, including infant mortality rate, percentage of low birthweight babies, proportion of babies immunized against childhood diseases, and rate of babies born to adolescent mothers.

Overall, about 20% of American children and youth live in families below the poverty level. Poverty is more prevalent among younger children; one in four infants and toddlers live below the poverty line. While the percentage of children in poverty has remained relatively steady since 1981, income disparities have grown significantly since 1980. The percentage of children living in families with high income and the percentage of children living in families with extreme poverty have risen, while the percentage of children living in families with medium income has fallen [Federal Interagency Forum on Child and Family Statistics 1998]. More important, the depth of poverty among poor children has increased. In 1975, 32% of all poor children ages 0 to 5 years lived in families with income 50% below the poverty threshold ("deep" poverty), and this percentage had increased to 47% by 1993 [Bronfenbrenner et al. 1996].

Children living below the poverty line are more likely to suffer from poor general health, to have high levels of blood lead, and to have no usual source of health care. They are also more likely to experience housing problems and hunger, less likely to be enrolled in early childhood education, and less likely to have a parent working full time all year. Children in poor families are less likely to be up to date with their immunizations than children with family incomes at or above the poverty level (69% compared to 80%). In 1996, low birthweight rates were the highest in two decades. The infant mortality continues to decline, however, mostly because the chances for highest risk infants to survive have improved substantially. Black infants continue to be at much higher risk of low birthweight and infant mortality than infants of other races [Federal Interagency Forum on Child and Family Statistics 1998]. Recent research consistently shows that persistent poverty has more detrimental effects on IQ, school achievement, and socioemotional functioning than short-term or transitory poverty, and that children experiencing both types of poverty usually fare less well than children who have never experienced socioeconomic disadvantage [McLoyd 1998].

Concerns about the adequacy of family contributions to children's development—heightened by increases over time in single-family homes, divorce rates, births to unmarried mothers, geographic mobility of families, and father absence—are fueling some of the nation's interest in policies and programs to support young children. For instance, survey data on the frequency of family practices known to help the development of children's reading and writing skills indicate that many children apparently are not experiencing literacy-rich environments at home. Specifically, in 1996, 57% of children ages 3 to 5 years were read aloud to by a family member every day in the last week, up slightly from 53% in 1993. Sixty-four percent of white, non-Hispanic children, 44% of black, non-

Hispanic children, and 39% of Hispanic children were read to every day in 1996 [Federal Interagency Forum on Child and Family Statistics 1998].

The Early Years Matter

There has long been adherence to the belief that the early years of life constitute a formative or critical period that shapes the course of human development. Recently the empirical base of this belief has expanded dramatically through the accumulation of evidence on the long-term effects of early childhood environments. An influential report on the early years issued by the Carnegie Corporation's Task Force on Meeting the Needs of Young Children [1994] summarizes the primary message of these studies in succinct fashion: "We can now say, with greater confidence than ever before, that the quality of young children's environment and social experience has a decisive, long-term impact on their well-being and ability to learn" [p. xiii].

A significant addition to scientific knowledge on lasting effects of the early years is research on brain functioning. Revolutionary developments in sophisticated tools for brain scans have enabled researchers to examine the impact of environments on the structure and functioning of the developing brain [Nelson & Bloom 1997]. Recent studies in molecular biology have discovered there is far more extensive brain development in the first year of life than previously recognized and demonstrate that adverse early environments substantially increase the risk of serious developmental problems. The Carnegie Task Force on Meeting the Needs of Young Children [1994] highlights five key findings from research on brain function and early intervention programs:

- The brain development that takes place in the first year of life is more rapid and extensive than previously understood.
- Brain development is more vulnerable to environmental influence than previously suspected.
- Early environments have long-lasting influence on brain development.
- The environment affects the number of brain cells, the number of connections among them, and also the way these connections are "wired."

- Early stress has a negative impact on brain function [pp. 7-8].

High-quality Early Childhood Programs Are Effective

Widespread interest in improving supports for the early childhood years is driven partly by research demonstrating that high-quality programs can have positive effects on young children's intellectual and social outcomes. Evaluations of early childhood programs have been conducted mostly with disadvantaged populations. The results indicate that, among children from low-income families, model early childhood programs yield significant gains in intellectual performance and socioemotional development by the end of a year of intervention. Model early childhood programs also have produced strong, positive effects on special education placement and grade retention, and they have had positive impacts on life success factors such as teenage pregnancy, delinquency, welfare participation, and employment (for a recent review, see Barnett [1995]).

Probably the best known study of preschool program effects is the Perry Preschool Project in Ypsilanti, Michigan. This experimental study has followed preschool (3 and 4 years of age) participants to age 27 years and found that program participants had half as many criminal arrests, higher earnings and property wealth, and greater commitment to marriage than their counterparts who did not attend preschool [Schweinhart et al. 1993]. Benefit-cost analyses at 27 years indicate the program produced economic benefits to participants and to the general public that greatly exceeded the costs of the program. Specifically, the benefit-cost ratio is in excess of 7:1; most of the benefits accrued to the general public largely through reductions in crime [Barnett 1993].

Most longitudinal studies of early childhood program effects on children from disadvantaged backgrounds report that early IQ gains often erode within three years of school entry and that academic gains "wash out" within five to six years. Length of preschool program participation [Campbell & Ramey 1994], lack of follow-up supports in elementary school [Reynolds 1994], and flawed research designs [Barnett 1992] may account for "fade out" effects. It also is unreasonable to expect early childhood programs to inoculate children living in high-risk circumstances from future negative influences.

Early Childhood Program Quality Is Generally Low and Unevenly Distributed

In 1995, six out of 10 children under the age of 6—more than 12.9 million—who had not yet entered kindergarten were receiving some type of child care and education on a regular basis from persons other than their parents [Federal Interagency Forum on Child and Family Statistics 1998]. Recent studies indicate that a majority of these children are in child care arrangements that are mediocre or substandard in quality. Only one in seven child care centers was found to provide a level of quality that researchers in one national study deemed to promote healthy development. Seven out of 10 centers provided poor to mediocre levels of quality, and almost half of the infant and toddler classrooms provided poor quality of care. The study sample was made up of 401 centers in four regions in the United States [Helburn 1995]. An earlier study of 227 licensed, full-day center-based programs in five metropolitan areas also found that most centers provided barely adequate services; only 12% of the classrooms met or exceeded a good level of quality [Whitebook et al. 1989].

About one-third of the child care arrangements used by employed mothers with children under 5 years of age are family child care homes with nonrelative providers or nonparent relatives (e.g., child's grandmother). An observational study of 226 providers of family child care and relative care in three communities in California, Texas, and North Carolina determined that only 9% of the homes were of good quality. Thirty-five percent were rated as inadequate quality, and the remaining 56% were rated as adequate custodial arrangements [Kontos et al. 1995].

Less is known about the quality of early childhood programs offered through public schools. One large study of early childhood classrooms sponsored by Head Start, public school, and private child care found that all programs generally provided adequate levels of quality, but none was rated as excellent and the amount of individual attention given to children was generally low across all settings [Layzer et al. 1993]. A study of public school early childhood programs in the late 1980s found wide variation in quality, and nearly one-fourth used developmentally inappropriate materials [Mitchell et al. 1989]. One statewide study of 103 public kindergarten classrooms found that only 20% were developmentally appropriate [Bryant et al. 1991]. An investigation of public school preschool programs in three major population centers of South Carolina revealed that large-scale programs can provide developmentally appropriate experiences [Frede & Barnett 1992].

A crucial message from recent analyses is that the quality of early childhood programs is not equitably distributed across families of different socioeconomic status in the United States. One analysis found that centers predominantly serving children from upper income families provided the highest quality of care, and centers predominantly serving children from middle-income families almost uniformly provided the poorest quality of care. The centers that served children from low-income families did not differ significantly in quality from centers serving children from upper-income families [Phillips et al. 1994]. A recent national study of 1,281 children found that infants from families at the highest and lowest income levels received higher quality center-based care than children from "near poor" and middle-income families [NICHD Early Child Care Research Network 1997]. The likely explanation here is that higher income parents can afford to pay for better quality care, and government subsidies or philanthropic contributions support a better level of quality of care in centers serving children from low-income families. In general, it is children from working poor and lower middle-class families who receive a lower quality of care because their families lack access to government subsidies or the financial capacity to purchase high-quality care [Phillips et al. 1994].

We Know How to Improve Outcomes

Much of the momentum for improving early childhood outcomes stems from the belief that a sufficient body of knowledge exists on how to improve the functioning of children at greatest risk of failure. Schorr and Schorr [1988] promoted this idea with a well-read book entitled *Within Our Reach* more than a decade ago. In contrast with the notion that educational and human service programs for disadvantaged populations are largely an exercise in "throwing money" at intractable problems, Schorr and Schorr assembled an impressive collection of data to document the huge public and private costs of ignoring vulnerable populations early in life, and to document that solutions lie "within our reach" for improving the early lives of several million American children growing up at risk. The thesis of the book's call for action is that a critical mass of research and experience is available to answer problems that dominate the American domestic agenda. Major policy reports issued in the past decade offer similar optimism about the resourcefulness of the knowledge now available for designing effective prevention and intervention programs.

How Can We Improve Child Outcomes?

A distinguishing characteristic of blue-ribbon committee reports on young children's outcomes issued in the past decade is the specificity of recommendations. No longer are reports comprised of vague generalities about the value of preschool education for children from disadvantaged circumstances. Recent recommendations focus in detail on discrete components of high-quality environments for young children, building on research knowledge that has expanded exponentially over the past 20 years. The essential ingredients in achieving and sustaining positive outcomes in early childhood fall into four areas: supports for families, early childhood program curricula, staff credentials and program standards, and schools that can flexibly respond to a diverse range of child abilities and backgrounds.

Families

Discussions of how to improve child outcomes typically begin with a recognition of families as the first and foremost influence on children's development. Major reports on ways to strengthen young children's well-being (see Table 3-1) typically recommend policies and programs focused on parents' contributions to children's outcomes. As noted in the report of the Carnegie Task Force on Learning in the Primary Grades [1996], "Any thought of how the institutions that shape children's lives can improve educational achievement must start with families" [p. 33].

Research supports the idea that families are the starting point for improving children's outcomes. There is compelling evidence on the enduring effects of early home environments on children's learning and development. Consider the results of a recent longitudinal investigation on children's everyday family experiences with language in the first three years of life. The quality of language and verbal interactions in the family—language diversity, feedback tone, symbolic emphasis, style of guidance, responsiveness—accounted for 60% of the variance in measures of child accomplishment (vocabulary skill and IQ score) at age 3 years and in receptive language and language development in third grade [Hart & Risley 1995].

In addition to language environment, research points to the following parent beliefs and practices as important contributors to children's outcomes:

- Parental teaching strategies that stimulate the child's own thinking and encourage active, verbal engagement of a task;
- The provision of reading and writing materials (e.g., picture dictionaries) and the parent's own reading behavior as supports for early literacy development;
- The parent's understanding of child development as a complex process that involves the child as an active contributor to his or her own development; and
- Appropriate parental expectations of the child's abilities.

Studies show that parental behaviors and attitudes are inextricably interwoven into daily exchanges with the child, and it is impossible to identify one of the parent's beliefs or behaviors as the single most important influence on children's outcomes (for a review, see Powell [1995]).

How might society ensure positive effects of parents on their children? A common response is to provide education and support programs to strengthen the quality of parents' interactions with their children and the conditions of the home environment. For example, the National Education Goals Panel calls for parents to have access to training and support that enables every parent to spend time each day helping the child learn. Parenting education is among the primary foci of the federal government's Head Start program, state-supported initiatives such as Minnesota's Early Childhood Family Education Program and Missouri's Parents as Teachers program, and numerous programs sponsored at local and regional levels through public and private funds. Program supports for responsible parenthood also emphasize early and comprehensive prenatal care as key to having a healthy baby.

The field of early childhood education has been a pioneer in developing innovative programs to support parents, and thus there is a useful set of program experiences and research knowledge to tap in answering questions about effective ways of working with parents. Early childhood programs that work directly with the child and also include systematic provisions for developing and sustaining supportive relationships with parents have been found to have positive effects on a range of parent outcomes (for a review, see Powell [1995]) and, further, parent involvement has been found to be associated with positive child outcomes (e.g., Reynolds [1992]). Outcomes are less robust for programs that work exclusively with parents. In particular, evaluations of home visiting programs focused on parents yield mixed results on the efficacy of work with parents (e.g., Olds & Kitzman [1993]). Because there are multiple and powerful determinants of parenting beliefs and practices that are not easily influenced, programs of minimal or even modest intensity in terms of duration or frequency of contact are unlikely to support meaningful change in parenting behaviors [Larner 1992].

Good practices in early childhood programs for engaging parents include the following:

- Program recognition of the role of staff and parent confidence in one another (e.g., staff believing parents want to do well by their children) as central to fostering supportive relationships;

- The use of multiple instructional methods for enabling adults to understand and practice parenting behaviors that support children's development and learning;
- Sensitivity to the situational contexts, needs, and interests of parents individually as well as collectively;
- Genuine opportunities for parents to help shape the content and methods of program attention to parenting issues; and
- Opportunities for parents to form mutually beneficial ties with parents and to gain access to community resources as a way of strengthening a family's informal and formal support system for child rearing.

Research, as well as sustained contact with families through program services, indicate that the vast majority of parents wish to do well by their children. This generalization holds true across economic strata (e.g., Hart & Risley [1995]), and is especially important to emphasize in discussions about strategies for working with lower income parents, who often are viewed as lacking sufficient interest in the responsibilities of child rearing. To the contrary, a profound commitment to being a good mother runs deep and wide among lower income women [Holloway et al. 1997]. This orientation provides a strong common ground for building authentic relationships with early childhood staff if given time and freedom to surface.

Conditions of family functioning such as poverty, unsafe neighborhoods, and stressful work situations are increasingly of interest to policymakers and professionals interested in supporting optimal environments for parenting and child development. Strategies for improving the existing contexts of parenting are part of the recent policy recommendations. The *Caring Communities* report of the National Association of State Boards of Education [1991], for instance, recommends that employers establish policies for parental leave as well as release time or flextime for parents to locate an early childhood program, help their child adjust to a new program, and to visit and volunteer in programs. The Carnegie Task Force on Meeting the Needs of Young Children [1994] envisions a community-level "culture of responsibility" for helping children get off to a good start in life. Recommendations for broad-based action for fostering family-centered communities include strong local leadership, community assessments of needs and existing program capacities, and an emphasis on results.

Curriculum

The goals and methods of early childhood programs have long been the focus of contentious debates generally framed via the juxtapositions of acceleration versus enrichment goals for children, child- versus teacher-driven classroom activities, didactic versus nondidactic instructional methods, and whole child versus domain-specific (e.g., cognitive) program emphasis. The debates are further complicated by a historical and now largely artificial split between child care (often viewed as a custodial arrangement for keeping children safe while parents work or attend school) and early childhood or preschool education programs (often seen as providing a half-day socialization and/or academic experience that helps prepare children for success in kindergarten and the elementary school grades).

While professionals as well as the lay public are far from reaching general agreement on *what* and *how* young children should be taught, recently there have been important advances in the specificity of recommendations and amount of research that directly address the goals and methods of early childhood programs.

In terms of recommendations, the National Education Goals Panel [1992] submits that high-quality environments in the early years should focus on five dimensions of early learning and development that prepare a child for school: physical well-being and motor development, social and emotional development, dispositional and stylistic approaches toward learning, language usage, and cognitive and general knowledge. In addition, Head Start, this nation's largest early childhood program, has refined its indicators of social competence (physical health, social and emotional behavior, and cognitive skills) as guides to program work with, and desired outcomes for, all children [Zigler 1998].

The concept of *developmentally appropriate practice* has been widely promoted as the standard for best practices in early childhood programs.

Guidelines for developmentally appropriate practice with young children were developed by the early childhood field's largest professional group, the National Association for the Education of Young Children, in the early 1980s [Bredekamp 1987] and a thorough revision was issued 10 years later [Bredekamp & Copple 1997]. In brief, the guidelines give attention to age and individual appropriateness, and call for curriculum emphasis on the whole child, active learning that flows from the child's interests, and concrete activities relevant to young children's lives. The guidelines are thought to represent consensus thinking among early childhood professionals about best practices in early childhood programs, and the concept has been incorporated into numerous standards statements, including the National Education Goal Panel legislation.

Positive child outcomes have been found to be associated with developmentally appropriate practice. Studies indicate that children in early childhood classrooms characterized by child-initiated activities score higher on measures of creativity, language outcomes, verbal skills, child confidence in cognitive skills, academic achievement in first grade, creativity, attitudes toward school, and stress behaviors in the classroom than children in early childhood classrooms characterized by didactic or teacher-directed activities. The available research is not uniformly supportive of developmentally appropriate practice. Some findings reveal no differences in children's social development in developmentally appropriate versus inappropriate classrooms, and one study found that literacy achievement was higher among preschool and kindergarten children in didactic classrooms compared to child-initiated classrooms (for a review, see Dunn & Kontos [1997]).

The National Research Council's empirically based recommendations for preventing reading difficulties in young children underscore the value of high-quality early childhood programs and, more specifically, recommend phonological awareness training for preschoolers who are at risk of reading difficulties [Snow et al. 1998]. A recent position statement on supporting the development of reading and writing in young children by the International Reading Association and the National Association for the

Education of Young Children [1998] recommends a variety of literacy experiences in the preschool years, including reading aloud to children, enhancing children's exposure to and concepts about print, and emphasizing the relationship between letters and sounds.

There is a good and growing research foundation, then, for guiding curriculum practices in early childhood programs that are likely to yield strong developmental and academic achievement outcomes for children. Whether these approaches eventually will prevail in the United States is a major question addressed in the final section of this chapter.

Credentials and Standards

A persistent myth in the United States is that the education and care of young children is not an intellectually challenging enterprise. Not surprisingly, state regulations for early childhood programs typically require staff to have minimal or no formal professional preparation in child development or early education. This is a serious mistake.

A growing research literature shows that teachers with higher levels of education and training have more positive interactions with children and that the children in their care have better outcomes (e.g. Whitebook et al. [1989]). A recent analysis of data from two major studies demonstrated that teachers with the most advanced professional preparation (a bachelor's or more advanced degree in early childhood education) were the most effective compared to teachers with lower levels of education. Teachers with associate (two-year) degrees and Child Development Associate certificates (a national competency-based, experiential learning in-service program) were more effective than teachers with some college or a high school diploma plus some workshops [Howes 1997]. A significant result of Howes's analysis is that sensitive and responsive teaching—often assumed to be a personality characteristic that can get lost or diminished through "too much" schooling—was highest among teachers with the most advanced level of teacher preparation. It seems that advanced professional education enables individuals to be appropriately responsive to all children. In a related vein, a study of family child care homes found that care provided by relatives (e.g., child's grandmother) to be of poorer quality, on average, than care provided by nonrelatives [Kontos et al. 1995].

The professional preparation of early childhood teachers needs to be a serious pursuit with rigorous standards. The National Research Council's report on the prevention of reading difficulties appropriately notes that the cognitive complexity and practical importance of development in early childhood should translate into a demanding and interesting major course of study in higher education, but seldom is preschool education presented in these terms [Snow et al. 1998, p. 280]. The lack of a coordinated system to develop well-trained and compensated staff in early education and care also is one of the weakest elements of the early childhood field nationally [Morgan et al. 1993]. Accordingly, the need to significantly upgrade the educational credentials of early childhood teachers is a central component of most policy recommendations on improving early childhood outcomes. The report of the Carnegie Task Force on Learning in the Primary Grades [1996], which devotes an entire chapter to early learning, endorses the establishment of a career ladder in the early childhood field that enables professional mobility and rewards advanced levels of professional preparation with pay and title. The report showcases impressive models of professional development and career ladders in the military and in selected states (e.g. Nebraska, Delaware). The Quality 2000 Initiative recommends a three-tiered approach to licensing all individuals who care for young children, including early childhood administrator, educator, and associate educator licenses [Kagan & Cohen 1997]. An associate or bachelor's degree is among the requirements of the proposed early childhood educator license. Because the Howes [1997] analysis shows that associate and bachelor's degree preparations are not equivalent in terms of effectiveness in working with children, it seems appropriate to require a four-year degree in early childhood education for an early childhood educator license.

Well-prepared teachers require supportive classroom conditions to produce positive child outcomes. The classroom condition that has been found to be particularly influential is the number of children per teacher, or child:staff ratio. Studies show that children's developmental outcomes are more positive in classrooms with a smaller versus larger number of children per teacher (for a review, see Hayes, Palmer, and Zaslow [1990]). It is generally the case that good things go together: better prepared teachers are in programs with good child:staff ratios [Phillips & Howes 1987]. Because both teacher background and child:staff ratio are cost-sensitive factors, a key policy question is whether the effectiveness of teachers with advanced levels of education and training is diminished when there are more children in the classroom. The Howes [1997] analysis suggests that more advanced levels of teacher education and training do not enable teachers to be as effective with less stringent child:staff ratios as less well-prepared teachers with more stringent ratios.

Ready Schools

Children's outcomes are improved when schools are prepared to work in flexible and effective ways with a heterogeneous population of children and their families. This theme is central to most policy recommendations issued in recent years. For example, the Carnegie Task Force on Learning in the Primary Grades [1996] submits that schools should provide varied learning environments that offer the highest quality of instruction for all children, including those of diverse linguistic and cultural backgrounds. Similarly, the *Ready Schools* report of the National Education Goals Panel calls for schools to be "committed to the success of every child" and to "alter practices and programs if they do not benefit children" [Shore 1998, p. 5]. The report recommends that schools be responsive to children's individual needs, including the provision of intensive help when needed.

Research evidence supports recommendations for school responsiveness to a range of educational needs. Continued intervention in the early school grades has been found to strengthen the effects of early childhood programs for children from disadvantaged backgrounds. A randomized study of the Carolina Abecedarian Project found that children's scores on cognitive and academic achievement measures increased as the duration of intervention increased [Ramey & Campbell 1987; Horacek et al. 1987]. The school-age intervention was a home/school resource teacher who prepared an individualized set of home activities to supplement the school's basic curriculum in reading and mathematics, helped families secure needed community services (e.g., adult literacy classes), and served as advocates for the child and family within the school and community. At 8 years of age, children who had received continuous intervention for the first eight years of life performed better in reading and mathematics than children who received preschool only. In turn, those who received the school-age supports only had reading and mathematics scores that were lower than the scores of children who received preschool. Follow-up data secured four to seven years after the intervention ended found that the school-age treatment alone was less effective than preschool alone or preschool plus school-age assistance [Campbell & Ramey 1994]. A study of more than 1,000 former Head Start children in Chicago also found follow-up intervention in school to be effective [Reynolds 1994].

Use of developmentally appropriate practice in kindergarten classrooms also has been recommended as a way for schools to accommodate a range of child abilities [Boyer 1991; National Association of State Boards of Education 1991]. Research findings indicate that children in developmentally inappropriate classrooms exhibit more overall stress (e.g., sucking fingers) than children in developmentally appropriate classrooms [Burts et al. 1992], and in first grade the children who participated in developmentally appropriate classrooms had higher reading comprehension scores than children from less appropriate kindergarten classrooms [Burts et al. 1993].

Expanding the kindergarten day beyond the usual half-day session is an approach that has had some modest academic effects on children, but the benefits for children from middle-class backgrounds are not consistent across studies [Karweit 1994]. One-on-one tutoring programs that use teachers rather than aides have been found to be effective [Wasik & Slavin 1993].

To date, there is no compelling evidence to support raising the age requirement of children entering kindergarten or adding an extra year of a "developmental kindergarten" or "junior kindergarten" for children who are at risk of academic failure. At best, the extra-year programs add a temporary boost in achievement that fades over time [Karweit & Wasik 1994].

How Can We Build on the Lessons of Improved Outcomes?

Promote Basic Understandings

Many lessons from efforts to improve early childhood outcomes are at odds with some widespread myths associated with the early years. Chief among these myths are the following: real learning does not begin until children enter school, poor child outcomes are the fault of bad parents, and the care and education of young children requires minimal intellectual ability on the part of adults. Ambitious public awareness strategies aimed at promoting basic understandings about the early childhood period seem essential to the eventual adoption of policies and practices that support healthy functioning in the formative years of life.

The early childhood years are a high-stakes opportunity for prudent investment in our society's future. Cost-benefit analyses of early childhood programs for children from disadvantaged backgrounds demonstrate a remarkable long-term return on program costs. Importantly, most of the benefits to society are in the form of significant reductions in crime-related expenditures. Moreover, most parents are not in a financial position to pay the actual expenses of a high-quality early childhood program and, further, high-quality programs require subsidies or in-kind donations over and beyond the revenues generated through parent fees. This state of affairs leads to calls for the expansion of publicly supported programs such as Head Start to serve more lower income children. While Head Start and most other public early childhood programs are free to families, the key point is that significant benefits accrue to society from investments in early childhood programs for disadvantaged populations.

Mothers have long been the target of blame when children's outcomes fall short of societal expectations. Typically, policymakers and the general public exhibit "considerable sympathy for young poor children who are viewed as innocent victims...(but) there has been precious little sympathy for their parents, whose plight is often seen as of their own making" [Zigler 1998, p. 12]. As noted earlier, research offers a strikingly different picture of parents overall in terms of profound interest in and big dreams for their children's futures. Yet stereotypes about the child-rearing motivations of lower income parents serve to inhibit funding for family-centered early childhood programs and, within early childhood programs, function as barriers to the development of healthy teacher-parent relationships.

The deplorable level of salaries for early childhood personnel and the general lack of state regulations for appropriately credentialed staff to work with young children reflect deeply entrenched ideas about the amount of rigor required of staff in early childhood programs. As described earlier, high-quality program experiences for young children require professionally trained teachers in early childhood education. New images of essential skills for competent work with young children are needed.

Still in development in the United States is a basic understanding of what constitutes quality learning experiences in an early childhood environment. Existing definitions of quality have been generated by professionals without parent contribution, and parents often use criteria in selecting an early childhood program that professionals generally do not consider in assessments of program quality. The concept of developmentally appropriate practice does not resonate with ideas about appropriate early childhood program goals and methods held by many parents. The developmentally appropriate practice concept described earlier in this chapter is particularly foreign to many parents of low income and ethnic minority status, who often prefer didactic approaches such as rote memorization, flash cards, and worksheets as the means of helping young children develop basic academic skills (for a review, see Powell [1997]). Thus, a superordinate challenge in a pluralistic society such as the United States is to craft an understanding of quality program experiences that is truly respectful of family traditions and expert knowledge. A focus on the ends—what knowledge and skills should young children possess—may prove to be a useful focus for discussions at local, state, and national levels.

Set and Enforce Standards

The title of the Quality 2000 Initiative report—*Not by Chance*—is an apt depiction of needed directions in ensuring a floor of quality in early childhood programs. Under current provisions, a high-quality program of early education and care is a chance occurrence that a majority of young children do not experience.

The best strategy for improving and maintaining program quality is to require all staff to be licensed, based on a degree in early childhood education, and for program licensing requirements to be carefully enforced with *all* programs available to the general public. Legal exemptions for certain types of programs (e.g., sponsored through church auspices) are common in most states and, as noted in the Quality 2000 Initiative report, serve to undermine public confidence in the quality of the early care and education field [Kagan & Cohen 1997]. The Quality 2000 Initiative report also wisely recommends financial and other incentives for programs to obtain voluntary accreditation through the National Academy of Early Childhood Programs, which is affiliated with the National Association for the Education of Young Children. Accreditation requirements probably will continue to be several notches above state licensing requirements, even in states with stringent requirements.

Some leaders propose parent choice as a strategy for improving the quality of early childhood programs. The assumption here is that parent-as-consumer demand for quality programs will stimulate upgrades in the program marketplace. However, the promise of parent choice as a viable policy strategy for improving the quality of child care in the United States, per professional standards, is diminished significantly by child care research indicating that parents are generally satisfied with their child care arrangements, typically engage in a cursory examination of various child care settings in relation to professional criteria, and usually include criteria that are in conflict with professional benchmarks of quality [Holloway & Fuller 1992]. Information services that help parents identify and select high-quality early childhood programs are valuable, but cannot be expected to single-handedly shape the motivations and orientations inherent in parents' decisionmaking about an arrangement for their child.

The daunting challenge is for society to marshal the resources needed for high-quality early childhood programs. The Quality 2000 Initiative recommends a broad array of groups, including business, government, parents, and community organizations, to generate the needed new funds for a quality early care and education system. Further, the Initiative calls for 10% of all public early care and education funds to be invested directly in an infrastructure and quality enhancements for early childhood programs. In addition, each state and locality is to form a permanent board charged with responsibility for the infrastructure and governance of early care and education [Kagan & Cohen 1997].

The latter part of the 20th century has been a productive period of marshaling research evidence and program experience toward thoughtful designs for improving early childhood outcomes. The agenda is now well formulated and there is a high level of optimistic energy in existing policy recommendations. As we embark on the new millennium, the biggest challenge is to realize a broad-based political will to achieve better futures for America's children.

References

Barnett, W. S. (1992). Benefits of compensatory preschool education. *Journal of Human Resources, 27,* 333-342.

Barnett, W. S. (1993). Benefit-cost analysis of preschool education: Findings from a 25-year follow-up. *American Journal of Orthopsychiatry, 63,* 500-508.

Barnett, W S. (1995). Long-term effects of early childhood programs on cognitive and school outcomes. *The Future of Children, 5*, 25-50.

Boyer, E. L. (1991). *Ready to learn: A mandate for the nation.* Princeton, NJ: Carnegie Foundation for the Advancement of Teaching.

Bredekamp, S. (Ed.). (1987). *Developmentally appropriate practice in early childhood programs serving children from birth through age 8.* Washington, DC: National Association for the Education of Young Children.

Bredekamp, S., & Copple, C. (Eds.). (1997). *Developmentally appropriate practice in early childhood programs* (rev. ed.). Washington, DC: National Association for the Education of Young Children.

Bronfenbrenner, U., McClelland, P., Wethington, E., Moen, P., & Ceci, S. (1996). *The state of Americans: This generation and the next.* New York: Free Press.

Bryant, D. M., Clifford, R. M., & Peisner, E. S. (1991). A comparison of frequencies of stress behaviors observed in kindergarten children in classrooms with developmentally appropriate versus developmentally inappropriate instructional practices. *American Educational Research Journal, 28,* 783-803.

Burts, D. C., Hart, C. H., Charlesworth, R., DeWolf, D. M., Ray, J., Manuel, K., & Fleege, P. O. (1993). Developmental appropriateness of kindergarten programs and academic outcomes in first grade. *Journal of Research in Childhood Education, 8,* 23-31.

Burts, D. C., Hart, C. H., Charlesworth, R., Fleege, P. Mosley, J., & Thomasson, R. H. (1992). Observed activities and stress behaviors of children in developmentally appropriate and inappropriate kindergarten classrooms. *Early Childhood Research Quarterly, 7,* 297-318.

Campbell, F. A., & Ramey, C. T. (1994). Effects of early intervention on intellectual and academic achievement: A follow-up study of children from low-income families. *Child Development, 65,* 407-423.

Carnegie Task Force on Learning in the Primary Grades. (1996). *Years of promise: A comprehensive learning strategy for America's children.* New York: Carnegie Corporation of New York.

Carnegie Task Force on Meeting the Needs of Young Children. (1994). *Starting points: Meeting the needs of our youngest children.* New York: Carnegie Corporation of New York.

Dunn, L., & Kontos, S. (1997). What have we learned about developmentally appropriate practice? *Young Children, 52,* 4-13.

Federal Interagency Forum on Child and Family Statistics. (1998). *America's children: Key national indicators of well-being, 1998.* Washington, DC: U.S. Government Printing Office.

Frede, E., & Barnett, W. S. (1992). Developmentally appropriate public school preschool: A study of implementation of the High/Scope curriculum and its effects on disadvantaged children's skills at first grade. *Early Childhood Research Quarterly, 7,* 483-499.

Hart, B., & Risley, T. R. (1995). *Meaningful differences in the everyday experience of young American children.* Baltimore, MD: Brookes.

Hayes, C. D., Palmer, J. L., & Zaslow, M. (Eds.) (1990). *Who cares for America's children: Child care policy for the 1990's.* Washington, DC: National Academy Press.

Helburn, S. (Ed.). (1995). *Cost, quality and child outcomes in child care centers.* Denver, CO: Department of Economics, Center for Research in Economic and Social Policy, University of Colorado at Denver.

Holloway, S. D., & Fuller, B. (1992). The great child-care experiment: What are the lessons for school improvement? *Educational Researcher, 21,* 12-19.

Holloway, S. D., Fuller, B., Rambaud, M. F., & Eggers-Piérola, C. (1997). *Through my own eyes: Single mothers and the cultures of poverty.* Cambridge, MA: Harvard University Press.

Horacek, H. J., Ramey, C. T., Campbell, F. A., Hoffman, K. P., & Fletcher, R. H. (1987). Predicting school failure and assessing early interventions with high-risk children. *Journal of the American Academy of Child Psychiatry, 26,* 758-763.

Howes, C. (1997). Children's experiences in center-based child care as a function of teacher background and adult:child ratio. *Merrill-Palmer Quarterly, 43,* 404-425.

International Reading Association and National Association for the Education of Young Children. (1998). Learning to read and write: Developmentally appropriate practices for young children. *Young Children, 53,* 30-46.

Kagan, S. L., & Cohen, N. E. (1997). *Not by chance: Creating an early care and education system for America's children.* New Haven, CT: Bush Center for Child Development and Social Policy, Yale University.

Karweit, N. L. (1994). Issues in kindergarten organization and curriculum. In R. E. Slavin, N. L. Karweit, & B. A. Wasik (Eds.), *Preventing early school failure: Research, policy and practice* (pp. 78-101). Boston: Allyn & Bacon.

Karweit, N. L., & Wasik, B. A. (1994). Extra-year kindergarten programs and transitional first grades. In R. E. Slavin, N. L. Karweit, & B. A. Wasik (Eds.), *Preventing early school failure: Research, policy and practice* (pp. 102-121). Boston: Allyn & Bacon.

Kontos, S., Howes, C., Shinn, M., & Galinsky, E. (1995). *Quality in family child care and relative care.* New York: Teachers College Press.

Larner, M. (1992). Realistic expectations: Review of evaluation findings. In M. Larner, R. Halpern, & O. Harkavy (Eds.), *Fair start for children* (pp. 218-245). New Haven, CT: Yale University Press.

Layzer, J. I., Goodson, B. C., Moss, M., & Farquhar, E. (1993). *Life in preschool. Volume 1 of an observational study of early childhood programs for disadvantaged four-year-olds.* Final report to the Office of Policy and Planning, U.S. Department of Education. Cambridge, MA: Abt Associates.

McLoyd, V. C. (1998). Socioeconomic disadvantage and child development. *American Psychologist, 53,* 185-204.

Mitchell, A., Seligson, M., & Marx, F. (1989). *Early childhood programs and the public schools: Between promise and practice.* Dover, MA: Auburn House.

Morgan, G., Azer, S. L., Costley, J. B., Genser, A., Goodman, I. G., Lombardi, J., & McGimsey, B. (1993). *Making a career of it: The state of the states report on career development in early care and education.* Boston: Center for Career Development in Early Care and Education, Wheelock College.

National Association of State Boards of Education. (1991). *Caring communities: Supporting young children and families.* Alexandria, VA: National Association of State Boards of Education.

National Education Goals Panel (1992). *The national education goals report: Building a nation of learners.* Washington, DC: U.S. Government Printing Office.

Nelson, C. A., & Bloom, F. E. (1997). Child development and neuroscience. *Child Development, 68,* 970-987.

NICHD Early Child Care Research Network, National Institute of Child Health and Human Development. (1997). Familial factors associated with the characteristics of nonmaternal care for infants. *Journal of Marriage and the Family, 59,* 389-408.

Olds, D. L., & Kitzman, H. (1993). Review of research on home visiting for pregnant women and parents of young children. *The Future of Children, 3,* 53-92.

Phillips, D. A., & Howes, C. (1987). Indicators of quality in child care: Review of research. In D. A. Phillips (Ed.), *Quality in child care: What does research tell us?* (pp. 1-19). Washington, DC: National Association for the Education of Young Children.

Phillips, D. A., Voran, M., Kisker, E., Howes, C., & Whitebook, M. (1994). Child care for children in poverty: Opportunity or inequity? *Child Development, 65,* 472-492.

Powell, D. R. (1997). Parents' contributions to the quality of child care arrangements. In C. J. Dunst & M. Wolery (Eds.), S. Reifel (Series Ed.), *Advances in Early Education and Day Care (Vol. 9), Family policy and practice in early child care* (pp. 133-155). Greenwich, CT: JAI Press, Inc.

Powell, D. R. (1995). *Enabling young children to succeed in school.* Washington, DC: American Educational Research Association.

Ramey, C. T., & Campbell, F. A. (1987). The Carolina Abecedarian Project: An educational experiment concerning human malleability of children. In J. J. Gallagher & C. T. Ramey (Eds.), *The malleability of children* (pp. 127-139). Baltimore: Paul H. Brookes.

Reynolds, A. J. (1994). Effects of a preschool plus follow-up intervention for children at risk. *Developmental Psychology, 30,* 787-804.

Reynolds, A. J. (1992). Comparing measures of parental involvement and their effects on academic achievement. *Early Childhood Research Quarterly, 7,* 441-462.

Schweinhart, L. J., Barnes, H. V., & Weikart, D. P. (1993). Significant benefits: The High/Scope Perry Preschool Study through age 27. *Monographs of the High/Scope Educational Research Foundation, Number 10.* Ypsilanti, MI: High/Scope Press.

Schorr, L. B., & Schorr, D. (1988). *Within our reach: Breaking the cycle of disadvantage*. New York: Doubleday.

Shore, R. (1998). *Ready schools*. Washington, DC: National Education Goals Panel.

Snow, C. E., Burns, M. S., & Griffin, P. (1998). *Preventing reading difficulties in young children*. Washington, DC: National Academy Press.

Wasik, B. A., & Slavin, R. E. (1993). Preventing early reading failure with one-to-one tutoring: A review of five programs. *Reading Research Quarterly, 28, 178-200.*

Whitebook, M., Howes, C., & Phillips, D. A. (1989). *Who cares: Child care teachers and the quality of care in America*. Final report of the National Child Care Staffing Study. Oakland, CA: Child Care Employee Project.

Zigler, E. (1998). By what goals should Head Start be assessed? *Children's Services: Social Policy, Research, and Practice, 1*, 5-17.

4 Building Relationships for Learning

Dorothy Rich

Only a few decades ago, parent involvement was considered nice but not really important. Today, thanks to educational research, experience, and common sense, parent involvement in children's education is considered vital for school improvement. It is identified as a major determiner of student success. Yet, just because we tell people about parent involvement—and even tell them what to do to make it happen—does not mean that they will take our good advice.

Those of us in the field produce long lists of parent involvement research studies, readings, and activities. For more than 30 years as a parent involvement "pioneer," I have been among the list makers and program developers. But, it was not until I created MegaSkills® in 1987 that I began to understand more about what adults need to make use of our data and our models, no matter how good they are.

The mightiest research and the greatest programs still depend on people's motivation to use them. They depend on adults' capacity to learn and their will to change. For people to take advice, even good advice, they need to feel able to take it and to want to take it. It is vital to develop this capacity... not just for children but for adults as well.

The Special Focus of the Home and School Institute

The "umbrella" concept for the programs and materials I have created for the Home and School Institute grow from these needs. This is, I believe, a two-part process: building competencies for learning and building relationships for learning

Schooling is made up of a complex set of relationships between children, teachers, parents, and the larger framework of the school organization. To get the most from this framework, children and their caring/teaching adults need key personal competencies that I call "MegaSkills®." These are the habits, the behaviors, and the attitudes needed to succeed in school and life. Children need adults who can teach these MegaSkills® and "connect" with the ways schooling is organized.

My work, which has evolved from research and experience, focuses on meeting the needs of learners—the adults and children involved—rather than on the administrative structure of schools. The changes I seek are personal changes (the MegaSkills®). These in turn create the learning relationships that build and sustain educational achievement. The role of the adult is a vital, often overlooked, educational key, and that is why I concentrate so strongly on meeting the needs of adults.

Parents and teachers across the nation have to feel and be personally capable. When it comes to education this doesn't always come naturally. Some may ask if we have time to care about adults when we have to educate children. I believe that we have no choice.

Headlines report growing anxiety about schools. The public is making their concerns known in tangible ways through the push for vouchers and the growth of charter and alternative schools. Schools have to pay attention. The goal of this chapter is to explore the basics for building personal capacities of educators, to discuss lessons learned, and to outline practical strategies that can be put into practice now.

From What Was to What Is

It used to be, we'd put a teacher, a set of books, and a set of tests in one room and say, "Go to it!" That's what happened to me as a beginning teacher. When I became a teacher in the 1950s, the words "family" and "community" were not mentioned in any of my teacher education courses. When I went into the classroom, I thought all I had to be was to be a fine teacher and my students would learn—and learn what I was teaching. What a naive period we were in. How comfortable it was. Today we are more knowledgeable and more realistic, and it certainly is not as comfortable. We have left the age of educational innocence.

Teaching has always been a demanding job. Until fairly recently, most of us didn't know how extraordinarily complex it really is: To impart knowledge (that part's relatively easy) and "to cause to learn" (that's the hard part). We did not know about the impact of the home and community on children's work in school. We know more now; we know better now. And it hurts ... because it all used to seem much easier, and now it seems so hard.

Throughout my career in parent involvement, the big question I kept asking myself (and still do) is this: What can every parent do at home to help every child learn and want to learn more? My interests in the role of the family and community in education started with teaching my first classes. Everyone said I was a really good teacher, and I got a lot of high grades for my work. But, I saw a number of my senior high students having problems in class, difficulties that they just didn't need to have. And I started asking myself and my fellow teachers a lot of questions.

At the same time in my own home in the early 1960s, I listened as my young children asked me questions about learning and knowledge—well before they were ready go for school. This was long before Head Start and preschools. It was still in that "dark ages" period when we thought that children started learning only when they entered the school door.

A "radical" idea started whispering in my head: "Children learn a lot outside of school. A home, every home, is an important learning place and parents can do a lot to help every child learn and do well in school ... not just at the beginning, but all the way through." This was definitely not a fashionable idea at a time when schools were supposed to be super institutions able to do everything.

Our New Point of Understanding

History, research, and experience bring us now to a new and heightened point of understanding. It's appropriate to ask what have we learned and to think about where we can be going. There was a long period in which the United States enjoyed almost effortless superiority in education. We are a nation of wondrous growth, optimism, and seemingly inexhaustible resources. Even during the Depression in the 1930s, faith in education, when all else failed, seemed to endure. In World War II, we scored a great victory over the most industrialized nations in the world. Education seemed almost effortless. In many ways it was. So much was supporting schooling that we did not recognize how it was being propped up by society—by outstanding teachers, who went into teaching because there were no other jobs available, and by a generally accepted work-hard ethic and a sweat-on-brow yearning for a better life.

A great change in public attitudes about how to live life has made an enormous difference in education. The message that used to go out to young people, and not so young ones, was work hard, wait, and maybe there will be a reward somewhere out there. Today, one of the overriding messages (certainly being sent by the media) is: "Do it now! Have it now!" And, this is especially hard on education. The stimulation outside the schoolroom walls far exceeds the usual happenings of the classroom. And there is really no way for the school to compete with the attractions of the Internet, the music ... all the vibrations of the outside world.

Until recently, schools were part of a set of intimately connected social and educational institutions—the family, the neighborhood, the church, and the community clubs and groups. A variety of players was involved on the educational team, putting across a consistent educational message. To be sure, not everybody was a great student in those good old days, and those good old days were really not so very good. Parents were told by an all-knowing school, "Hands off education ... leave it to us. You don't know what you are doing." And many parents willingly heeded those unwise words.

Today the vital web of community, social, and educational institutions (really the safety net for education) is punctured with gaping holes. There is a lot of discussion about community and the role of the family—but it's often about how they are not doing their job. Teachers and parents are under attack and many are discouraged and demoralized. Yet if education wasn't so good in the good old days, it stands to reason that it is not so bad today. We have higher expectations for serving more children. We say to ourselves, "We have to do more. We have to do better."

Today, parent involvement is encouraged and supported as never before. The studies of researchers—including the late James Coleman, Herbert Walberg, Joyce Epstein, James Comer, Lawrence Steinberg, and more—fill many a library shelf and web page. The US Department of Education sponsors national parent and community partnership initiatives and a phone line (1-800-USA-LEARN) where any time day or night, teachers and parents can request a multitude of studies and materials. When it comes to parent involvement, what we didn't know or care about not so long ago is virtually axiomatic now.

When Knowing More Is Not Enough

Yet, just because we know more doesn't mean that parents or educators today are using what's been learned. Even though the importance of involvement is widely trumpeted, nearly one-third of the students in Lawrence Steinberg's study "Beyond the Classroom," say their parents have no idea how they are doing in school [1996]. About one-sixth of all students believe that their parents don't care whether they earn good grades in school. Even if students are underestimating their parents' concern, the fact that so many think their parents have little interest in their schooling is evidence of a problem of tremendous significance.

Steinberg's study reports that only 20% of parents today consistently attend school programs. More than 40% never do. Membership in the National PTA is half today of what it was 30 years ago [1996].

As for homework, research indicates American parents are not enthusiastic about their children being assigned great amounts of homework. Reading and intellectual activities often take a back seat to going to the mall, watching TV, hanging out with friends, buying or thinking about the latest clothes, records, cars, etc. This isn't new. What is new is that these anti-school pursuits appear to start at a younger age and many parents increasingly are feeling more and more helpless to do anything about them.

All of this is going on *outside* of school. Inside schools, and mostly in discussion about schools, it's as if we're in another world. It's a world filled with words like goals, standards, evaluation and testing. Schools are in what I call the "Goal Rush."

What's worrisome is an assumption that just because there are goals, students will automatically rush out to meet them. Knowing something about human nature, we have to know that just having goals is not enough. And having evaluations are not enough. Certainly, we need better tests. But just because we have a better tape measure won't keep people from getting wider waist lines.

Hugh Price of the National Urban League states the issue well:

> Classroom standards are only half the story, and the easy half at that. Children have little chance of clearing the higher academic bar if we concentrate only on how high it has been set. The crucial, but as yet unanswered, question is whether the adults in children's lives will do what's necessary to equip them to clear the bar. [Price 1996]

The Fundamentals of Learning

The true fundamental that makes the difference in education is not found in stores or promulgated in educational documents. It's the message that needs to come across to students in the classroom and in the home. This message comes through relationships and through role modeling. It comes, even today, the old fashioned way—person to person.

The key to helping children do their best is perhaps too mundane to be believed. It's this—to improve education, we have to use what the research tells us to do: to find more ways to involve mature, positive adults in the lives of children. Schools used to be as isolated as islands. Today, schools and families are inextricably linked. When these links work, we have a Learning Community. When they do not connect, we suffer the irreparable loss of "social capital." As generally optimistic Americans, we tend to look for fast, active panaceas. Machines are appealing, partly because they look so efficient. No matter how good they look, however, the breakthrough in education they have to make is in the toughest place to reach— the heart of the student.

This is true even in science. Anderson and Lee write:

> No matter how tightly students' classroom behavior is controlled and guided by teachers and curriculum materials, students always retain personal control over their attention and effort. Eventually, the success of science teaching depends on creating social bonds in which the teacher and the curriculum lead the students to identify the goal of scientific understanding as their own personal goal. [Anderson & Lee 1997]

Of course we need fine facilities and up-to-date materials. But what we need more is what it takes to get to the inner core of the student that says, "I want to read this book, I want to study this material, I believe I can succeed; I know it takes hard work; I believe it's worth it."

The reality is this: We can change the books, put in more teachers, fix buildings. But kids won't learn unless they want to learn, unless they have the will to learn. Research shows that children do learn how to read in early elementary grades. What they don't do is to continue to read. The National Assessment for Educational Progress (NAEP) indicates that while almost all American high school graduates can do simple arithmetic, they can't do the increasingly complicated mental tasks needed for employment.

In school, test scores tell us that students today are scoring about as well as they did in the 1970s. But, what was good enough for the seventies, as we recognize, just isn't good enough anymore. In the workplace, employers are alarmed. Today's graduates, they say, are only marginally prepared for job success. The problem is not just literacy. Students have trouble acquiring and demonstrating disciplined work habits.

At home, parents see children struggling to deal with the growing complexity and often overwhelming choices in their daily lives. Younger and younger children have to cope with emotional and dangerous problems such as divorce, sex, drugs, and AIDS. They are asked to be grown up when they are not grown up.

The clock won't turn back; all moms won't go home to the kitchen; broken marriages won't get restored. We have to find some new ways to connect kids with adults, and adults with adults. Many parents feel isolated and, frankly, don't know what it takes to help themselves and their children become successful in and out of school. Teachers and administrators, in urban and suburban settings, need help to do their job with families and communities when pressures outside the school threaten to destroy the work of even the best schools.

The Different Fundamentals of MegaSkills®

In many established parent involvement programs, the focus is on the school, on the teacher's role, on the organization. MegaSkills® may well be the only program* focusing on the qualities, behaviors, habits, and attitudes, combined with academics, that individuals need to be prepared for school and to do well in school.

It used to be assumed that children came to school ready to learn, that they were prepared with the attributes it takes to be a successful learner. This can't be assumed any longer. What is now taught at home, in the community, and in the media, is not preparing our children to be the kinds of learners they need to be.

MegaSkills® is focused on the child as learner and involves families as the messengers and models for children so that every child knows it takes to succeed. This is carried out through practical, everyday activities that parents use with children at home, and that teachers use in the classroom. These are not traditional school exercises. Instead, they use home and community resources and settings to provide multiple ways to learn.

MegaSkills® works to answer the question: What does it take to enable us to learn, to achieve, to succeed? The answers lie in the attributes we all know are important: Confidence, Motivation, Effort, Responsibility, Initiative, Perseverance, Caring, Teamwork, Common Sense, Problem Solving, and Focus. Gleaned from school report cards and job evaluation forms, the 11 MegaSkills® make up what I call "The Never-Ending Report Card."

* For more information about the MegaSkills® Program, contact the author at http://www.megaskillshsi.org

As a teacher, I have always believed that we can teach these attributes. We can provide the practice that children need to learn them, and we can do it by involving families and teachers working together with children. MegaSkills® did not develop overnight. They grow from this basic question that I continue to ask: Beyond the forces of luck and innate talent, what holds most people, including children, back or propels them forward? What is it that most people can learn that can enable them to succeed?

In the 1960s, when I started the Home and School Institute, we were told that schools are "it," that they can and will do everything. I was emphatically told I didn't need to worry about what *families* do or don't do. In the 1990s, things turned about. We are told that schools are weak, and that families are important in education, but that there is no one out there to work with.

It is somewhat startling to me, and yes, reinforcing, to be able to say that I believe today the same as I believed in the 1960s. I believe that both school and home are powerful institutions (working in a more amorphous but powerful context of community) and that the real, the best, and only hope for improving education is to unite the educational forces of school, home, and community in working together.

This is more complex than adding an hour to the school day, more complex than vouchers or putting computers in every classroom. While these may be worthy objectives, they do not answer concerns about student motivation, perseverance, and love of learning. When I speak of the family's educational role, it sounds old-fashioned, similar to what parents have always done. But it is quite contemporary, because many parents today never learned or have forgotten what they have to do at home to pave the way for their children's success in school.

When I first said the word "MegaSkills®" in the midst of a presentation to a group of educators in 1987, I said it in a whisper. I had formulated this word in my mind to identify the important basics that students need to learn to succeed. I did not know if it would mean anything to others. At the end of my talk, I heard a voice at the back of the room ask, "What are those MegaSkills®?"

From that one voice has come many voices from across the nation and the world. I didn't know it then, but I had defined a concept more powerful than I could have believed. Listed below are the MegaSkills®:

- Confidence: feeling able to do it
- Motivation: wanting to do it
- Effort: being willing to work hard
- Responsibility: doing what's right
- Initiative: moving into action
- Perseverance: completing what you start
- Caring: showing concern for others
- Teamwork: working with others
- Common Sense: using good judgment
- Problemsolving: putting what you know into action
- Focus: concentrating with a goal in mind

For the third edition of the book, *MegaSkills®* [1998], I added the MegaSkill *Focus* to the list. We don't have to be psychologists to understand that emotional health undergirds academic strength. The family and the community are keys not only to academic achievement but to the emotional maturity children bring into the classroom.

MegaSkills®: Building Competencies for Learning

The goal of MegaSkills® is to enable children and their caring adults to build capacities they need to be able to learn whatever they have to or want to learn...in and out of school. This demands an integration of academics and emotions. MegaSkills® develops both the academic and the emotional "muscles" simultaneously.

When I developed the original MegaSkills® Program, I had not even thought about how much adults would gain from it. It was only through feedback from parents and teachers about themselves that I began to see the value of MegaSkills® for the adults caring for and teaching children. Teachers and parents reported changes in their own lives, often with more impact than the changes for their children. Among them: "I now have the *Confidence* to apply for a job. I now know how to talk with my boss, to have the ambition I need in my own life, to be the parent my child can be proud of..." These reports, in person and on paper, have become the driving force for building my understanding about what adults need in order to help children learn.

Four basic principles undergird the MegaSkills® Process:

- All children can learn what it takes to succeed. All teachers can learn. All parents can learn.
- MegaSkills® are superbasic assets of attitudes and behaviors that can be taught.
- MegaSkills® can be learned through practical activities linked to academics.
- To teach most effectively, we need to remember the closeness of the head and the heart.

Evolution of MegaSkills® Training Programs

Throughout my career, my work has focused on translating research into practical action. This led me to two key strategies: teacher training and home curricula. In 1988, the first edition of *MegaSkills®* was published, and it enjoyed a strong reception in the book stores. But, to reach the families who might not otherwise receive this kind of help, I became convinced it was important to go beyond the bookstores and in 1989 designed the MegaSkills® Workshop Program.

The new role for teachers today is to be connectors between the classroom and the world. This requires training to work in partnership with parents and as catalysts to build community support for schooling. MegaSkills® trains teachers to be leaders in mobilizing the work of parents and community.

The earliest Home and School Institute teacher training programs, started in 1972, were full semester courses offered both as in-service and as a college master's degree in School and Family-Community Involvement.

In an effort to speed the programs to communities nationally, MegaSkills® training is conducted in accelerated one- and two-day seminars with a follow-on practicum conducted by teachers for parents in the community.

The on-site process works in this way: First, the Institute trains a corps of leaders at local sites. They follow a detailed curriculum to conduct workshops for families in schools, in libraries, in churches, and even in prisons. The sessions take one to two hours each and provide hands-on activities for demonstrations and families working together. Parents go home from these workshops to do learning "recipes" with their children.

By far the most popular programs I have ever designed are what I call "home learning recipes." These are school-to-home curricula. They do not duplicate the school but extend and supplement the school. I have to admit that when I first started developing "recipes" and talking about how spoons and clocks and bikes and all the usual paraphernalia of home can help teach children important skills, I mumbled the word "recipes" under my breath, almost apologizing for it. It sounded too homespun to be educationally significant, certainly compared to formal education studies and treatises. (See sample "recipes" on the next two pages.)

I've stopped apologizing. The parents and the children in our Home and School Institute programs opened my eyes. They told me and my colleagues and anyone else who would listen that doing these "recipes" (which take only a few minutes a day) with their children help to change their lives at home. I was surprised when I heard parents tell about their experiences in words like these: "I see my kids in a new way," or "Now my kids talk to me." The children have a more poignant response. Over and over they say, "These recipes made my parents have time for me."

Program Impact: The Parent Workshops

The MegaSkills® Program grew from these experiences. When I started developing "recipes," I knew I had to design a system small enough to handle, that's active, that gets people to do things together, and to experience success together. I said to myself: "Make it practical. Make it enjoyable. Remember, it doesn't take a lot of time to do a lot of good." Children need to be able to apply what they learn in school. "Recipes" help parents

Promises! Promises!

Recipe for Early Elementary Level

Why Do It

To help children become more personally responsible.

This activity helps children follow through on their promises. It helps children realize what keeping promises involves.

Materials Needed

Thinking minds

How to Do It

- Talk about what happens when people don't do what they're responsible for. Examples: Plants that don't get water will wilt. Animals (and children) that don't get fed will whine. Garbage that isn't taken out will smell bad.
- Discuss the consequences for others when tasks are not done. Is it fair to expect others to do our work? Is it responsible?
- Decide together on tasks for each family member to do. Should people be able to do only the things they like? Yes or no? Talk together about this.

More Ideas

When children argue about not doing their assigned tasks, ask them to think about what would happen:

- If parents decided they didn't want to shop or cook meals?
- If the bus driver stayed home, or the movie projectionist didn't show up for work?

Helpful Hint

Turn a household task into a game. Decide how long it will take to do the job. Then time yourselves against the clock. To add more fun, turn on the radio or a record and do the job to music. This helps the work get done and go faster, too.

Free Time Choices

Recipe for Middle School/Intermediate Level

Why Do It

To help children make good choices about the use of free time. This activity helps youngsters delve into their own interests so that they can figure out how to spend time on what they really care about.

Materials Needed

Thinking minds, newspaper and magazine articles on hobbies and sports.

How to Do It

Help your children take stock of their interests. Examples: music, sports, dance, or history. Read newspaper articles. Talk together. For some youngsters these interests actually might be reading, writing, or math.

Figure out together how to take one of these interests and pursue it. Are there clubs to join, hiking or chess groups? Are there people to check with who are already doing these things?

Think together about new skills to learn. Examples: skating, swimming, dancing, or drawing.

Sign up for a class or program together. Make this a parent and child effort to learn a new skill or even a foreign language.

More Ideas

Talk together about your own interests when you were a child and what they are now that you are an adult. This gets a world of conversation going and helps children see parents in a new light.

Helpful Hint

Some free time is needed for just plain "goofing off," but too much of that can lead to laziness and passive TV watching. Free time is a great opportunity to extend and develop interests. Some of these may be connected with school, but others may be quite different from schoolwork. There is a world of opportunity in community and recreational programs, often free or low cost. They are waiting to be tapped.

know that sorting the laundry or setting the table are terrific ways to reinforce skills needed for reading. And they get chores done at home. Children need ways to feel successful at home and use what they have learned in school.

To date, the MegaSkills® Program has trained more than 10,000 leaders who come from 48 states. They in turn have provided programs for over 100,000 families. Program impact is encouraging. Memphis State University researchers, report that TV watching for children in the program decreased. Time not spent watching TV was spent on homework. In Austin, Texas, school district research indicated that MegaSkills® students showed higher scores in national and statewide achievement tests. Across the nation, principals report the rate of discipline incidents for MegaSkills® students is lower and that the program is reaching parents who had not previously been involved with the school.

An analysis of the MegaSkills® School in Louisville, Kentucky, identified consistent positive changes in student attitudes and behavior. Teachers said that students had become more respectful and considerate of others (92%), more able to work cooperatively (93%), more responsive (93%), and more confident and self-reliant (86%) [Edge 1996]. In San Diego, California, MegaSkills® Programs are being integrated with success in the Comer School Process [Fernandez 1998].

Surveys taken after each training and in on-site assessments by the Home and School Institute reveal that families really like the program and activities. Teachers recognize a positive change in the atmosphere of the classroom and an increased ability of children to be self-disciplined and to use MegaSkills® for managing their own behavior. Principals report increased student achievement. MegaSkills® are accepted and found to be important by teachers and parents across class, race, ethnic and age lines. Studies are continuing as MegaSkills® programs are offered in Spanish, Vietnamese, Hmong, Korean, and, in some California sites, in Chinese and Armenian.

Program Impact: The MegaSkills® Classroom Program

The MegaSkills® Classroom Program, started in 1992, owes its birth and growth to teachers who asked for a MegaSkills® Program to use directly with children.

Principal Tom Catlett in Richmond, Indiana, identified the need children have for a common language. "Now," he said, "We are all on the same page." As he explains, the staff had assumed until teachers started teaching the MegaSkills® that students knew what it was to be Responsible, to make an Effort, to use Common Sense. It wasn't until they started teaching the MegaSkills® that they realized that the students really had not understood what these concepts meant in action.

Velda Correa, principal of Rico School in Weslaco, Texas and her staff have integrated MegaSkills® throughout their Title I school with the highest poverty rate in a small community near the Mexican border. Mrs. Correa reports: "This is the first year that I feel proud as a principal that the scores are where they need to be. We have used a lot of programs. MegaSkills® is different. It had us live at a different degree. It has taken us to a different level of humanness with one another."

School test scores [Texas Education Agency 1998] reveal marked improvements over a one-year period for third-grade reading (69% to 91%) and math (75% to 95%) [Correa 1998]. Advances are reported for fourth grade reading and math. Fourth-grade writing strongly increased from 85% to 96%. "The reason I believe that MegaSkills® has helped us with achievement and discipline," says Correa, "is because it puts us all on the same wave length."

In evaluating the MegaSkills® School in Louisville, Professor Denzil Edge of the University of Louisville reports that the number of involved parents has doubled. Children, he says, are learning from each other and actively identifying their own and other's MegaSkills® in the classroom and on the playground.

Teachers are using the MegaSkills® Classroom Programs in a wide variety of ways, from special sessions, almost like clubs, to integration of MegaSkills® directly into academic lessons. The classroom initiative also serves to bolster parent involvement. The program has been specifically designed so that teachers can simultaneously teach MegaSkills® in reading, language arts, science, math, and critical thinking.

Teachers as Learners

To keep up and stay abreast in today's knowledge explosion, teachers need abilities not just to teach but to learn. Recognizing the needs of educators as adult learners, I piloted at the 1998 Phi Delta Kappa Gabbard Institute, a one-day staff development training program entitled "MegaSkills® for Educators Personal and Professional Development." This program has evolved into the newest Institute training: "Nurturing the Educational Leader Within You." Just as parents need increased learning competencies, so do teachers. This program builds teachers' capacities for continued learning.

Building Relationships for Learning: Recommendations for Practice

We wish we knew everything (or even more than we know) right now. But just as in medicine, while we await certain cures, we just can't wait. Herbert Walberg writes: "We'd like to have randomly assigned treatment and control groups with pretests and posttests. Other information, such as parent, teacher, and student interviews and observations, may be valuable. This takes considerable will power, energy, and funds, and a few programs have proven themselves by this test." Yet, just as in the war on cancer, we don't wait before we take action. We move forward, learning as we go. To use the findings I have made to date, here are three key recommendations for practice. Whatever programs we select for our schools, educators need:

- To remember the importance of relationships between the individual student and family with the school. To use programs and strategies that provide specific, practical ways to build ongoing relationships for learning.
- To seek out programs that simultaneously build the capacities of adults while building the abilities of children. To remember that parents and teachers need their own MegaSkills® (or by whatever name used to refer to the capacities it takes to learn and teach well).
- To focus on the real basics of education today: building capacities and competencies for learning. To have the patience and ongoing commitment it takes, not just for more immediate test scores, but to help children and their caring adults become stronger learners for longer lives.

What's needed now is a new kind of support for the educational role of the family. It is increasingly clear that priority attention must be given to developing the kind of participation that directly involves families in enhancing the education of their own child and themselves. This is the approach that offers the greatest opportunity for equity and for widespread and sustained involvement. It's the approach that appeals to the most basic parental motivation for involvement in the first place—the desire to help one's child do better and to help one's self. This adult involvement may or may not show up on immediate student test scores. Rather, it lays the base for success and many more tests all through students' longer, learning lives.

Moving Forward

When I am asked about the key factor that makes students like school, study hard, and stay in school, the answer is a "C" word, but it's not "Curriculum." The word I choose is "Caring." Students have to feel needed. Parents have to feel needed, teachers, too. This is the human element in education. Connectedness is a protective factor in children's lives. Schools have to find ways of helping everyone feel important, essential, and connected.

Figure 4-1 on page 91 illustrates my Relationships of Learning concept. It would be better if this could be shown on a web site or on TV so that the constant motion of these interactions would be evident. This is a static representation of an energetic and always-in-motion learning enterprise.

It's all very well to talk about test scores. But, we have to remember that we build test scores by building people, children and adult included. I am not talking abut vapid self-esteem concepts, but specific competencies. Education is a very human, "messy" enterprise. Even in the age of computers, education is still a person-to-person connection.

The Human Element

Parent involvement, while honored in theory, is, as we know, fragmentary, modestly budgeted for most schools, and dependent on the volatility of funds and the differing interests of administrators.

In our age, enamored of technology and seeking tangible evidence of forward motion in the schools, it's tempting to spend funds on a computer

Figure 4-1. Relationships for Learning

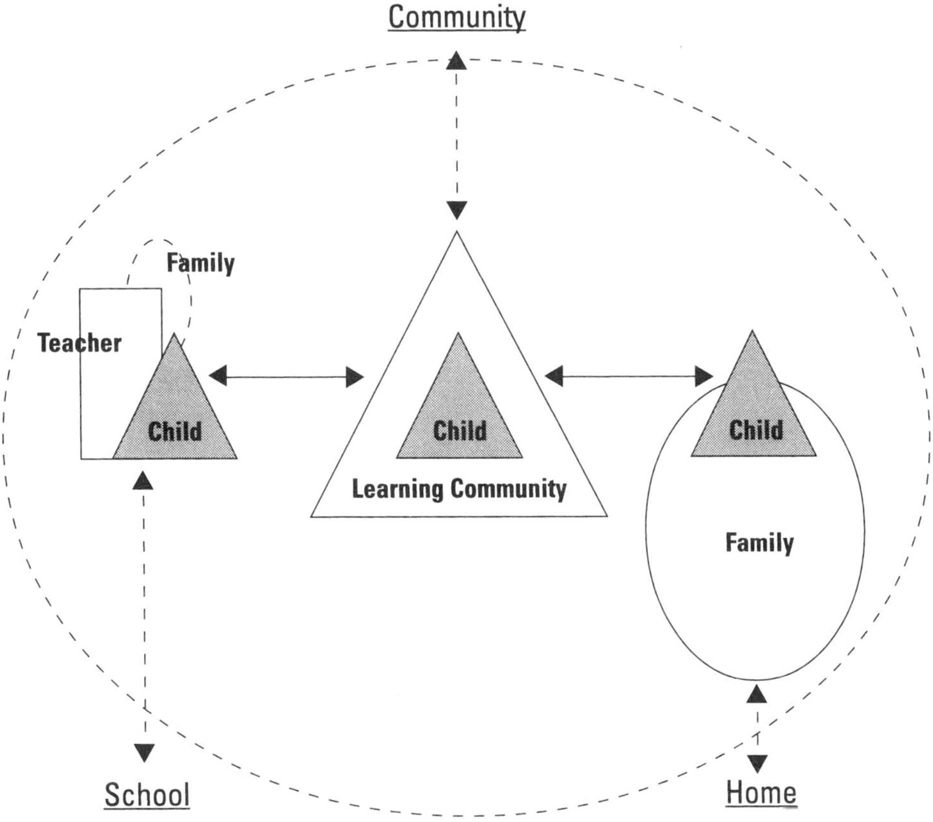

lab rather than on training for staff and parents. Computers may crash, but they do not require seeking substitutes or providing lunch on training days.

There is a dream, a fond hope that somehow there is a quick fix in education—if only we could find it. There's been a tendency to have faith in machines, in retooling the system rather than in retooling people.

When the first machine can raise a warm hand to greet a child in the morning, or phone home without using a prerecorded message, I'll be glad to rethink my investments in caring adults.

Parents and teachers might wish that each could do the job alone. Yet, today's schools need parents and today's parents need the school. And children need them both more than ever. In many ways, this is our greatest hope for change.

In a period of growing expectations, worry about the future, and taxpayer unrest, it is more important than ever to use the resources on hand. Luckily, the most at-hand resource in education is people. The continuing issue teachers face is how to mobilize people to help themselves and their children...and moreover, to sustain these efforts.

Throughout this chapter, I have emphasized the strategic importance of building the capacities to learn and the will to change—of the teachers and parents in children's lives. We can no longer overlook adult needs or think it's inappropriate to focus on adults when we have to focus on children.

The concern now is that our children, to become successful learners and workers in the 21st century, need more. To extend the work of MegaSkills® beyond the training programs. I have developed a new parent program entitled, *What Do We Say? What Do We Do?®* (Forge Publishers 1997) The book and parent study guide focuses on the everyday crises and disappointments that are part of the school/home connection. It's about critical issues in this relationship and development of personal MegaSkills® for children and their parents.

There's an old, old saying, really a cliché that still bears repeating. "Catch me a fish and I'll eat today. Teach me to fish and I'll eat for the rest of my life." This must be a basic underlying theme of all that we do when we connect home and school.

It's the theme, the focus of the MegaSkills® Programs, which are keyed to enabling and empowering families to help themselves and their children. Regardless of what program is used, what educators need is a systematic, sustained way to teach parents what they need and want to know about how to help themselves and their children.

References

Anderson, C., & Lee, O. (1997, May). Will students take advantage of opportunities for meaningful science learning? *Phi Delta Kappan, 78,* 9, 720-724.

Barton, P. E., & Coley, R. J. (1992). *American's smallest school: The family*. Princeton, NJ: Educational Testing Service.

Bloom, B. (1981). *All our children learning: A primer for parents, teachers, and other educators*. New York. McGraw-Hill.

Comer, J. P. (1988). Educating poor minority children. *Scientific American, 259* (5), 42-48.

Correa, V. (1998). *Evaluating the impact of the MegaSkills® Program*. Audiotape report. Welasco, Texas.

Edge, D. (1996). Maupin MegaSkills® school-wide final evaluation. University of Louisville, Louisville, Kentucky.

Epstein, J. (1991, January). Paths to partnership. *Phi Delta Kappan, 72* (5), 344-349.

Fernandez, B. (1998). Report on MegaSkills®/Comer process in the San Diego schools. San Diego, California.

Fruchter, N., Galletta, A., & White, J. L. (1992). *New directions in parent involvement*. New York: Academy of Educational Development.

Henderson, A., & Berla, N. (1994). *A new generation of evidence: The family is critical to student achievement*. Washington, DC: National Committee for Citizens in Education.

Price, H. (1996). Keynote address given at the annual conferences of the National Urban League, August 11, 1996.

Rich, D. (1998). *MegaSkills®: Building children's achievement for the information age*. Boston: Houghton Mifflin.

Rich, D. (1994). *The new MegaSkills® bond*. Washington, DC: DRA Press.

Rich, D. (1997, August 6). Seven habits of good teachers today. *Education Week*, 16 (41), 53 & 57.

Rich, D. (1997). *What do we say? What do we do?* New York: Forge Publications.

Steinberg, L. (1996). *Beyond the classroom: Why school reform has failed and what parents need to do*. New York: Simon and Schuster.

Texas Education Agency. (1998). Third grade reading and math scores. Austin: Author.

Walberg, H. (1984). Families as partners in educational productivity. *Phi Delta Kappan*, *65*, 397-400.

Walberg, H. (1998, June 3). Personal communication with author.

5 School-Family Partnerships

*Evanthia N. Patrikakou, Roger P. Weissberg, and Michelle I. Rubenstein**

Parent involvement has surfaced during the recent years as an important influence on a child's schooling. Researchers and policymakers compellingly emphasize the importance of making parent involvement a priority in American education. Research has provided mounting evidence that parent involvement plays a crucial role in a student's academic progress [Dauber & Epstein 1993; Eccles & Harold 1996; Keith 1993; Patrikakou 1996, 1997; Reynolds & Walberg 1991, 1992], and policymakers included parent participation in the National Educational Goals of 2000, supported by all 50 governors. Goal 8 states that, "By the year 2000, every school will promote partnerships that will increase parental involvement and participation promoting the social, emotional, and academic growth of children" [National Education Goals Panel 1995, p. 13].

From the onset of the child's life, the parent-child relationship is one of the most profound catalysts of social, emotional, and cognitive development. From the critical first attachment of the child to the parents to the later years of adolescent development, parents—through their behaviors, attitudes, and parenting practices—exert an enormous influence on the child's social, emotional, and cognitive growth [Parke & Buriel 1998]. For example, a toddler's social and language development is influenced

---

* This paper was supported, in part, by a grant from the Laboratory for Student Success at Temple University, Center for Research in Human Development and Education. Correspondence about this manuscript may be sent to Dr. Eva Patrikakou at the Department of Psychology (M/C 285), The University of Illinois at Chicago, 1007 West Harrison Street, Chicago, IL 60607-7137.

strongly by the nature of the relationship she has with her parents. Even during adolescence when the views of parents and adolescents seem to differ on several issues, conflicts frequently facilitate further social and emotional development [Holmbeck & O'Donnell 1991].

Families are the first socialization system in which parenting styles interact with the child's development, and through this interaction children grow into social maturity [Santrock 1996]. Once children enter the stage of formal schooling, strong parental influences extend to the child's academic progress. Parenting styles continue to have a great impact on the child's academic achievement even in late adolescence [Dornbusch et al. 1987], and parent attitudes and behaviors also continue to have a great impact on the adolescents' academic and life choices [Patrikakou 1996, 1997; Reynolds & Walberg 1991, 1992; Steinberg et al. 1992].

Numerous studies have indicated that parent involvement in children's education is the catalyst predicting student success from preschool through high school [Reynolds 1989; Steinberg 1996]. The importance of parent involvement at school becomes even more pronounced when one reviews results from studies examining early school adjustment of low-income, minority children. The striking majority of studies indicate that from the very early stages of schooling, parent participation enhances academic achievement and school adjustment [Reynolds & Bezruczko 1993]. The role of parent involvement has been identified as a key component of effective early childhood prevention programs since the creation of Head Start and Follow Through [Olmsted 1991; Schweinhart & Weikart 1988; Zigler & Muenchow 1992]. Specifically, effective interventions include parent activities in their repertoire and, therefore, "allow children greater opportunities to develop scholastic and social skills necessary for sustained [intervention] effects" [Reynolds 1994, p. 14]. By including parent involvement activities, intervention programs enhance children's adjustment in primary grades and, because such adjustment is crucial for later school success, give children a better chance for achieving long-term cognitive, academic, and social benefits. All this evidence makes the inclusion of parents, especially in early childhood in intervention school programs, imperative.

Due to the mounting evidence that emphasizes the important role that parents can play in their child's academic, emotional, and social development, as well as their impact on the effects of school interventions, researchers and educators alike have been calling for systematic efforts to increase parent involvement in children's education. Nevertheless, parent involvement still remains largely an "untapped resource" [Moles 1993].

Parents are the obvious participants in "parent involvement," but teachers are an equally important element in the equation. The question, "Which is more important for a student's academic progress and social adjustment, the school or the family?" is rhetorical. Researchers recognize the overlapping influence of the two institutions, and theoretical as well as empirical models indicate that both school and home play an influential role in the development of a child [Bronfenbrenner 1986; Epstein 1987; Patrikakou 1996]. As Epstein [1992, p. 1] noted, the term school-family partnerships should be used instead of parent involvement, as it "emphasizes that the two institutions share major responsibilities for children's education."

In the present chapter, we will (1) present a broader theoretical framework in which school-family partnerships can be conceptualized, (2) summarize parent and teacher views on the most important aspects for the development and maintenance of school-family partnerships, (3) review a sample of school-family partnership programs, and (4) discuss the implications of this analysis for future policy and practice.

A Theoretical Framework of School-Family Partnerships

> Whatever the socioeconomic level, ethnic group, or type of family structure, we have yet to meet a parent who is not deeply committed to ensuring the well-being of his or her child. Most families are doing the best they can under difficult circumstances; what we should try to do is change the circumstances, not the families. [Bronfenbrenner 1979, p. 849]

According to Bronfenbrenner's ecological theory [1979, 1986, 1989], it is the broader environment with its values, regulations, and traditions, that serves as a dynamic force in development. The ecological theory provides one way to conceptualize interactions between home and school and how they relate to academic achievement. Within this framework, all the different sources that affect academic achievement are interacting constantly with the characteristics of the individual, forming circles of influence around him/her (see Figure 5-1). The individual is in the center of the system, the family follows in the next concentric circle, with school, peers, and other community influences to be found next. All influences experienced by the individual in any given setting (e.g., home or school) belong to what is called the *microsystem.* Influences and interrelations among microsystems are depicted in the second level, which is called *mesosystem.* Therefore, the mesosystem is composed of interacting microsystems. Every time an individual enters a new microsystem, the mesosystem expands to include the new entry. All participants, other than the individual, in interacting settings are part of the interconnections depicted in the mesosystem. The structure of the mesosystem is where family and school, especially parents and teachers, interact to contribute to the child's academic, emotional, and social development, and it is within this system that school-family partnerships can be cultivated. The existence of strong reciprocal links between home and school can have a positive influence on a child's development, whereas the lack of such links may become a risk factor in development [Weissberg & Greenberg 1998].

The next level is the *exosystem,* in which influences from broader social groups and institutions (e.g., school board or community services) are included. While these settings do not include the individual directly, events occurring within them may have an effect on the child. For example, changes in school policies may significantly affect a child's schooling and progress, and alter interactions among microsystems and mesosystems.

Finally, one encounters the outermost level, the *macrosystem,* which is where values, traditions, ideologies, cultural characteristics, and institutional patterns can be found. Influences within this system include the effects of major historical events (e.g., wars) or more gradual socioeconomic changes, such as the globalization of the economy. These broader issues

Figure 5-1. An Ecological Perspective of School-Family Partnerships

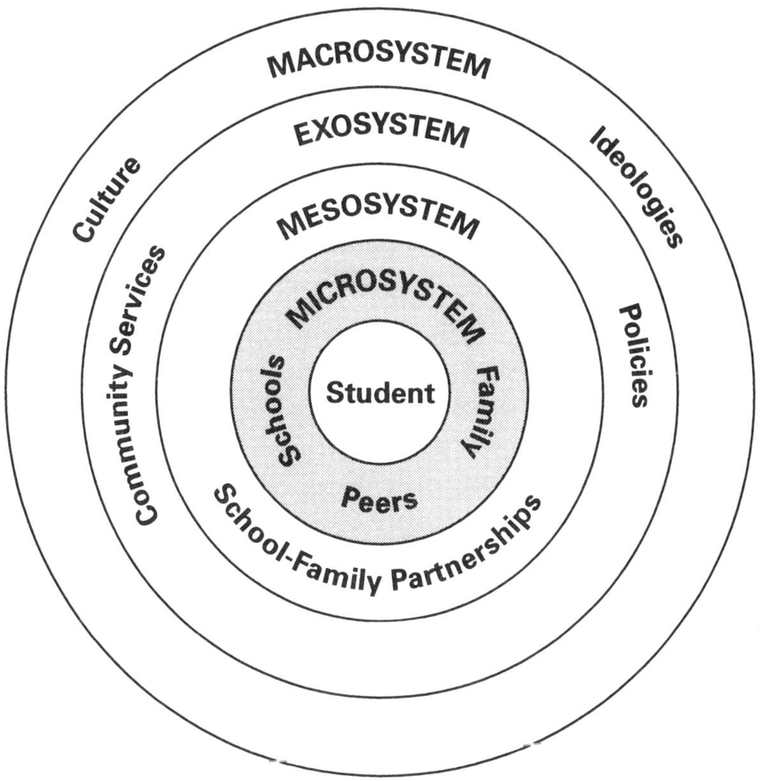

can have a great impact on lower systems, including the mesosystem where school-family partnerships are to be found. For example, if a global economic crisis trickles down to the U.S. economy, causing significant budget cuts for school programs, school-family partnership programming, as well as other parent involvement initiatives, will be affected by receiving smaller funds.

Within this framework, school-family partnerships can be conceptualized as sociological influences that affect a child's academic and socioemotional development. Specifically, two components can be identified within this set of systems: the sociological component, which consists of various forms of parent and teacher beliefs and practices with regard to school family partnerships, and the psychological component, which concentrates on the perception of such parental influences by the student, as well as the individual's psychological characteristics.

The student is in the center of the system and, in general, psychological factors are to be found within the circle of the individual, whereas sociological influences are represented in outer circles. The filtering circle around the individual represents the child's perceptions of various events which, in accordance with previous theoretical work (e.g., Eccles [1983] and Eccles and Harold [1996]), are instrumental in influencing outcomes related to academic achievement [Patrikakou 1996, 1997].

Another reason that this framework provides a good fit for conceptualizing school-family partnerships is the emphasis developmental theorists have placed on the importance of the relationships between settings such as home and school. Almost two decades ago, before the issue of parent involvement became so popular, Bronfenbrenner [1979] recognized the increasing isolation of school from home, relating it to the progressive decline of achievement scores. In addition, he noted that this alienation between the home and school environments had an effect not only on the academic progress of children, but also on their socioemotional development, citing increasing rates in child delinquency. What was then speculation based just on the "convergence between incomplete theory and incomplete data" [p. 848], today is unfortunately a confirmed hypothesis on sad statistics.

School and family are two of the most important contexts of child development and by bringing them closer, we will provide students with a structure and a continuity that fosters for their cognitive and socioemotional competence. In Bronfenbrenner's words [1979, p. 848], "The developmental potential of a child-rearing setting [family or school] is increased as a function of the number of supportive links between that setting and other contexts involving the child or persons responsible for his or her care. Such interconnections may take the form of shared activities, two-way communication, and information provided in each setting about the other."

Closely related to the ecological framework is the notion of "overlapping influence" proposed by Epstein [1987, 1992]. She places home and school influences in spheres that, although related, can be brought together or pulled apart depending on practices applied in each environment. Factors such as the child's developmental changes, as well as environmental ones, are the crucial mediators that bring the spheres closer or alienate them. In this model, as in that of the ecological theory, the child plays a central role. It is assumed that students are not passive recipients of the benefits that a good home-school relationship can provide. Instead, they are considered active players working towards their success at school. When home and school work as partners, both emphasizing the importance of education, and facilitating and coordinating necessary resources to assist students in their efforts, the "student's own work is legitimized by this process of mutual support" [Epstein 1992, p. 3]. Disparity between home and school can impede children's development, learning, and academic performance [Dauber & Epstein 1993], while continuity between family interactions and classroom interactions lead to higher achievement [Hansen 1986].

The influences of school and family are interrelated and can reinforce each other's efforts to help children succeed in school. In school-family partnerships parents, teachers, and students are brought to work together towards the shared goal of the child's success. Overall, parents and teachers seem to agree that parent involvement is an essential ingredient in school success [Weissberg et al. 1997]; however, parent involvement still remains an unexploited resource [Moles 1993]. Eliminating this discrepancy between attitudes and action is a major goal of school-family partnership programs. With respect to specific issues, do parents and teachers see eye to eye on how parent involvement can be implemented and the barriers lifted? The following two sections attempt to paint the picture from the parents' and the teachers' perspective.

School-Family Partnerships from the Parent's Perspective: Benefits and Barriers

> "It is easy for me to be involved in her education because her teacher lets me know what is going on, what she has learned, and what she needs to learn." (A parent from an inner-city Chicago Public School)

One of the goals of school-family partnerships is to increase the involvement of parents in their child's education. Although parents seem to have generally positive attitudes toward their child's school and consider their goals to be similar with those that teachers have for students, parents believe that schools can do more to involve them in their child's learning [Epstein 1986]. It is important to note that parent attitudes are highly correlated with the school's practices to involve parents; parents who believe that the school is actively trying to involve them in their child's education are more likely to consider the school a good one and report that the school has a positive climate [Dauber & Epstein 1993]. In general, parents tend to give higher ratings to teachers and schools when they perceive that they are invited to participate in their children's education frequently [Epstein 1986].

For school-family efforts to be effective and therefore successful in increasing parent involvement, schools must assess, among other things, the characteristics and the needs of the parent population they serve [Epstein 1995]. In this way, starting points for intervention can be identified and discussion on needs and implementation of school-family-partnership activities can be triggered [Epstein 1995]. One way to guide assessment efforts and assist in a more comprehensive structuring of school-family partnerships is the use of parent and parent-involvement typologies. Using these conceptual organizers, schools can target various levels of school-family partnerships, assess current practices at each level, and focus on areas of weakness with more precision.

There have been many typologies of parents and parent involvement in education [Bauch 1994]. Parent-involvement typologies have been widely used in research and program development efforts, whereas parent typologies—although important elements in the school-family partnership equation—do not appear that often.

Parent Typologies

What is a parent typology? It is a way of categorizing parental attitudes and actions in regard to school and educational activities. Usually such behaviors are based on the parent's own experience with schooling and the educational system, current level of functioning, as well as other events that may affect a parent's involvement in the child's education. Berger [1995] offers the following parent typology: (1) Parents who systematically avoid participating in school activities, (2) parents who participate after some encouragement from the school, (3) parents who readily respond to a school's invitation, (4) parents who enjoy school involvement and take initiatives, and (5) parents who enjoy exercising power and can dominate school activities.

Another parent typology is used by the School-Family Partnership Project at the University of Illinois at Chicago [Patrikakou et al. 1998]. This categorization is based both on the parents' skills and life events that may influence their participation in their child's education (microsystem), as well as their school-family attitudes and practices (mesosystem). Although not mutually exclusive, the following four parent types have been identified:

- Parents who have positive attitudes toward, and the necessary skills for, active and constructive involvement in their children's education.

- Parents who want to help their children, but need some guidance, support, and reassurance to participate effectively in their children's education.

- Parents who would like to participate in their child's education, but who face a basic skills barrier, such as illiteracy or limited knowledge of English. Once the issue is addressed through special programs (e.g., adult literacy) they can then become more actively involved in their children's schoolwork.

- Parents who have serious personal problems (e.g., substance abuse) that interfere with their daily functioning and impede them from participating in their child's education prior to resolving those issues.

Clearly, programs geared to attract the participation of one group of parents will not necessarily meet the needs of another. Recognizing the target audience of a given program and making an effort to ultimately reach all types of parents is critical. This may require additional program components or a merging of several programs.

Parent Involvement Typologies

Parent involvement typologies are descriptive of the role that parents can play in various environments, such as home and school. Although typologies vary on certain aspects, it is important to note that there is a significant overlap among them. Two typologies that offer different levels of parent participation and of how schools can facilitate different and more extensive forms of involvement are those of Bloom [1992] and Epstein [1987, 1995].

According to Bloom's [1992] typology, parents can play seven roles along three levels. Specifically, the three levels are involvement, participation, and advocacy. Within the first level a parent can assume the type of "spectator" where he/she monitors the child's school progress but does not actively facilitate the learning process at home, nor does he/she reinforce the school routine and curriculum. It is the parent as "teacher" who actively assists the child with homework and establishes learning routines at home.

The second level of participation encompasses three types of parent involvement. The first, "parent-as-accessory-volunteer," provides assistance to the teacher in the form of a chaperone for field trips, conducting fundraisers, or other nonclassroom support services. The second type, "parent-as-educational-volunteer," involves parents as teacher-aides in the classroom checking homework, reading to the children, or tutoring them. The third type within the participation level is "parent-as-employee," in which a parent is paid by the school to perform any of the above-mentioned activities in this level.

The third level of involvement is advocacy. Within this category, parents can play an important role in administrative procedures and decisions by participating in school councils, organizing other parents, or evaluating the results of programmatic changes. The second role that parents can assume within this level is that of "mover-and-shaker," where a parent can initiate, implement, monitor, and evaluate basic structural changes of school systems on a local or wider basis.

Epstein's typology [1987, 1995] is the most well-known, as it is frequently cited in various studies in the broader area of school-family partnerships. The six types of involvement, or "six types of caring" as she calls them [Epstein 1995, p. 704] are listed below:

- **Type 1: Parenting.** The basic obligations of the family, such as establishing positive home conditions to encourage school success.
- **Type 2: Communicating.** The communication between home and school that facilitates the flow of information about school curriculum and the child's progress.
- **Type 3: Volunteering.** The recruitment of parents to act as volunteers to help and support school initiatives and functions.
- **Type 4: Learning at Home.** Parental involvement at home, such as helping children with homework and other learning activities, based on the information schools provide.
- **Type 5: Decisionmaking.** The active parent involvement in school decisions and extend advocacy to lobbying for school improvements.
- **Type 6: Collaborating with the community.** The identification and dissemination of a network of available resources and services in the community to assist parents and schools in their efforts to better their children's education.

As mentioned at the beginning of the present section, typologies can serve as effective guides for needs assessment and as useful tools to identify the strengths and limitations of home-school interactions (mesosystem). Based on the various parent-involvement typologies, several measurement instruments have been developed (for example see Epstein & Salinas [1993], Hickman et al. [1995], and the School-Family Partnership Project [1997]). Such instruments assist schools in evaluating the present status of school-family partnership activities and target specific areas of involvement for intervention. These measurement tools can also be used to monitor a program's effectiveness and guide future modifications. In general, typologies are necessary theoretical tools, extremely helpful in assisting researchers and practitioners to organize their thinking and work in the field of school-family partnerships. But in practice, what challenges does reality hold that can interfere with the implementation of parent participation activities? What are some of the dynamics developed within microsystems and between microsystems that affect the mesosystem's home-school interactions? The following section presents what beliefs and barriers parents identify as they try to be involved in their child's education.

Beliefs and Barriers

> Families today are just not like we used to know them...times and people have changed but the public school system hasn't changed...we need a system that fits new needs. (a teacher cited in Leitch & Tangri [1988])

Although a striking majority of parents and teachers agree that parent involvement is an important element in education [Weissberg et al. 1997], actual parent involvement "is surprisingly minimal" [Swap 1993, p. 13]. What contributes to this discrepancy between beliefs and practice? During the past two decades there has been a rapid change in family and related societal demographics. For example, a high percentage of mothers of school-aged children are working out of the home [Berger 1995], single-parent families have doubled since 1970 [Braun & Swap 1987], teen pregnancy has increased dramatically in the past decade [National Center of Health Statistics 1991], the number of families living in poverty has increased [Braun & Swap 1987], and a significant increase in linguistic and cultural diversity of students has taken place, which requires special attention [Berger 1995]. These rapidly changing demographics have made it more difficult for parents to participate in school activities and in their child's education in general.

The three major barriers that parents identify are time, and lack of knowledge of what is expected of them and of what specific ways they can help their children at home, and various sociocultural biases in the school environment.

Time

Time seems to be a major barrier impeding parents from participating in school activities and assisting their children with schoolwork at home. In a survey by the School-Family Partnership Project [Weissberg et al. 1997] of more than 650 families whose children attended Chicago public schools, parents reported lack of time or schedule conflicts as the two most important barriers of parent involvement; in general, 55% felt that parent activities at school are at inconvenient times.

With the increase in single-parent households and the dramatic change in the work force, with mothers of school-aged children entering it in great numbers [Berger 1995], time has become a valuable commodity for parents who struggle to make ends meet. It is important that schools recognize and adapt to this need by surveying parents about convenient times for activities, offering alternative means of communication, and most of all, understanding that it is not the parent's fault if he or she cannot participate due to employment, family responsibilities, or other time restrictions. For example, parents reported having difficulty attending parent-teacher conferences during the day due to inflexible work schedules. Whenever schools made adjustments to accommodate parents' time restrictions, parents were responsive, offering greater cooperation and support for teachers and the school. As Epstein [1986] indicated, parents are appreciative of any parent involvement and outreach efforts schools make, and they give high marks to teachers who incorporate parent involvement in their regular educational activities.

Child care responsibilities also influence the parents' capacity to participate in their child's education. More than 80% of parents participating in a school-family partnership survey [Weissberg et al. 1997] reported that they had more than two children living at home. If it is hard for parents to attend the parent-teacher conference for one of their children, it is self-evident that the degree of difficulty increases tremendously for two or more. Espinoza [1988] reported that many families did not have child care resources or a live-in caregiver, which imposed a big obstacle for their participation in school activities. Alternative child care and after-school programs offered by community organizations can offer parents a helping hand so they can attend school events. Berger [1995] also suggested that schools should provide some form of child care on days that parent participation is essential, such as for parent-teacher conferences. In that way parents can have the opportunity to participate and actively contribute in their child's education.

Lack of Knowledge

An important ingredient to parent involvement and successful school-family partnership practices is consistent communication between parents and teachers [D'Angelo & Adler 1991; Dornbush & Ritter 1988; Patrikakou et al. 1998]. Most parents report that they would like to know what their children are learning at school and how they can be involved in their education [Epstein 1992]. Parents feel that schools should inform them about their curricula as well as about ways to assist their children at home. Chavkin and Williams [1987] reported that 90% of parents believe that parent involvement in their children's school would increase if they had more information and understood better what their children were learning. Epstein [1992] found that 90% of parents of elementary and middle-school students believe that the school should tell them how to get involved and help their children at home. Even providing parents with general information can be sufficient to trigger noticeable change. Dornbusch and Ritter [1988] reported that by merely informing parents through a newsletter that parent participation is associated with higher academic achievement, attendance rates at school events increased dramatically.

Biases and the School Environment

Ethnic and cultural diversity is increasing in the United States and the ability of schools to prepare minority students for full participation in American life and society has been questioned. During the past decade, researchers have investigated the issue of parent participation and differences among various cultural groups [Patrikakou 1997; Steinberg et al. 1992]. The number of children up to 17 years old whose primary language is other than English is expected to triple by the year 2000, and underachievement of minority or "disadvantaged" school children has been extensively discussed (see, for example, International Academy of Education [1995]).

Disadvantaged children often experience adverse conditions in a variety of settings such as poverty and lack of resources in the family, school, or the community. In addition, parents of such children often have limited education and negative personal experiences with the educational system, leading them to mistrust and often fear the school environment [Menacker et al. 1988]. Such attitudes pose a serious obstacle in parent involvement and may, furthermore, influence the children's perceptions and their school performance. To make matters worse, teachers tend to communicate with parents primarily when there is a problem at school. This association between school and bad news only reinforces the parents reluctance to get involved and fuels their defensiveness when dealing with the school system [Moles 1993]

Cultural differences, in general, impose a variety of barriers for school-family partnerships and increase the perception gap between parents and teachers. Linguistic differences that include not only English as a second language, but also nonmainstream English dialects, can lead to various problems, such as paternalism and lower expectations for disadvantaged parents and their children [Moles 1993]. By expanding the opportunities for positive interaction, remediating negative perceptions, and increasing parent and teacher skills on school-family partnerships, the process of regaining faith in education and the school system can begin. The development of positive, trusting attitudes toward the school is a slow process, however, that requires constant attention, systematic and methodical structuring, frequent evaluation, and most importantly, the school's commitment to establish and maintain a constructive partnership with parents. Teachers and schools also identify several issues that can restrict their involvement in school-family partnerships. The following section presents what teachers identify as important issues when discussing parent involvement outreach efforts.

School-Family Partnerships from the Teacher's Perspective: Benefits and Barriers

> Our school can extend itself more to the parent. Sometimes the parents need a little push or motivation. If the parent can't come to the school to support their child, we must go to them. (a Chicago public school teacher)

Successful implementation of parent involvement in schools depends on teacher perceptions and practices on the issue. "The teacher is the glue that holds the [school-family] partnership together" [Moore 1991, p. 19]. However, little has been done to explore the relationship between teachers' perceptions of parent involvement behaviors and student outcomes, such as academic achievement and social adjustment.

Teacher perceptions of parent involvement not only affect the teachers' participation in such programs, but also play an instrumental role in influencing the teacher's relationship with the student. Positive perceptions can promote a "teacher's relationship with students in the way of greater attention or increased expectations for their school success" [Reynolds et al. 1992, p. 616] (also see Kohl, Patrikakou, Weissberg, Reynolds, & Kasprow [1998]). Therefore, understanding the relationship among teacher perceptions, sociodemographic factors, and child outcomes is important not only for the successful implementation of school-family partnerships, but also because teachers' views of the parent's involvement are closely related with the child's daily functioning in the classroom.

An overwhelming majority of teachers agree that parent involvement contributes to more successful students and a more positive school climate. However, only 32% feel that it is their responsibility to involve families [Connors & Epstein 1994], and only half believe that they can change parent behaviors [Dornbusch & Ritter 1988; Epstein 1992; Epstein & Dauber 1991]. This indicates that teachers do not perceive themselves as effective agents of change and, therefore, may not be actively involved in parent involvement efforts. Since they don't believe they can improve parent participation, teachers may not contribute adequately to this cause.

Training

The reluctance on the part of the teachers to actively involve parents may be partially due to insufficient training in developing the necessary skills [Chavkin & Williams 1989; Moore 1992]. The role of teachers has changed, and current societal trends call for them to work not only with children but also with adults. Armed only with traditional training, teachers, when out in the field, face problems for which they feel unprepared. Specific courses targeting the issues of parent involvement and school-family partnerships should be offered in undergraduate and graduate programs to assist future educators redefine their professional role by acquiring necessary skills for being effective partners [Epstein 1995].

Teachers themselves report that additional training on the issue of parental involvement is necessary in order for parental involvement efforts to be implemented successfully and for teachers to learn how to better connect with their students' families [Connors & Epstein 1994]. However, as Chavkin and Williams [1989] indicated, in spite of the fact that 87% of teachers and 92% of administrators believe that special training is necessary to work with parents effectively, little teacher training in parent involvement takes place as part of prospective teachers' curriculum. For example, only 4% of the teachers had taken a course on parent involvement as undergraduates, while 37% have had only one class session devoted to the topic [Chavkin & Williams 1989].

As the body of evidence supporting the importance of parent involvement in education grows, the need for teacher colleges to include relevant courses in their required curriculum becomes even more pronounced. Teacher colleges should orient undergraduates to current findings on the importance and benefits of parent participation and provide them with strategies to reach out to parents more effectively and make the most out of this important resource [Rich 1988]. In addition, in-service training and relevant support should be offered to practicing teachers to provide them with the opportunity to enhance their skills in involving parents and effectively utilize this significant agent of improvement.

Urbanism

Teachers working in urban areas are especially in need of additional skills for working with high-risk families [Moore 1992]. Teachers in urban schools report that, although they want parents to be involved in several learning activities, parents do not respond accordingly [Epstein 1992; Epstein & Dauber 1991]. Burton [1992a, 1992b] found that teachers in inner-city public schools often display relatively negative attitudes toward parents and school-based programs to support parents. Interestingly, although few schools have specific programs to help parents understand how they can get involved in those learning activities, teachers tend to blame parents for the latter's low level of involvement [Epstein 1992; Epstein & Dauber 1991]. In addition, teachers in inner-city Chapter 1 schools indicate that most parents are not involved in their children's education, and they don't seem to have the intention to be [Dauber & Epstein 1993].

Parent Demographics

As discussed earlier in this chapter, there has been a rapid change in societal demographics in recent years. Teacher perceptions of parents and families seem to be partially influenced by demographic factors, such as the parents' education, SES, or marital status. Not surprisingly, better educated parents receive higher teacher ratings on parental involvement [Epstein 1990]. Initial evidence indicates that other sociodemographic factors, such as the child's age, gender, race, family structure, and/or mobility, are critical in shaping teachers' perceptions of parental involvement. For example, Epstein [1990] noted that teachers do not feel single parents are sufficiently involved in their child's education at home, despite indications that single parents were spending more time than married parents helping their children with homework. In addition, grade level was an important factor in the Epstein [1990] study, as teachers of younger children tend to give parents higher ratings, viewing them as more helpful than did teachers of older students.

Too Much to Do, So Little Time

Although increased parent involvement has major and obvious advantages, from the teachers' perspective, more contact with parents increases teachers' and other school personnel's responsibilities and raises various concerns about time and heavy work load. Both issues need to be addressed to improve teacher perceptions and practices of parent involvement [Becker & Epstein 1982; Burton 1992a; Chavkin & Williams 1989; Moore 1992; Purnell & Gotts 1985]. Teachers feel overburdened, with limited resources available to them and view parent involvement efforts as being outside their expertise [Burton 1992a]. Often, teachers do not know how to involve parents effectively or how to use them as a resource. Consequently, they resist playing a family-related role and may display a negative attitude toward parent involvement efforts. In a teacher's own words, "People seem to want teachers to take on psychologist, counselor, and social worker jobs. If I try to be the best in all, I will no longer be a teacher" [Burton 1992a, p. 41].

The previous two sections examined parent and teacher views on school-family partnerships, and from each side's perspective there are important issues that may interfere with the implementation of school-family partnership programming. The following section presents examples of school-family partnership programs and how they attempt to address some of the issues raised by parents and teachers in order to facilitate the mesosystem's interactions

Bringing Parents and Teachers Together: School-Family Partnership Programs

School-family partnership programs try to bridge differences in perceptions and address practical issues and barriers that emerge when parents enter the education stage as active participants in their children's learning. There is a great variety of programs in the broader area of school-family partnerships that vary tremendously in their scope, strategies, targeted population, and use of evaluation. In this section we will present three programs that try to address some of the barriers raised by parents and teachers as impeding the development of home-school partnerships.

The School-Family Partnership Project at the University of Illinois at Chicago

The School-Family Partnership (SFP) project at the University of Illinois, Chicago, is a federally funded effort through a grant from the Mid-Atlantic Laboratory for Student Success, Center for Research in Human Development and Education at Temple University. The project's mission is to develop and implement strategies and materials that will enhance two-way communication between parents and teachers, as well as increase parent involvement both in home and school learning activities. In this phase, the SFP project targets primarily teachers and parents of elementary-school grades. Based on the theoretical frameworks and empirical findings presented earlier in this chapter, as well as the issues of lack of time, knowledge, training, and the need for the creation of a positive school environment that parents and teachers often raise, the SFP project has identified several essential ingredients of school-family partnership programs that it has integrated in the project's philosophy and scope [Patrikakou & Weissberg 1999]. Although these components also appear in other partnership programs, their integration within a comprehensive theoretical framework, and their inclusive application to the program's strategies and materials, is a relatively new approach. Some of the project's essential elements are outlined below:

- Assessing parents' needs, views, and practices on parent involvement at the beginning of the school year is an essential first step with twofold benefits:

  - it assists teachers to plan their parent outreach more effectively, and

  - it conveys an important message to parents that their perspective is useful and respected by the school.

  Assessment is most productive when it continuously monitors the effectiveness of partnership strategies and use of materials throughout the school year. An end-of-the-year (summative) evaluation will help get closure to the year's efforts as well as provide valuable information for the upcoming year's planning.

- Creating a school environment that welcomes parent involvement and conveying positive attitudes toward school-family partnerships is another important ingredient. In this way, the message that parents are valuable contributors to the child's education can be reinforced for both parents and teachers.

- Providing ongoing training and materials to educators is of paramount importance. It is the striking minority of teacher colleges that offer a course on parent involvement, and therefore, most teachers are underprepared to engage in school-family partnerships [Chavkin & Williams 1989]. Therefore, providing guidance to teachers is key for the success of a school-family initiative. In this way, teacher perceptions regarding roles that parents can play in their children's education can be expanded, and the parent outreach repertoire used by teachers can be enriched significantly.

- Establishing and maintaining a regular two-way (reciprocal) communication between home and school is an essential part of a successful partnership. Parents who perceive teachers to make systematic efforts to communicate with them are more likely to be involved in their child's education both at home and at school [Patrikakou & Weissberg, in press]. Regular home-school communication strengthens the connection between parents and teachers, and facilitates a reciprocal exchange of information that leads to increased benefits for children's learning.

- Offering specific information to parents about ways in which they can be involved in their child's education both at school and at home is a key to keeping parents informed and actively participating in learning activities in which they can engage with their children. By sharing ways with parents in which they can extend learning from the classroom to the home and beyond, their involvement becomes more meaningful, and, in this way, parents can share the learning process with their children and maximize their academic, emotional, and social development.

Based on these important factors [Patrikakou & Weissberg 1999], the School-Family Partnership project has created a series of materials including brochures*, measurement tools, as well as a "Teacher's Guide" to the program's implementation. The guide covers three major areas: home-school communication, parent involvement at home, and parent involvement at school. In addition to a general overview of school-family partnerships, the Guide provides teachers with specifics for each of the three areas, including strategies, their rationale, and ready-to-use materials designed to enhance the degree of the program's implementation and its effectiveness. In this systematic way, the several issues raised by teachers as barriers for school-family partnerships are addressed, and through the use of the program's planning and implementation tools educators can more actively involve parents and maximize the benefits from their interactions with the student's family.

Chicago Child-Parent Center and Expansion Program

The Chicago Child-Parent Center (CCPC) and Expansion Program is an early childhood educational intervention for children at risk for academic underachievement and school failure [Reynolds 1994, 1997, 1998; Reynolds et al. 1990; Reynolds & Bezruczko 1993; Reynolds & Gill 1994]. The program is federally funded through Title 1 of the Elementary and Secondary Education Act, and is the second oldest federally funded early childhood intervention program for disadvantaged children [Reynolds 1994]. The expansion program began in 1967 and there are currently 24 Chicago Child-Parent Centers operated by the Chicago public schools

* For obtaining parent and teacher brochures on the topics of parent-teacher communication, report card sharing, and homework you can contact the Laboratory for Student Success services at 1301 Cecil B. Moore Ave., Philadelphia, PA 19122-6091; telephone: 800/892-5550, visit the LSS website at http://www.temple.edu.lss, or contact the School Family Project at the University of Illinois at Chicago, c/o Dr. Eva Patrikakou, Department of Psychology M/C 285, 1007 West Harrison Street, Chicago, IL 60607-7137; fax: 312/355-0559.

[Reynolds 1997]. This program provides educational and family support services for disadvantaged children and their families and provides a maximum of six years of continuous intervention services from ages 3 to 9. The goal of the program is to foster children's social development, school readiness, and academic achievement. The major focus is the expansion of parent involvement opportunities primarily at school, including classroom volunteer, parent room activities, participation in school activities, and educational and vocational opportunities. Parent participation at least one half-day per week of parent involvement in child-parent center is required.

Program participants displayed higher reading and math achievement as compared to non-CCPC children, and this difference remained significant through eighth grade. Program participants also had significantly fewer incidences of grade retention and special education placement as compared to children in the nonintervention group failure [Reynolds 1994, 1997, 1998; Reynolds et al. 1990].

The CCPC program, with its emphasis on parent involvement at school provides parents with an opportunity to improve their educational and vocational skills, and it creates a school climate that is welcoming for parents, fostering positive relationships between them and teachers. These gains in parent involvement lead to higher parent satisfaction with the quality of their children's schooling and higher academic achievement [Reynolds & Gill 1994]. The implementation of the CCPC program has indicated that by addressing issues such as those described earlier in this chapter (i.e., lack of knowledge, urbanism, and parent demographics) school-family programming can be effective in improving parent involvement attitudes and practices, and in increasing the chances for children's school success.

The School Development Program

One of the most well-known models is Comer's School Development Program (SDP). The goal of the SDP is to strengthen the alliance between parents and teachers and to foster greater continuity between home and school to enhance children's learning and achievement [Comer 1989, Comer & Haynes 1991]. The SDP aims to establish a positive school climate that acknowledges the strengths of all families and facilitates home-school communication [Ascher 1993; Cauce et al. 1987]. The SDP reflects a true partnership approach and emphasizes the shared responsibility of parents and teachers in supporting children's learning. The project began as a collaborative initiative between the Yale Child Study Center and the New Haven Public Schools, and was initially piloted in two public elementary schools in 1968 [Comer 1980]. Currently the SDP program is being implemented in 721 schools throughout the country [Comer et al. 1996].

The SDP utilizes a nine-component process model that includes three mechanisms, three operations, and three guiding principles. The three mechanisms include a School Planning and Management Team (SPMT), a Student and Staff Support Team, and a Parent Program. The School Planning and Management Team is responsible for implementing the three operations that are the creation of a comprehensive school plan, staff development activities, and periodic assessment and modification. The three guiding principles include a "no-fault" approach, consensus decisionmaking (rather than voting), and collaboration among the participants on the SPMT and the principal.

Several studies have demonstrated that program participation is associated with increased academic performance in reading and math, improved behavior and school adjustment, enhanced self-concept, more positive ratings of classroom climate, and decreased parent-teacher conflict [Cauce et al. 1987; Comer 1980; Comer & Haynes 1991].

The SDP assesses a range of issues that parents and teachers feel are important for school-home relations. The program places an emphasis on the communication between parents and educators, and through the "guiding rules" it establishes a well-defined basis for everyone involved in a child's education to work together. It recognizes that well-informed parents can be important contributors to the educational process and in this way it addresses the issue of lack of knowledge that many parents often raise with regards to helping their child with schoolwork.

All three programs that were described above attempted to address some of the issues affecting home-school relationships. The School-Family Partnership program targets primarily teachers and works toward remediating their concerns about training, time, and the changes in parent demographics. The program also addresses two of the major points raised by parents: the school climate and the lack of knowledge of what is taking place at school, and the ways in which they can assist their children achieve. The Chicago Child-Parent Center and Expansion Program targets parents and offers them opportunities for active school participation, as well as educational and vocational training. In this way, the program's training improves parenting skills and keeps parents informed about ways they can be involved in school activities. The third program presented in this section of the chapter, the School Development Program, calls for changes in the school's climate and offers a structure within which positive changes can occur. The program offers opportunities for positive interactions among the adults involved in a child's education and places an emphasis on the importance of communication and home-school collaboration.

Concluding Remarks and Future Directions

School-family partnerships can serve as facilitators within a child's mesosystem where the two most important microsystems in a student's life (family and school) interact. Effective home-school relationships take a long time to form and become established. The process of developing positive, trusting attitudes toward the school is a slow one and requires commitment, systematic planning, and persistence. Based on theoretical and empirical advances during recent decades we have a better understanding of the important factors that contribute to the formation of an effective school-family partnership program, as well as their consequences.

In the present chapter, we presented a broader theoretical framework in which school-family partnerships can be conceptualized, we summarized parent and teacher views on several important aspects for the development and maintenance of school-family partnerships, and we reviewed a sample of school-family partnership programs that attempt to address the issues raised by parents and teachers. It is important to note however, that although certain elements of partnerships are common across programs and school-family activities, each school constitutes a unique environment with specific needs and chemistry between parents and teachers. Therefore, prior to the implementation of any kind of partnership program, it is imperative that an initial assessment be conducted to evaluate current practices and areas that require improvement. In this way, the activities of a school-family partnerships program will be responsive to specific needs and will address issues with more precision, increasing the probability of success.

For school-family partnerships to produce long-lasting positive effects for parents, teachers, and students, several changes must occur. Schools need to view parents as valuable allies and prioritize school-family partnerships as a necessary ingredient for student success. School-family partnership programs can guide parents and teachers through the process, enhance communication, increase parent involvement, and, ultimately, affect student achievement positively. But for this mesosystem process to occur and succeed, exosystem changes should take place. School-family partnerships cannot exist in isolation. There are parts of a multisystem that is affected by other lower and higher level systems. For example, although state and federal policies that encourage school-family partnerships may exist (exosystem), the mechanics and funding support for such policy implementation are lacking. Specifically, if teacher colleges continue not to include parent-involvement training as part of their curriculum, the capacity of prospective teachers to implement parent-involvement policies effectively will be diminished. If training is not offered for those educators already in the field, how can they respond to the call for increases in parent involvement? The skills that teachers need to interact successfully with parents are not innate, but must be demonstrated and modeled as an integral part of their training. Therefore, exosystem changes must occur to facilitate the implementation of school-family partnerships in the mesosystem.

Parent involvement and school-family partnerships have emerged as crucial factors in enhancing children's development and education. But as Cole noted, "Ideas are only as important as what you do with them" [Bronfenbrenner 1979, p. vii]. School-family partnership programs have illustrated ways in which parents and teachers can work together constructively and maximize the benefits for children's education. By prioritizing such programming in schools, as well as initiating change in other systems that affect the school-family partnership process, we can put this great idea of parent involvement into practice.

References

Ascher, C. (1993). *Changing schools for urban students: The School Development Program, Accelerated Schools, and Success For All.* Washington, DC: Office of Educational Research and Improvement. ERIC Document Reproduction Service No. ED 355 313.

Bauch, J. P. (1994). Categories of parent involvement. *School Community Journal, 4* (1), 53-60.

Becker, H. J., & Epstein, J. L. (1982). Parent involvement: A study of teacher practices. *The Elementary School Journal, 83*, 85-102.

Berger, E. H. (1995). *Parents as partners in education* (4th ed.). Columbus, OH: Prentice-Hall.

Bloom, J. (1992). *Parenting our schools: A hands-on guide to educational reform.* Toronto, ON: Little Brown and Company.

Braun, L., & Swap, S. (1987). *Building home-school partnerships with America's changing families.* Boston: Wheelock College.

Bronfenbrenner, U. (1979). Contexts of child rearing: Problems and prospects. *American Psychologist, 34* (10), 844-850.

Bronfenbrenner, U. (1986). Ecology of the family as a context for human development: Research perspectives. *Developmental Psychology, 22*, 723-742.

Bronfenbrenner, U. (1989). Ecological systems theory. In R. Vasta (Ed.), *Annals of Child Development, 6.* Greenwich, CT: JAI Press.

Burton, C. B. (1992a). Family as a focus for early education reform: The implications of public school teacher perspectives. *Journal of Research in Childhood Education, 7*, 37-45.

Burton, C.B. (1992b). Defining family-centered early education: Beliefs of public school, child care, and Head Start teachers. *Early Education and Development, 3*, 45-49.

Cauce, A.M., Comer, J. P., & Schwartz, B. A. (1987). Long-term effects of a system oriented school prevention program. *American Journal of Orthopsychiatry, 57*, 127-131.

Chavkin, N. F., & Williams, D. L. (1987). Enhancing parent involvement: Guidelines for access to an important resource for school administrators. *Education and Urban Society, 19* (2), 164-184.

Chavkin, N. F., & Williams, D. L. (1989). Low-income parents' attitudes toward parent involvement in education. *Journal of Sociology and Social Welfare, 16*, 17-28.

Comer, J. P. (1980). *School power: Implications of an intervention project.* New York: Free Press.

Comer, J. P. (1989). Parent participation in the schools: The School Development Program as a model. *Family Resource Coalition Report, 2*, 4-14.

Comer, J. P., & Haynes, N. M. (1991). Parent involvement in schools: An ecological approach. *Elementary School Journal, 91*, 271-277.

Comer, J. P., Haynes, N. M., Joyner, E. T., & Ben-Avie, M. (1996). *Rallying the whole village: The Comer process for reforming education.* New York: Teachers College Press.

Connors, L. J., & Epstein, J. L. (1994). *Taking stock. Views of teachers, parents, and students on school, family, and community partnerships in high schools.* (Research Report). Washington, DC: Office of Educational Research and Improvement, ERIC Document Reproduction Service No. ED 380 524.

D'Angelo, D. A., & Adler, C. R. (1991). Chapter I: A catalyst for improving parent involvement. *Phi Delta Kappan, 72*(5), 350-354.

Dauber, S. L., & Epstein, J. L. (1993). Parents' attitudes and practices of involvement in inner-city elementary and middle schools. In N. F. Chavkin (Ed.), *Families and schools in a pluralistic society* (pp. 53-71). Albany, NY: State University of New York Press.

Dornbusch, S. M., & Ritter, P. L. (1988). Parents of high school students: A neglected resource. *Educational Horizons, 66*(2), 75-77.

Dornbusch, S. M., & Ritter, P. L., Leiderman, D. F., Roberts, D. F., & Fraleigh, M. J. (1987). The relation of parenting style to adolescent school performance. *Child Development, 58*, 1244-1257.

Eccles, J. (1983). Expectancies, values, and academic behaviors. In J. T. Spence (Ed.), *Achievement and achievement motives* (pp. 75-145). San Francisco, CA: Freeman.

Eccles, J. S., & Harold, R. D. (1996). Family involvement in children's and adolescents' schooling. In A. Booth & J. F. Dunn (Eds.) *Family-school links* (pp. 3-24). Mahwah, NJ: Lawrence Erlbaum.

Epstein, J. L. (1986). Parents' reactions to teacher practices of parent involvement. *Elementary School Journal, 86*(3), 277-294.

Epstein, J. L. (1987). Parent involvement: What research says to administrators. *Education and Urban Society, 19*(2), 119-135.

Epstein, J. L. (1990). Single parents and the schools: Effects of marital status on parent and teacher interactions. In M. T. Hallinan, D. M. Klein, & J. Glass (Eds.), *Change in societal institutions* (pp. 91-121). New York: Plenum.

Epstein, J. L. (1992). *School and family partnerships: Report No. 6*. Baltimore, MD: Johns Hopkins University, Center on Families Communities, Schools and Children's Learning, ERIC Document Reproduction Service No. ED 343 715.

Epstein, J. L. (1995). School/family/community partnerships: Caring for the children we share. *Phi Delta Kappan, 76*(9), 701-712.

Epstein, J. L., & Dauber, S. L. (1991). School programs and teacher practices of parent involvement in inner-city elementary and middle schools. *Elementary School Journal, 91*, 289-303.

Epstein, J. L., & Salinas, K. C. (1993). *School and family partnerships: Surveys and summaries*. Baltimore, MD: John Hopkins University, Center on Families, Communities, Schools and Children's Learning.

Espinoza, R. (1988). Working parents, employers, and schools. *Educational Horizons, 66*(2), 63-65.

Hansen, T. D. (1986). An eco-structural intervention in family-school conflict. *Journal of Family Psychotherapy, 7*, 23-30.

Hickman, C. W., Greenwood, G., & Miller, D. (1995). High school parent involvement: Relationships with achievement, grade level, SES, and gender. *Journal of Research and Development in Education, 28*, 125-133.

Holmbeck, G., & O'Donnell, K. (1991). Discrepancies between perceptions of decision making and behavioral autonomy. In R. Paikoff (Ed.) *Shared views of the family during adolescence* (pp. 51-70). San Francisco: Jossey-Bass.

International Academy of Education. (1995). Families and schools. A handbook for practitioners [Special issue]. *School Community Journal, 5.*

Keith, T. Z., Keith, P. B., Troutman, G. C., Bickley, P. G., Trivetter, P. S., & Singh, K. (1993). Does parental involvement affect eighth-grade student achievement? Structural analysis of national data. *School Psychology Review, 22*, 474-496.

Kohl, G. O., Patrikakou, E. N., Weissberg, R. P., Reynolds, A. J., & Kasprow, W. J. (1998). Teacher perceptions of parent involvement in urban elementary schools: Sociodemographic and school adjustment correlates. Manuscript submitted for publication.

Leitch, M. L., & Tangri, S. S. (1988). Barriers to home-school collaboration. *Educational Horizons, 66*(2), 70-74.

Menacker, J., Hurwitz, E., & Weldon, W. (1988). Parent-teacher cooperation in schools serving the urban poor. *The Clearing House, 62*, 108-112.

Moles, O. C. (1993). Collaboration between schools and disadvantaged parents: Obstacles and openings. In N. F. Chavkin (Ed.), *Families and schools in a pluralistic society* (p. 21-49). Albany, NY: State University of New York Press.

Moore, D. R. (1992). The case for parent and community involvement. In G. A. Hess, Jr. (Ed.), *Empowering teachers and parents: School restructuring through the eyes of anthropologists* (pp. 131-155). Westport, CT: Bergin & Garvey.

Moore, E.K. (1991). Improving schools through parental involvement. *Principal, 71*, 19-20.

National Center for Health Statistics. (1991). *Advance report of final natality statistics, 1989. Monthly Vital Statistics Report, 40.* Hyattsville, MD: Public Health Service.

National Education Goals Panel. (1995). *The national education goals report. Building a nation of learners.* Washington, DC: Government Printing Office.

Olmsted, P. P. (1991). Parent involvement in elementary education: Findings and suggestions from the follow through program. *Elementary School Journal, 91*(3), 221-231.

Parke, R. D. & Buriel, R. (1998). Socialization in the family: Ethnic and ecological perspectives. In W. Damon (Series Ed.) & I.E. Sigel & K. A. Renninger (Vol. Eds.). *Handbook of child psychology: Vol. 4. Child psychology in practice* (5th ed., pp. 463-552). New York: Wiley & Sons.

Patrikakou, E. N. (1996). Investigating the academic achievement of adolescents with learning disabilities: A structural model approach. *Journal of Educational Psychology, 88*, 435-450.

Patrikakou, E. N. (1997). A model of parental attitudes and the academic achievement of adolescents. *Journal of Research and Development in Education, 31*, 7-26.

Patrikakou, E. N., & Weissberg, R. P. (February 3, 1999). *Seven P's to promote school-family partnership efforts. Education Week*, 34 and 36.

Patrikakou, E. N., & Weissberg, R. P (in press). Parents' perceptions of teacher outreach and parent involvement in children's education. *Journal of Prevention and Intervention in the Community.*

Patrikakou, E. N., Weissberg, R. P., Shanahan, T., Anderson, L., & Rubenstein, M. (1998, April). Strategies to enhance school-family partnerships. Paper presented at the American Educational Research Association Conference in San Diego, CA.

Purnell, R. F., & Gotts, E. E. (1985). Preparation and the role of school personnel for effective school-family relations. (Research Report). ERIC Document Reproduction Service No. ED 262 000.

Reynolds, A. J. (1989). A structural model of first-grade outcomes for an urban, low socioeconomic status, minority population. *Journal of Educational Psychology, 81*, 594-603.

Reynolds, A. J (1994). Effects of a preschool plus follow-on intervention for children at risk. *Developmental Psychology, 30*, 1-17.

Reynolds, A. J. (1997). *A longitudinal study of extended early childhood intervention.* Madison, WI: Institute for Research on Poverty.

Reynolds, A. J. (1998). The Chicago Child-Parent Centers and Expansion Program: A study of extended childhood intervention. In J. Crane (Ed.), *Social programs that work* (pp. 110-147). New York: Russell Sage Foundation.

Reynolds, A. J. & Bezruczko, N. (1993). School adjustment of children at risk through fourth grade. *Merrill-Palmer Quarterly, 39*, 457-480.

Reynolds, A. J., & Gill, S. (1994). The role of parental perspectives in the school adjustment of inner-city black children. *Journal of Youth and Adolescence, 23*, 671-694.

Reynolds, A. J. & Bezruczko, N., Mavrogenes, N. A., & Hagemann, M. (1990). *Longitudinal study of children at risk: 1985-1990. Summary report.* Chicago, IL: Chicago Public Schools.

Reynolds, A. J., & Walberg, H. J. (1992). A structural model of science achievement and attitude: An extension to high school. *Journal of Educational Psychology, 84*, 371-382.

Reynolds, A. J., & Walberg, H. J. (1991). A structural model of science achievement. *Journal of Educational Psychology, 83*, 97-107.

Reynolds, A. J., Weissberg, R. P., & Kasprow, W. (1992). Prediction of early social and academic adjustment of children from the inner-city. *American Journal of Community Psychology, 20*, 599-624.

Rich, D. (1988). Bridging the parent gap in education reform. *Educational Horizons, 66*, 90-92.

Santrock, J. W. (1996). *Child development.* Chicago, IL: Brown & Benchmark.

School-Family Partnership Project. (1997). *Parent and teacher questionnaires*. Chicago, IL: Author.

Schweinhart, L. J., & Weikart, D. P. (1988). The High/Scope Perry Preschool Project. In R. H. Price, E. L. Cowen, R. P. Lorion, & J. Ramos-McKay (Eds.), *14 ounces of prevention: A casebook for practitioners* (pp. 53-65). Washington, DC: American Psychological Association.

Steinberg, L. (1996). *Beyond the classroom.* New York: Simon & Schuster.

Steinberg, L., Dornbusch, S. M., & Brown, B. B. (1992). Ethnic differences in adolescent achievement. *American Psychologist, 47*, 723-729.

Swap, S. M. (1993). *Developing home-school partnerships: From concepts to practice.* New York: Teachers College Press.

Weissberg, R. P., & Greenberg, M. T. (1998). School and community competence-enhancement and prevention programs. In W. Damon (Series Ed.) & I. E. Sigel & K. A. Renninger (Vol. Eds.), *Handbook of child psychology: Vol. 4. Child psychology in practice* (5th ed., pp. 877-954). New York: Wiley & Sons.

Weissberg, R. P., Schultz, T., Izzo, C., Shanahan, T., Hancock, M., Patrikakou, E. N., & Giller, B. (1997, March). *Teacher and parent perceptions of promising school-family partnership practices.* Paper presented at the American Educational Research Association Conference in Chicago, IL.

Zigler, E., & Muenchow, S. (1992). *Head Start: The inside story of America's most successful educational experiment.* New York: Basic Books.

6 Using Motivational Theory to Guide School Reform

*Carol Midgley and Martin L. Maehr**

Achievement has been—remains—a prime concern of captains of industry, politicians, and the proverbial "person on the street." It is the object of repeated reports in the popular media. In most such reports, the ultimate concern is with societal achievement: national power, the enhancement of prestige, and ensuring the financial well-being of the citizenry. While societal achievement may be the ultimate concern for many engaged in this conversation, it is widely recognized that the key to societal success is education. School achievement is at the heart of whatever a society or a person becomes. Employers believe this. So do parents. Thus there have been a surfeit of reports on school achievement. The call for "educational standards" has been as regular and persistent as the call for reforms to meet these standards. Almost everyone has their favorite approach to school reform, including the application of technology, improved teacher education, school "restructuring," and a host of others. But at the heart of it all, it must be recognized that schools do not achieve. Students do. While technology may help, good teachers and materials are necessary, and school restructuring may not hurt—in the final analysis, the investment of a student in learning is the sine qua non. How persons come to invest in any-

* Sincere appreciation is extended to the principal and teachers who collaborated with us and who contributed to the understandings and insights described in this chapter. The writing of this chapter, which is based on work described in detail in *Transforming School Cultures* [1996] by Martin L. Maehr and Carol Midgley, and published by Westview Press, was funded in part by the William T. Grant Foundation.

thing (in this case learning) is the object of serious and continuing concern by motivational psychologists. And, in recent years their attention has been drawn not only to understanding student motivation and achievement but toward applying that understanding to school reform designed to enhance students' engagement in learning. This chapter is concerned with such efforts. While building on extensive research and practical experiences by colleagues, we concentrate especially on our own recent collaborative work with selected schools.

Approaches to Enhancing Student Motivation and Learning

It is difficult to imagine that one could be concerned with school reform and not be concerned with student motivation. Sadly, more often than not, that has been the case. Part of the reason is that motivation research has only recently made it possible and reasonable to view the nature of school and schooling as a manipulable factor in determining student motivation and learning. There have been at least as many approaches to enhancing student motivation and achievement as there are theories of motivation. One cannot easily review them all. However, it is possible to provide a kind of taxonomy of approaches that suggests the options available and provides an illustrative example or two.

Treating Individuals

Historically, the study of motivation and achievement began with the study of individual differences in achievement. Motivation was treated essentially as a "personality trait" that was acquired, usually in childhood. Changing this trait in the case of "underachievers" meant reversing a pattern of long standing, providing the individual with counter experiences or new understandings, much like that which is done in the course of psychotherapy. But above all, the problem was viewed as residing in the individual and the individual had to be changed.

A number of programs were developed early on following this basic perspective. These programs included, for example, summer camps that concentrated on re-socializing the child to adopt new motivational orientations, new affective responses to learning activities, and a willingness to accept challenge. They also included special types of educational programs to enhance views of competency and self-esteem in particular areas. But regardless of what specific facet was the focus of attention—feelings, thoughts about self, or behavioral patterns—the emphasis was on changing the person.

Often children were taken out of the classroom and given special treatment with the expectation that they would then be able to return and function well. This individual treatment was expensive in time and effort—and probably in terms of money as well. It is also questionable whether it had a lasting effect or even persisted when the child returned to the classroom. Moreover, there is the issue to which we are much more sensitive today than before: The message that was conveyed to the child as a result of being pulled out of the classroom because of "special needs." This is not to suggest that these approaches have no place, only that they have a limited place in most school settings—for a host of reasons.

Designing Situations for Individuals with Similar Needs

It was inevitable that attention would be drawn to the classroom situation as a whole, separating out children with different "needs" into different classrooms designed to meet these needs. This option is perhaps implicit in much of the "tracking" that is still practiced in schools; it is hardly an option that has been shown to be justified by motivational research. This principle is also embodied in the work of Eccles and Midgley and their colleagues [1989, 1993] in which children's stage of development rather than individual differences in motivational orientation is the basis for establishing an appropriate match of situation to persons. In their work, an argument has been made that adolescents share certain needs or orientations that often are not met by the learning environments they experience at that stage of life. For example, the quality of the teacher/student relationship deteriorates just as young adolescents are looking for positive adult relationships outside the home, and the opportunity for decisionmaking declines just as young adolescents express a desire for more input into their lives both at home and at school. This research resulted in specific recommendations for improving middle level schools (e.g., Carnegie [1989]). This focus on the facilitating aspects of the learning environment for students at a certain stage of life was a catalyst for taking the nature of school environments seriously in working programmatically toward enhancing the investment of children in learning.

Toward the Concept of an Optimum Learning Environment

The early work of Eccles and Midgley was a major step toward reinforcing the direction of effort in defining an optimum environment for learning. A second major step in this regard was a motivation intervention study conducted by Richard de Charms and his colleagues [1976]. Briefly, de Charms and his group set out to assist teachers working in inner city schools with presumably "unmotivated" students. The operative theory was that if and as students came to view themselves as origins of their action and not simply pawns of fate, they were likely to be more motivated and less passive in the school setting. Basic research had yielded some principles regarding the circumstances that encourage the development of a sense of personal control, and these researchers set out to operationalize these principles in selected classrooms. There was also the realization that if teachers were to treat their students as origins of their actions, then teachers must experience a similar environment.

This early attempt was only partially successful in achieving its goals. Nevertheless, it led the way to new conceptions of motivational causes and motivational change. Specifically, it led to an understanding that students' perceptions of their classrooms, specifically their perceptions of themselves as responsible actors in the learning process, were at the heart of motivation. Further, it opened up a new range of possibilities regarding precisely how instructional practices likely affected this perception. Clearly, the learning environment was put forth as a factor that could be manipulated in determining the motivation and achievement of students. A significant step was taken to move beyond treating "unmotivated" individuals, to reforming school settings to enhance student learning. At about the same time, there was a major theoretical development in the conceptualization of motivation, which provided an additional impetus. Increasingly, motivation was viewed in social cognitive—instead of "dynamic"—terms. The motivation to achieve, especially to do well in school, was viewed less and less as determined by needs and motives established in early childhood, and more and more as determined by thoughts associated with, constructed in, the immediate situation. In particular, "achievement goal theory" emerged as an important approach to conceptualizing motivation.

A Goal Theory Perspective on Motivation Change

Over the last several decades, goal theory has emerged as a major new direction in motivational research (e.g., Dweck & Leggett [1988], Maehr [1989], and Nicholls [1989]). This theory has developed within a social-cognitive framework that focuses on the aims or purposes that are pursued or perceived in an achievement setting. Goal theory departs markedly from many previous notions about motivation. Rather than conceiving of students as possessing or lacking motivation, the focus is on how students think about themselves, their tasks, and their performance [Ames 1987]. Goals provide a framework within which individuals interpret and react to events, and result in different patterns of cognition, affect, and behavior [Dweck & Leggett 1988]. Theorists have described two achievement goals in particular: the goal to develop ability (variously labeled a task goal, learning goal, or mastery goal), and the goal to demonstrate ability or to avoid the demonstration of lack of ability (variously labeled a performance goal, ego goal, or ability goal). Although there are some differences among achievement goal theorists regarding the exact nature and functioning of these two types of goals, for the most part there is considerable overlap among these different conceptions.

Task and performance goals represent contrasting purposes in pursuing a course of action (see Table 6-1). Performance goals relate especially to

Table 6-1. Definitions of Task and Performance Goals

	Task	Performance
Success defined as...	Improvement, progress, mastery, innovation, creativity	High grades, high performance compared to others, relative achievement on standardized measures, winning at all costs
Value placed on...	Effort, attempting difficult tasks	Avoiding failure
Basis for satisfaction...	Progress, mastery	Being the best; success relative to effort
Work/performance context...	Growth of individual potential; learning	Establishing performance hierarchies
Reasons for effort...	Intrinsic and personal meaning of activity	Demonstrating one's worth
Evaluation criteria...	Absolute criteria; evidence of progress	Norms; social comparisons
Errors viewed as...	Part of the growth process; informational	Failure, evidence of lack of ability or worth
Competence viewed as...	Developing through effort	Inherited and fixed

Source: This table builds on earlier analyses by Ames and Archer [1988] and is from Maehr and Midgley [1996].

social competition and demonstrating one's ability to outdo or outperform others. In a learning situation, this takes the form of demonstrating that one is "smart"—actually, "smarter" than others, or that one is not "dumber" than others. Task goals relate especially to progress and mastery; the intrinsic and personal meaning of performing a task is central. Students espouse this goal as they refer to the excitement in acquiring a new skill; the belief that all can learn; and the importance of effort, improvement, and understanding.

Generally, in schools as in most achievement situations, individuals will be more or less inclined toward one or the other of these two goals. Ask students why they study, and they are likely to give reasons that reflect definitions of task or performance goals. Unfortunately, in many cases students will say that school is not so much about learning as about performing, coming up with the right answers, completing work on time, and being at the top of the class or at least not at the bottom of the class. In more concrete terms, one child leaves for school saying, "I want to get the highest score on the math test. At least I hope I do better than Susie." Another child says, "I want to see if I can figure out how to do those new algebra problems." The importance of these goals for healthy development and for school reform derives from two streams of research. The first is concerned with the patterns of affect, cognition, and behavior associated with these differing goals. The second has to do with the role of the learning environment in focusing students on one goal or the other.

Achievement Goals and Healthy Development

When we use the term "healthy development," we are including both academic and emotional well-being, since they are inextricably linked. What is remarkable is the consistency of the research associating a task goal orientation with a host of positive outcomes (see Urdan [1997] for a review). Children who are oriented to task goals feel good about themselves, their academic potential, and their future lives. They believe that if they work hard, they can be successful. They are less likely to be absent from school, to engage in disruptive behavior, and to feel angry and alienated. This is true for students across the "ability" continuum. Where one stands on the ability continuum is no longer salient. All children can work hard, learn skills, think deeply, and develop intellectually. In contrast, the research on performance goals has been somewhat inconsistent (e.g., Harackiewicz, Barron, & Elliot [1998]). There is considerable evidence, however, that the goal to demonstrate ability relative to others, or to hide lack of ability, is associated with emotional stress, maladaptive behavior, and disengagement from deep thinking and learning.

The Influence of the Learning Environment on Achievement Goals

The question then becomes, what is it that influences whether students espouse task or performance goals? Certainly, some children may be more "competitive" than others. Parents and early experiences undoubtedly influence a child's goal orientation, though there is little research on this relationship. However, there is growing evidence that the goals that children espouse arise in, are fostered by, and vary with the achievement situation experienced (e.g., Meece [1991], Nicholls, Patashnick, & Nolen [1985], and Roeser, Midgley, & Urdan [1996]). If students are in a class where the "best" papers are posted, grading is on a curve, high achievers receive special privileges, and the teacher reminds students frequently of the importance of high grades and mistake-free papers, it make sense that they would be oriented toward demonstrating their ability (or hiding their lack of ability). On the other hand, if students are in a class where understanding is emphasized, mastery is the criterion, and effort and improvement are recognized, it makes sense that they would be oriented to developing their ability. We call the emphasis on achievement goals in the learning environment the "goal structure." As shown in Figure 6-1, the goal structure in the learning environment influences students' personal goal orientation, which in turn is related to their engagement in learning and their emotional well-being. Unfortunately, many schools and classrooms in this country orient children to demonstrating their ability rather than developing their ability. Indeed, the recent call for standards, national tests, and "recognizing excellence" reflects this emphasis on performance rather than on learning.

Changing the Learning Environment to Influence Goal Orientation

Can the learning environment be changed so that task goals are emphasized, students espouse task goals, and positive emotional and academic

Figure 6-1. Relationship of School Goal Structure to Personal Goals and Engagement in Learning

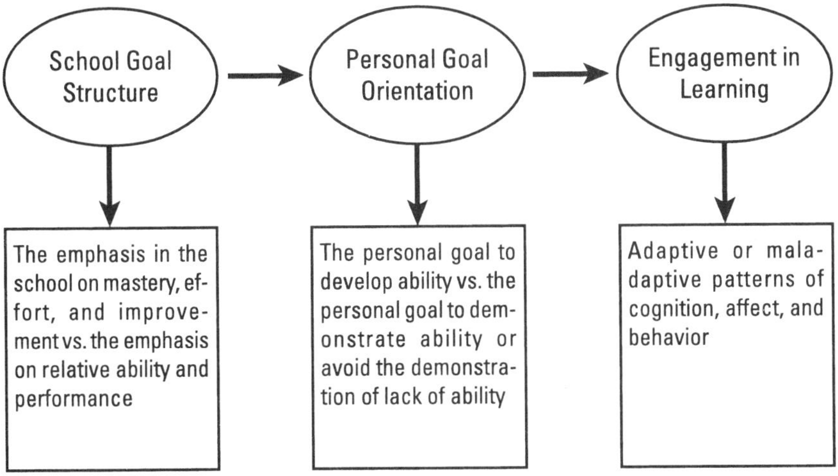

Adapted from Maehr & Midgley [1996]

well-being are enhanced? Carole Ames first demonstrated that this was possible about a decade ago. She worked with teachers to develop specific strategies that are conceptually consistent with a task or mastery orientation.

> The assumption underlying this intervention was that a mastery goal orientation is not dependent on a singular set of strategies or a particular instructional method—instead, it involves a constellation of strategies that are conceptually related to a common achievement goal [Ames 1990].

The Ames intervention focused on six dimensions of the learning environment: Task, Authority, Recognition, Grouping, Evaluation, and Time. These categories were first identified by Epstein [1988] using the acronym TARGET. Ames worked with teachers to develop specific strategies within each of these TARGET areas that were conceptually consistent with a task orientation. At the end of one year, children in the classrooms in which the strategies were introduced reported that their classrooms were more task focused than did children in control classrooms. In addition, at-risk students in treatment classrooms showed a stronger preference for challenging work, had more positive attitudes toward math and school, had higher self-concepts of ability, were more intrinsically motivated, and used more effective learning strategies than did peers in control classrooms [Ames 1990].

We replicated this program in five elementary schools in southeastern Michigan during the 1990-91 school year. During the course of this intervention, teachers occasionally mentioned that schoolwide policies or practices conflicted with strategies they were implementing in the classroom. For example, the school honor roll that recognized students for achieving all A's was perceived by teachers as undermining their efforts in the classroom to recognize students for improvement, participation, and effort. Or a schoolwide program to offer rewards to students who read the most books was perceived as undermining efforts by teachers to encourage students to take on challenging work. We began to see the need to change policies and procedures at the school level as well as at the classroom level.

Just as Ames and her colleagues identified classroom factors that influence the saliency of different goals, we identified the broad range of school-level policies, practices, and procedures that define learning and thus influence students' motivational orientation (see Table 6-2). It should be noted that many of these elements, although guided by policies at the school level (such as a policy on evaluation), are put into operation at the classroom level. Our goal has been to work with teachers and administrators to examine and change a wide range of policies and practices in a way that moves the school as a whole toward an emphasis on task mastery, problem solving, effort, challenge, and academic progress and away from an emphasis on competition, relative ability, and comparative performance.

Using Motivational Theory to Guide School Reform: In Practice

We spent several days each week for three years collaborating with the principal and teachers in Riversedge Elementary School (see note on page 140). The school building is old, outmoded, and scheduled for replace-

Table 6-2. Strategies to Move Toward a Task-Focused School Environment*

School Structures	Move Away From	Move Toward
Grouping	Grouping by ability	Grouping by topic, interest, student choice; frequent reformation of groups
Competition/ Cooperation	Competition between students; contests with limited winners	Cooperative learning
Assessment	Using test data as basis for comparison; overuse of standardized tests	Using test data for diagnosis; alternatives to tests, such as portfolios
Grading	Normative grading Public display of grades	Grading for progress, improvement Involving students in determining their grades
Recognition/Rewards/ Incentives	Recognition for relative performance; honor rolls for high grades; overuse of praise, especially for the completion of short, easy tasks	Recognition of progress, improvement; an emphasis on learning for its own sake
Student Input	Decisions made exclusively by administrators and teachers	Opportunities for choice, electives; student decisionmaking, self-scheduling, self-regulation
Approaches to the Curriculum	Departmentalized approach to curriculum	Thematic approaches/interdisciplinary focus; viewing mistakes as a part of learning; allowing students to redo work; encouraging students to take academic risks

Table 6-2 (continued)

School Structures	Move Away From	Move Toward
Academic Tasks	Rote learning and memorization; overuse of work sheets and textbooks; decontextualized facts	Providing challenging, complex work to students; giving homework that is enriching, challenging; encouraging problem solving, comprehension
Remediation	Pull-out programs; retention	Cross-age tutoring, peer tutoring; enrichment

* These strategies serve as examples. Strategies will depend on the characteristics of the school, the identified needs, and the preferences of the school staff. Strategies such as cross-age grouping, block scheduling, small house, and team teaching, although not listed here, are recommended as enabling mechanisms.
Source: Midgley & Urdan [1992]

ment if funding is approved. Across the street from the school is a sprawling and dilapidated public housing complex, often the site of the worst that children can experience: violence, drugs, poverty, neglect. While the physical facilities suggested little potential for enhancement, the leadership and staff at the school showed a potential for taking charge and taking action—against high odds!

It was evident to us that the staff believed that something different needed to be done in the school—though the struggle to define "different" was ongoing. Indeed, this probably figured into their decision to form a partnership with us. In our initial meetings, the staff expressed many concerns, including student motivation (or lack thereof), discipline, safety and well-being, lack of parental involvement—and of course, perennial financial

Note: We also collaborated with the staff of a middle school in the same district. A description of the collaboration at the middle school level, as well as a more detailed summary of the process, outcomes and understandings that resulted can be found in Maehr and Midgley [1996] and in Urdan, Midgley, and Wood [1995]. "Riversedge" is a pseudonym.

limitations. They had been working to address some of these problems. They had established special "self-esteem days" that they hoped would expand the horizons of students, made regular use of "motivational speakers," and had tried various strategies to involve more parents in the daily activities of the school.

The Collaborative Process

We entered this collaboration with some essential conceptions of how school-university collaborations could and should work. Generally, we saw collaboration as just that ... multiple individuals, perhaps in this case reasonably defined as two different groups, bringing separate biases, strengths, and weaknesses to the table. In an important sense, the school staff had the power to decide and to act. It was their school and they had to live with the action taken. We had to become acquainted with, as well as respectful of, the structures, processes, and values already operative in the school. But we did not assume that we had to remain silent and passive if and when confronted with policies and practices that appeared to be in conflict with enhancing task goals and minimizing performance goals. The fact that we entered this undertaking with a commitment to a vision of schooling meant that we would not be satisfied with any change. Our objective was change of a particular type.

Year One

Our first interactions were with members of the Riversedge state-mandated "school improvement team." This team had been working together to suggest school improvements for five years. During the first few meetings, we discussed the theory on which the project was based and the process that would be used to make changes. The discussion of theory seemed tedious to some at first. Occasionally someone from either team would stumble onto a metaphor or an example that seemed to stimulate discussion or crystallize understanding. To distinguish between a performance-orientation and a task-orientation, someone offered the example of a child coming home from school and telling her mother she had a great day because she got an A, or because she did better than her best friend. That was contrasted with a child saying she had a great day because she read a wonderful story about India, or finally solved a really difficult math problem. In discussing how one orientation or the other might influence a person's behavior, an apparently common educational experience prompted a lively discussion: deciding not to take a course in college because it might lower one's grade point average. One teacher said, "I've always wanted to learn chemistry, but I didn't take it because I was afraid I wouldn't do well. Wouldn't it be wonderful if we could just think about what we want to learn and not worry about whether we will get a high grade?"

At the end of one meeting a teacher said, "I'm beginning to get the idea—you are helping *us* to think about learning differently so that the *children* will think about it differently." Clearly this person sensed that school change might reside in thought change. These are examples of positive moments in the process. But not everything was that positive, especially in the early stages. At one meeting, a teacher complained: "I'm tired of talking about theory and want to get on with it—to do something more concrete." This need to move quickly was a recurring theme during the first year. In this case, we decided to hold a brainstorming session to identify problems and changes that could be undertaken to address those problems. In the course of the discussion, someone from the university team suggested that it might be helpful to select one of the possible changes for extended discussion, developing it as a prototype of the kind of change that would be in accord with the theory. This was agreed to, and the Riversedge team selected the design and operation of their "education fair" as a case for discussion.

This education fair was similar in form and design to a science fair, and had once been that. The event was held annually, and was a major school function. Parents were encouraged to help their children develop a project but not to do the work for them. Projects were judged and those deemed best received awards and were placed prominently in the hall; the remaining projects were displayed in the classrooms. The team began by discussing the strengths and weaknesses of the fair. Teachers mentioned that some parents, in spite of guidelines, did much of the work because they wanted their child to win, while other parents did not become involved in any way so that some children were unable to participate. Teachers spoke about the disappointment many children experienced when they didn't win, and the tendency of parents and other visitors to focus in particular on the winning projects on the night of the fair. From the university team's perspective, the education fair provided an excellent case for prompting an examination of the rationale for the collaborative project. For the Riversedge team, it very quickly became more than that. Questions of "What if ... ?" became "Why not ... ?" Participants talked about eliminating the judging and giving all participants a ribbon. One teacher offered to contact the high school to see if students could be recruited to provide guidance to Riversedge students whose parents were unable to help. Other ideas were suggested for making parents feel more comfortable about getting involved and providing support for children who needed it. Someone suggested putting the fourth and fifth grade students' projects in the hallways, and the other projects in the classrooms.

At that point, someone from the university team mentioned that we were discussing this only as a way to illustrate and understand the theory. This was quickly brushed aside. A teacher turned to the principal and said - "Well—can we do this or not?" After the meeting, plans were formulated and action was taken that did change many essential features of the education fair. In particular, changes were made that were substantially in accord with what we believed would serve to enhance a task goal orientation. Competition was minimized. All children were encouraged to try hard and to take on a challenging project; all were given an opportunity to demonstrate what they had accomplished. The changes were well-received by students and their parents. This first policy change was by all accounts a success.

At the meeting immediately following the education fair, members of the university team suggested that it might be good to spend some time discussing how the changes that had been made were consistent with the theory. What the staff team rejected in the case of the fair were practices that in only slightly different form were found in many other places and processes at Riversedge. However, there was little inclination to engage in a theoretical discussion. They wanted action. As a member of the school improvement team put it: "This is taking so long. How are we going to make all those changes we listed on the board if we move this slowly?" This need "to get on with it" was a feeling shared by most of the teachers on the team, and also by the principal.

As the next area to examine, the Riversedge team selected the "retention problem." Most seemed quite convinced that retaining students for a second year in the same grade was not a good solution to problems of underachievement. "But what are the alternatives?" asked participants. Two teachers suggested that something like an ungraded classroom, at least in the early grades, might be useful to consider. These two teachers mentioned that they had always wanted to team teach, and that combining students of more than one grade level might give them this opportunity. All agreed that "immature" students sometimes blossom later, and that strict age-graded structures are somewhat inflexible. Importantly, what was at first a suggestion for a structural change quickly prompted a set of instructional issues. What and how do you teach in an ungraded or multi-age classroom? Those particularly interested in these questions began reading, discussing, and occasionally visiting other schools where multi-age classrooms were in place. Much of this work occurred outside the context of the weekly meetings, but the fruits of the work dominated the discussions for a considerable period. We stressed that multi-age grouping did not automatically translate into a more task-focused school; rather, it provided a mechanism within which task goals could flourish.

By the end of the first year of our collaboration, four teachers had decided to participate in the multi-age classroom program. Other teachers were interested, but wanted to observe the classrooms in practice. The multi-age classrooms acquired a name, "MAGIC," for Multi-Age Grouped and Individualized Classrooms. The MAGIC teachers spent countless hours planning together on weekends and over the summer. They attended workshops to learn new teaching methods. They purchased books, educational materials, and professional literature. They designed a brochure to describe these classrooms to parents. Significantly, this brochure described the classrooms as "helping to emphasize self-improvement, not competition." What became increasingly evident was that introducing multi-age classrooms was more than an organizational innovation. It provided an opportunity for reconsidering the nature of the teaching and learning process.

In a sense, the organizational change was not that important. It was the fact that it presented new challenges, produced new thinking, and provided an opportunity for putting theory into practice. Increasingly the MAGIC teachers talked about the need to de-emphasize relative ability and to emphasize effort, understanding, and intellectual development. They examined and evaluated what they had been doing in the classroom, and planned what they would do differently in the new program. The move to multi-age classrooms was suggested by the teachers and had never been a part of our thinking. We learned that organizational change can stimulate instructional change, and that instructional change can indeed lead to a more task-focused school environment. School staff had taken over the process in a significant way.

Year Two

Riversedge Elementary School opened in the fall of year two with four MAGIC classrooms; two consisting of first, second, and third graders, and two consisting of third, fourth, and fifth graders. At first the MAGIC teachers talked about feeling overwhelmed. They were exhausted from long hours of planning and the myriad of practical details they needed to resolve. By November, the classes were functioning reasonably well. The teachers' frustrations changed to cautious optimism as they saw the benefits of their new approach reflected in their students' motivation and learning.

Meanwhile, the university team and an expanded group of teachers began to meet again on a regular basis, with a commitment to focus on the school as a whole, not just on the MAGIC classrooms. Student assessment was identified by the teachers as the next issue to be considered. The discussions were wide-ranging, with questions raised about assessing, reporting, and recognizing student progress. A pressing concern for the teachers in the MAGIC classrooms was the approaching "marking period" and how to report to parents. While this was certainly, first of all, the concern of the MAGIC teachers, it was recognized as a schoolwide issue. Teachers in the multi-age classrooms had decided that report cards using letter grades emphasized differences in ability among children, and were not appropriate in classrooms with children of different ages. They were certain that both students and parents interpreted grades as measures of relative performance, rather than as measures of effort and progress. They agreed that letter grades convey little information about what a student has mastered and where improvement needs to be made.

A group of teachers began meeting to develop a new report card for the MAGIC classrooms. They collected report cards from other schools and adapted them to suit their objectives. More than once, they expressed concern about the reaction to this change by the superintendent's office. It turned out that their concerns were unfounded. One of the assistant superintendents expressed his support and offered to help them design the new report card on his portable computer. It was evident to us that the resulting report card represented a move toward an emphasis on task goals. The principal made it clear, however, that the school as a whole was not yet ready to adopt the new report card.

In contrast, new ideas regarding ways to recognize student achievement were seen as affecting not just the MAGIC classrooms but the school as a whole. A visible change in schoolwide policy was the removal of the honor roll. In this case, the principal made a unilateral decision not only to remove the honor roll from its prominent place in the front hall, but to eliminate the practice of honoring children for their grades. She said that she had come to realize that the honor roll defined the goal of learning as outperforming others, rather than in terms of effort and improvement. The principal explained that she had not before considered how the awards served as a disincentive for the children who never received them, as well as the wrong incentive for higher achieving students. But not all parents and teachers agreed with the decision! Some teachers believed that an extrinsic reward of some kind was essential to get children to do their work. Some parents mentioned that they had taken pride in the honor roll certificates their children brought home, and had displayed them prominently. In response to this pressure, the principal promised that the honor roll, at least for a time, would be replaced with a new form of recognition.

At the team meetings, the discussion turned to ways of recognizing students. The group agreed that recognition in and of itself is not harmful and that the important issue is the basis for recognition. The group labored long and hard to come up with a list of "Principles of Recognition." In developing this list, teachers debated important issues relevant to goal theory. They frequently asked, "What kind of message will that give to students about how success is defined in this school, and what is valued here?" One of the parents who had been attending the meetings said that the articulation of the Principles of Recognition was a turning point for him and that he now clearly understood the difference between a task focus and a performance focus. He became a strong advocate for the changes, and since he was also a member of the School Board, his endorsement was especially valuable. The Principles of Recognition that were developed by the teachers are presented in Table 6-3.

Year Three

During the third year of the project, two new multi-age classrooms were added, one including first and second grades, the other including third and fourth grades. Parents who had children in the multi-age classrooms the previous year were quite vocal in their support, so that recruiting children for these classrooms was no longer a problem. In addition, a special effort was made to inform all the teachers in the school that it was not necessary to teach multi-age classrooms to move toward a learning environment that emphasized mastery, effort, improvement, and understanding, rather than relative ability and comparative performance. The principal assured her staff that, while it had been necessary to focus a lot of attention on the multi-age classrooms in the beginning, she was now committed to supporting changes in the "single-age" classrooms. Special funds were made

Table 6-3. Principles of Recognition—Elementary Coalition

1. Recognize individual student effort, accomplishment, and improvement.
2. Give all students opportunities to be recognized.
3. Give recognition privately whenever possible.
4. Avoid using "most" or "best" for recognizing or rewarding—as in "best project" or "most improved." These words usually convey comparisons with others.
5. Avoid recognizing on the basis of absence of mistakes. For example, avoid giving awards for students who get "less than five words wrong on a spelling test."
6. Avoid using the same criteria for all students. For example, avoid giving an award to "all students who get an A on the science test," or "all students who do four out of five projects."
7. Recognize students for taking on challenging work or for stretching their own abilities (even if they make mistakes). This gives a powerful message about what is valued in the classroom.
8. Recognize students for coming up with different and unusual ways to solve a problem or a novel way to approach a task. Again, you are telling students what you value.
9. Try to involve students in the recognition process. What is of value to them? How much effort do they feel they put in? Where do they feel they need improvement? When do they feel successful? How do they know when they have reached their goals?
10. It's OK to recognize students in various domains (behavior, athletics, attendance, etc.), but every child should have the opportunity to be recognized *academically.*
11. Try to recognize the quality of students' work rather than the quantity. For example, recognizing students for reading a lot of books could encourage them to read easy books.
12. Avoid recognizing grades and test scores. This takes the emphasis away from learning and problemsolving.
13. Recognition must be real. Do not recognize students for accomplishing something they have not really accomplished, for improving if they have not improved, or for trying hard, if that is not the case. The important factor is letting students know that they have the opportunity to be recognized in these areas.

Source: Midgley & Urdan [1992]

available so that all teachers who so desired could attend workshops on interdisciplinary approaches to the curriculum, cooperative learning, using manipulatives in math, whole language approaches to reading, and assessing student progress with portfolios.

At the after-school meetings, a number of topics were discussed and some substantive changes were made in approaches to discipline, the Young Authors Program, the field day, and the annual recognition ceremony for graduating fifth graders. In general, however, an awareness emerged that there was a need to reflect on and to consolidate the changes that had been made, rather than to move in many new directions. As one example, the Riversedge staff spent many sessions describing the negative effects on children of standardized testing. The university team urged them to communicate with central administrators and the school board, and to investigate alternative ways of assessing student progress. A consultant from the University of Michigan involved in "work sampling" approaches to assessment was invited to make a presentation at a meeting. There was interest among the staff, but also an awareness that this would involve a major commitment of time and energy. They simply couldn't take this on in addition to all the other changes that were underway. In addition, the teachers seemed to feel that this was an area (standardized testing) over which they had little or no control. In one of the meetings the principal said, "Someone else will have to fight that battle."

A Change in Thinking

Teachers began to talk about having a vision for their school, knowing now where they were headed and what they wanted for their students. A few teachers still expressed the belief that competition is what makes the world go around and that students need to have rewards for which to strive. But in general, the staff seemed to be pulling together. At the end of one meeting, the principal reminded the staff that the annual contest to select the best essay on the history of Riversedge School was coming up, and they should convey this information to their students, and remind them that they could win the trophy. One of the teachers looked at her in amazement and said, "That's not what this school is all about. How can we make all these changes and then do something like that? It makes no sense. No, we can't do that." Clearly the most important changes were in thinking. At the end of the year (and the project), we celebrated at the home of one of the teachers. Some of the teachers expressed some anxiety about moving ahead without the university team. However, most seemed to believe that they now had a vision of schooling that would help them make decisions in the future, as well as provide a basis for evaluating new educational "innovations" as they became fashionable.

Evaluation of the Program

There was widespread agreement that Riversedge had changed during the three years of our active collaboration, and that students had benefited from this change. Concrete examples of changed policies, the oral and written impressions of participants (students, teachers, parents, researchers), and the anecdotes and stories that reflected changed thinking provided compelling documentation. However, our mandate from the agency funding this project was that "rigorous quantitative methods" were to be used to assess change. Our preference would have been to conduct this quantitative investigation at the end of five or even seven years rather than at the end of three. We were well aware that the first year of collaboration had been spent, for the most part, discussing theory and establishing a trusting relationship between researchers and school staff. We were also cognizant that significant changes were still in the planning stage when the "postcollaboration" data were collected. And, we were especially mindful of the literature on school change that warns against premature evaluation. However, there was a mandate to be fulfilled and a final report to be written. To satisfy these requirements, we identified another elementary school in the same district to serve as a comparison school. Surveys were administered to first- through fifth-grade students and their teachers at Riversedge and the comparison school before the project began and during the third year of the collaboration. Rigorous studies were undertaken to examine whether students and teachers at Riversedge changed in ways predicted by the theory, in comparison to students and teachers in the school that was serving as a control.

Students

We were concerned about using survey methodology to document changes in the beliefs, perceptions, and behaviors of the students at Riversedge, in comparison to the students at the other school. We are experienced in survey administration, and do not feel that surveys are an appropriate way to gather data from students in the early elementary grades, even when they are administered individually. As it turned out, there was no meaningful pattern of evidence indicating that Riversedge students experienced a greater task-oriented school environment over time than did their peers at the comparison school—nor did they as yet exhibit different patterns of motivation and learning. Many of the scales that emerged from the data collected from children in the first, second, and third grades were found to be of questionable reliability. The reasons were partially clarified as we queried the children. For example, they told us that they "liked the high end of the scale." Other researchers have had similar experiences with young children. In any event, the survey approach was insufficient for the purpose of providing an independent, perhaps more "objective," reading on whether the changes that we could sense were occurring actually reached down in a significant way to the world of the child.*

Teachers

We expected the survey data from teachers to be more fruitful, and it was. We began our analysis by comparing the responses of teachers in Riversedge and the comparison school at the "start" and at the "end," following accepted statistical procedures. After controlling for initial differences, Riversedge teachers perceived that the school emphasized task goals more than did comparison school teachers. There was also an indication that Riversedge teachers increased their use of task-focused instructional prac-

---

* We did find evidence of differential change in students moving to the participating middle school as compared to students moving to the comparison middle school (see Anderman, Maehr, & Midgley [in press]).

tices (such as using cooperative learning and encouraging students to monitor their own progress) more than did comparison school teachers. But the results were not strong nor pervasive. They were at best marginal in terms of accepted statistical standards of significance.

Knowing what we did about the process of change, however, we were certain that this first overall analysis missed the point a bit. We knew that certain teachers were not participating at all in the change process. Their lack of involvement in the nature and direction of the change efforts was known to their colleagues and to us. Given this reality, we decided to look at the survey results again, comparing the patterns of change of "involved" and "uninvolved" teachers. As we suspected, these two groups presented distinctly different profiles. Most importantly, the involved group did exhibit evidence of the kind of change that the collaborative activities were designed to bring about. Highly involved teachers exhibited more change over time toward a task focus and away from a performance focus than did comparison school teachers. This was exhibited in their reports of changes in their instructional practices, their pedagogical beliefs, and the goals they held for their students.

In summary, systematic comparisons of data derived from an established survey instrument [Midgley et al. 1996] as well as informal and formal observations and interviews converged on a central point: Change had occurred, at least for those teachers who were highly involved in the process. At the end of less than three years, there was a basis for concluding that at least a certain portion of the teachers had shifted toward bringing a task-focused vision of school into being. They not only increasingly held a task-focused view of schooling and expressed themselves in different language, but were apparently also redesigning their teaching and classroom management accordingly. All of this held promise for the ultimate emergence of a task-focused school culture for students.

An Afterword

When the period of our active collaboration ended, we knew that Riversedge had made important changes consistent with an increased emphasis on task goals and a decreased emphasis on performance goals. We were heartened that many of the parents of Riversedge students were strong advocates of the changes and expressed their support and gratitude to the hard-working teachers. But we were unsure what would happen over time. In so many school reform programs, participants "burn out," lose sight of the original goals, or are pressured by powerful parents or district administrators to water down the changes they have made. Remarkably, the story of Riversedge is one of continuing effort directed toward ends established in the earliest stages of the collaboration.

While we are no longer involved in a continuing programmatic effort, we have remained in close contact with the principal and teachers. We have been called upon to assist them in developing funding proposals and in implementing instructional changes. For example, when the school staff decided to focus on the improvement of science instruction at the fourth and fifth grade levels, we assisted by providing demonstrations that would suggest how this might be done in concert with a task goal emphasis. But it should be emphasized that in this and other such cases, we acted as their (willing) servants, providing expertise, proposing options, making a suggestion or two here or there. It was theirs to design and to implement. Their asking for help was by no means a sign of dependency, but rather a testimony to their commitment to provide a task-focused learning environment for their students.

The multi-age classroom program has continued to expand. Importantly, the concepts that framed the original MAGIC classrooms are continuing to find their way into the single-age classrooms, often at the insistence of parents. The staff continues to pull together, overcoming what was once perceived as a separation between the MAGIC teachers and the other teachers in the school. They have renewed vigor, recently submitting a proposal to a major corporation for the establishment of an early childhood center to provide students with special health and social services. But there is more to be noted in this case. In 1996, Riversedge was named an "Exemplary Title 1 School" by the State of Michigan. To become an exemplary school, a school must show significant progress in the academic achievement of its students. In addition, the Riversedge teachers were asked if they would be willing to mentor other Title 1 schools and to describe their program at Title 1 conferences. In 1998, Riversedge was recognized by the U.S. Department of Education as a "Title 1 Distinguished School," again based on gains in student achievement. The superintendent of schools, in a letter to us, said the following:

> I want to personally thank you, the School of Education, and the University of Michigan at large for providing the wisdom, guidance, and focus which clearly played a major role in the phenomenal success that (Riversedge) students have realized.... Your efforts prompted our entire staff to develop an insatiable desire to provide quality educational experiences for students. The desire you created among those who serve children at (Riversedge) remains as pervasive as ever. The efficacy of your efforts is indelibly chronicled in the results of the children's (standardized achievement test scores) but more importantly, in their realization of self-worth, sense of cooperation, and vision which they evince on a daily basis.

We are grateful for these wonderful words of appreciation. We are grateful, in particular, for the opportunity to put theory into practice in partnership with a hard-working, committed, intellectually keen, and creative school staff. They have proven that motivational theory can indeed be used to guide school reform.

Putting Theory into Practice—and Practice into Theory

So what, in retrospect, was accomplished by this major expenditure of time and energy? One school moved away from an emphasis on performance goals and toward an emphasis on task goals, and good things happened. This is gratifying for the participants. Hopefully it will be useful for those who wish to follow a similar path. But are there broader implications? We think so. There is considerable discussion about the failure of research to inform practice, and practice to inform research. We believe that this partnership shows that both can and should happen.

First, it is clear that the abstractions of motivation theory, especially goal theory, can serve not only as a lens to evaluate school practices—but more importantly, to frame practices. It was no small feat to translate the abstractions of goal theory into everyday activities in schools. Note how we researchers initially missed the implications of doing something about the "Education Fair" and didn't come up with the idea of examining school retention policies. Working daily in schools at the business of school reform is the sine qua non for translating theory into practice. The efforts we have described do not provide a "cookbook" of directions to follow in enhancing the investment of students in learning, but they do possibly serve as a useful heuristic in this regard.

Without question, some of the most crucial achievement experiences occur within the context of schools. It is here where the child spends a major portion of the day. It is here where activities inevitably relate to realizing one's potential, to becoming the best person that one can be. It is here that children learn how to deal with "success" and "failure" and their multiple definitions. It is here that society places some of its highest expectations. And it is through schools that society expects children to become productive, adaptive, healthy, and happy adults.

There is another equally important implication of this work, perhaps a bit more subtle, but arguably no less important: Working to change practice can serve to enrich theory. New information acquired in the course of practice, and hypotheses tested by practitioners, can contribute to the development of theory. This exchange between theory and practice can be of great service to both researchers and practitioners.

Our partnership with Riversedge Elementary School has heightened our interest in the role of self-beliefs in the goal theory model, the applicability of this framework to students from different cultural and socioeconomic backgrounds, and the diverse influences on the development of goal orientations. The challenges of the classroom present some of the most interesting and fruitful opportunities for testing our understanding of the human being in social context.

Researchers find it easy to accept Kurt Lewin's [1952] wisdom that there is nothing so practical as a good theory. But as Cartwright [1978] later reminded us, Kurt Lewin should also have taught us that there is nothing so theoretical as a good practical problem.

Generalizing Beyond Schools

Of course, in today's world it is not only schools that need to change; other, perhaps all, agencies, institutions, and organizations must adapt to an everchanging world. The change needed is not just in markets, tools, and technology; it is a change in how all those in the organization think and act. The change demanded is so immediate that a gradual turnover in personnel won't do. The same persons must be enabled to learn and do new things, act in new and different ways. As a result, today's organizations—business, social service, or educational—must all be "learning" agencies. To us, that suggests that everyone in the organization be viewed as important resources—resources to be cultivated and enabled with a view to meeting the new challenges. Accepting this diagnosis of organizations more generally, is it likely that not just schools, but many other agencies and institutions might benefit from our perspective on the organizational culture of a school. Indeed, it would seem that any organization concerned with the personal growth of its human resources, most especially one also specifically devoted to enhancing the personal development of its clientele, as in the case of social service agencies, might well benefit from our experiences.

One might assume that social service agencies should ultimately be concerned with the personal growth of their clientele. And, as they deal with parents in particular, they need to be concerned with how family contexts do or do not facilitate the development of children. Obviously, our work in schools and instruction should be of direct significant to those assisting individuals in practicing effective parenting. But it also seems possible, perhaps likely, that those who lead and direct these agencies might find something in our work to guide them in designing their approach to providing services. Insofar as growth is indeed the objective, it seems increasingly clear that task goals should be stressed in dealing with individuals who, for example, are challenged with finding their way out of poverty or who are expected to demonstrate more acceptable life patterns of one type or another. Without specifically employing a theory such as employed in our work, social service agencies and professionals in fact often exhibit the value of a "task approach" in dealing with "problem" persons and families. It would seem that the theory and research associated with task and performance goals might enhance the conceptual framework that guides their work. Thus, those who work with clients do well to develop and stress individual growth and progress indicators and reflect this in their own evaluations, judgments, and actions.

Perhaps all work organizations would do well to consider the relative emphasis they place on a task orientation in the work lives of their employees, evaluating and recognizing more in terms of growth and less in terms of social comparisons in levels of attainment. Certainly, there is reason to believe that any organization that becomes too interpersonally competitive will not only run the risk of demoralizing a substantial portion of their employees but reduce the cooperation needed to meet organizational goals. Moreover, creating a competitive environment does not—just as has been found to be the case in schools—seem to be the best way to capitalize on the fullest potential of employees to learn, to innovate, and to grow in their contributions to the overall welfare of the organization as a whole [Amabile 1996]. While the theory out of which our approach to school reform has evolved has not as yet been extensively applied to the broader organizational world, some overtures in this direction have in fact been made (e.g., Button, Mathieu, & Zajac [1996], Maehr & Braskamp [1986], and Tzeng [1997]). We suggest that this is possibly an interesting new frontier that needs to be examined more in the future.

References

Amabile, T. M. (1996). *Creativity in context: Update to "The Social Psychology of Creativity."* Boulder, CO: Westview Press.

Ames, C. (1987). The enhancement of student motivation. In D. A. Kleiber & M. L. Maehr (Eds.), *Advances in motivation and achievement, Vol. 5: Enhancing motivation.* Greenwich, CT: JAI Press.

Ames, C. (1990, April). *Achievement goals and classroom structure: Developing a learning orientation.* Paper presented at the annual meeting of the American Educational Research Association, Boston.

Anderman, E., Maehr, M. L., & Midgley, C. (in press). Declining motivation after the transition to middle school: Schools can make a difference. *Journal of Research and Development in Education.*

Button, S. B., Mathieu, J. E., & Zajac, D. M. (1996). Goal orientation in organizational research: A conceptual and empirical foundation. *Organizational Behavior and Human Decision Processes, 67*, 26-48

Carnegie Council on Adolescent Development. (1989). *Turning points: Preparing American youth for the 21st century.* Report of the Task Force on Education of Young Adolescents, New York.

Cartwright, D. (1978). Theory and practice. *Journal of Social Issues, 34*, 168-180.

de Charms, R. (1976). *Enhancing motivation: Change in the classroom.* New York: Irvington.

Dweck, C. S., & Leggett, E. L. (1988). A social-cognitive approach to motivation and personality. *Psychological Review, 95*, 256-273.

Eccles, J. S., & Midgley, C. (1989). Stage/environment fit: Developmentally appropriate classrooms for early adolescents. In C. Ames & R. E. Ames (Eds.), *Research on motivation in education, Vol. 3* (pp. 139-186). New York: Academic Press.

Eccles, J. S., Midgley, C., Wigfield, A., Buchanan, C. M., Reuman, D., Flanagan, C., & MacIver, D. (1993). Development during adolescence: The impact of stage/environment fit on young adolescents' experiences in schools and families. *American Psychologist, 48*, 90-101.

Epstein, J. L. (1988). Effective schools or effective students: Dealing with diversity. In R. Haskins & D. MacRae (Eds.), *Policies for America's public schools: Teacher equity indicators* (pp. 89-126). Norwood, NJ: Ablex.

Harackiewicz, J. M., Barron, K. E., & Elliot, A. J. (1998). Rethinking achievement goals: When are they adaptive for college students and why? *Educational Psychologist, 33*, 1-21.

Lewin, K. (1952). *Field theory in social science: Selected papers by Kurt Lewin.* Edited by D. Cartwright. London: Tavistock Publications.

Maehr, M. L. (1989). Thoughts about motivation. In C. Ames, & R. Ames (Eds.), *Research on motivation in education, Vol. 3: Goals and cognitions.* New York: Academic Press.

Maehr, M. L., & Braskamp, L. (1986). *The motivation factor: A theory of personal investment.* Lexington, MA: D. C. Heath.

Maehr, M. L., & Midgley, C. (1996). *Transforming school cultures.* Boulder, CO: Westview Press.

Meece, J. L. (1991). The classroom context and students' motivational goals. In P. Pintrich & M. L. Maehr, (Eds.), *Advances in motivation and achievement, Vol. 7; Goals and self-regulatory processes.* Greenwich, CT: JAI Press.

Midgley, C., Maehr, M. L., Hicks, L., Roeser, R., Urdan, T., Anderman, E., & Kaplan, A. (1996). *Manual: Patterns of Adaptive Learning Survey (PALS).* Ann Arbor, MI: University of Michigan at Ann Arbor.

Nicholls, J. G. (1989). *The competitive ethos and democratic education.* Cambridge, MA: Harvard University Press.

Nicholls, J. G., Patashnick, M., & Nolen, S. B. (1985). Adolescents' theories of education. *Journal of Educational Psychology, 77*, 683-692.

Roeser, R., Midgley, C., & Urdan, T. (1996). Perceptions of the school psychological climate and early adolescents' self-appraisals and academic engagement. *Journal of Educational Psychology, 88*, 408-422.

Tzeng, H.-M. (1997). *The influence of staff nurses' perceptions of organizational culture on inpatient satisfaction with nursing care.* Unpublished doctoral dissertation, The University of Michigan, Ann Arbor.

Urdan, T., Midgley, C., & Wood, S. (1995). Special issues in reforming middle level schools. *Journal of Early Adolescence, 15*, 9-37.

Urdan, T. (1997). Achievement goal theory: past results, future directions. In M. L. Maehr & P. R. Pintrich (Eds.), *Advances in motivation and achievement: Vol. 10* (pp. 99-141). Greenwich, CT: JAI Press.

7 Promoting Safe Educational and Community Environments

*David W. Johnson and Roger T. Johnson**

Frances Hodgson Burnett, in her book, *The Secret Garden*, stated, "Where you tend a rose, a thistle cannot grow." By enhancing the positive development of children and youth (i.e., tending roses), the development of children and youth who are antisocial and pathological is prevented. Schools, families, and communities should tend roses to prevent thistles from developing. Doing so may be difficult. Many cities and towns have become what criminologists have described as criminogenic communities—places where the social forces that create predatory criminals are far more numerous and overwhelmingly stronger than the social forces that create virtuous citizens. Many children and youth are now growing up surrounded by teenagers and adults who are deviant, delinquent, or criminal and who may abuse, neglect, or criminally prey upon the young. This is not just an urban problem. Many suburban and rural children and adolescents are also neglected or preyed upon by members of their family and neighborhood.

It is difficult to change the nature of a family, neighborhood, or city. It is less difficult to change the nature of the school experience. A school community may be created to enhance the positive development of children and youth, prevent disruptions to healthy development, and restore order after a disruption has taken place.

* For more information, contact David Johnson, Department of Educational Psychology, University of Minnesota, 60 Peik Hall, 159 Pillsbury Avenue, Minneapolis, MN 55455, telephone: 612/624-7031, fax: 612/626-1395; e-mail: johnso10@maroon.tc.umn.edu.

Positive Development

There are many definitions of positive development from Freud, Erikson, Piaget, and others. To the authors, healthy social development includes six elements [Johnson 1975, 1997; Johnson & Johnson 1989].

- The first is the **ability to manage interdependence with others**. Children and youth need to learn how to assess the cooperative and competitive forces in a situation and respond appropriately, cooperating skillfully with others, competing for fun and enjoyment, and working autonomously on their own.
- The second is an **overall balance of trust** rather than distrust toward other people. Most people should be perceived to be trustworthy. They should believe that most people are trustworthy most of the time.
- The third is the **ability to view situations and problems from a variety of perspectives**. Children and youth need to recognize the limitations of their idiosyncratic perspective and learn to assume the perspectives of others.
- The fourth is a **meaningful sense of direction and purpose in life**. Children and youth need to develop a sense of "where I am going" that is valued by others and that is similar to the goals of the significant people in our lives.
- The fifth is an **integrated and coherent sense of personal identity**. Every person needs a strong, integrated, and distinct image of him- or herself as a certain kind of person who is differentiated and discernible from others.
- Finally, children and youth need **a positive process for deriving self-esteem**. Conclusions about self-esteem can be derived through reflected self-acceptance (seeing oneself as others see one), basic self-acceptance (seeing oneself as being intrinsically worthwhile), conditional self-acceptance (seeing oneself as being of value when one meets the external standards and expectations of others), self-evaluation (estimating how positively one's attributes compare with those

of peers), and real-ideal congruence (the correspondence between what one thinks one is and what one thinks one should be).

When students, faculty, and staff (as well as parents and neighborhood members) (1) are involved in cooperative efforts, (2) manage conflicts constructively, and (3) base their actions on civic values, a school community is created in which positive development of children and youth is enhanced.

The Three Cs Program

Healthy and positive development of children and youth are built on the three Cs: Cooperative community, constructive conflict resolution, and civic values (see Figure 7-1). This is true of the family and community as well as schools, but it is the school setting that is the focus of our work. The school is a cooperative system in which faculty/staff, students, and parents work together to achieve mutual goals concerning quality education. Sometimes conflicts arise over how best to achieve goals and coordinate actions. These conflicts have to be resolved constructively if the community is to survive. Both a cooperative community and constructive conflict resolution are based on civic values that recognize and support the long-term benefits of working together and contributing to the welfare of others and the common good as well as working for one's own well-being.

Working cooperatively with peers, resolving conflicts constructively, and internalizing prosocial values are experiences that all students need. Ideally, all students in a school and a school district will engage in these activities. These experiences are both primary prevention and a secondary intervention for children and adolescents who may be at risk for future problems, as well as essential for the positive development of all children and adolescents. The Three Cs Program, described below, has been implemented in a wide variety of schools throughout North America and many other parts of the world. It has been used with inner-city, lower class students, with upper-class private school students, and with everyone in between. It has been used in schools in third world countries as well as in North America and Europe.

Figure 7-1. The Three Cs of Effective Schools

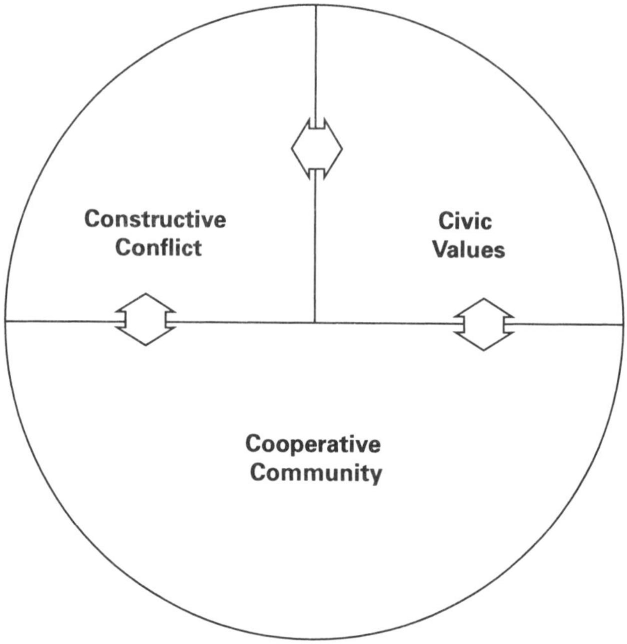

The First C: Cooperative Community

The Nature Of Community and Social Interdependence

Positive development of children and youth begins with establishing a learning community based on cooperation (i.e., working together to achieve mutual goals). Scholarship and learning do not exist in isolation; they are products of a community and a culture characterized by mutual respect and trust. Community is a group of people who live in the same locality and share common goals and a common culture. The school community is made up of the faculty and staff, the students, their parents, and members of the neighborhood. Broadly, the school community includes all stakeholders: central administrators, college admission officers, and future employers.

The heart of community and culture is social interdependence. Social interdependence exists when each individual's outcomes are affected by the actions of others [Deutsch 1949; Johnson & Johnson 1989]. Social interdependence may be positive or negative. Positive interdependence (cooperation) exists when individuals work together to achieve mutual goals, and negative interdependence (competition) exists when individuals work against each other to achieve a goal that only one or a few may attain. Social independence, where the outcomes of each person are unaffected by others' actions, is characterized by individualistic actions.

To create a learning community, positive interdependence (i.e., cooperation) must be structured at all levels of the school: Learning group, classroom, interclass, school, school-parent, and school-neighborhood. Members of the community must see themselves to be partners, not adversaries. The school cannot be a learning community if students are pitted against each other in the classroom or if students are isolated with no friends in the classroom. Just as the family is the beginning of community in society, the learning group is the beginning of community in the school.

The Power Of Cooperation

During the past 100 years, more than 550 experimental and 100 correlational studies have been conducted by a wide variety of researchers in different decades with different age subjects, in different subject areas, and in different settings (for a detailed review of the research on cooperative, competitive, and individualistic efforts, see Johnson & Johnson [1989]). In our own research program at the Cooperative Learning Center of the University of Minnesota, we have conducted more than 90 research studies over the past 30 years to refine our understanding of the nature of cooperation and how it works. Research participants have varied as to economic class, age, sex, nationality, and cultural background. A wide variety of research tasks, ways of structuring cooperation, and measures of the dependent variables have been used. Many different researchers have conducted the research with markedly different orientations working in different settings, countries, and decades. The research on cooperation has a validity and a generalizability rarely found in the educational literature.

Working together to achieve mutual goals can have profound effects on the individuals involved. The type of interdependence structured among individuals determines how they interact with each other which, in turn largely determines outcomes. Structuring situations cooperatively results in individuals promoting each other's success (individuals help, assist, support, and encourage each other's efforts). Structuring situations competitively results in individuals opposing each other's success (individuals obstruct and block each other's efforts). Structuring situations individualistically results in no interaction among individuals (individuals ignore each other and work alone) (see Table 7-1). These interaction patterns affect numerous variables, which may be subsumed within the three broad and interrelated outcomes of (see Figure 7-2) [Johnson & Johnson 1989]:

- **Effort exerted to achieve.** Higher achievement and greater productivity, more frequent use of higher-level reasoning, more frequent generation of new ideas and solutions, greater intrinsic and achievement motivation, greater long-term retention, more on-task behavior, and greater transfer of what is learned within one situation to another.

- **Quality of relationships among participants.** Greater interpersonal attraction, liking, cohesion and esprit-de-corps, valuing of heterogeneity, and greater task-oriented and personal support.

- **Psychological adjustment.** Greater psychological health, greater social competencies, higher self-esteem, a shared identity, and greater ability to cope with stress and adversity.

Effective cooperation requires that five basic elements be carefully structured into the situation [Johnson & Johnson 1989; Johnson, Johnson, & Holubec 1998a] (see Table 7-1):

- First, there must be a strong sense of positive interdependence, so individuals believe that they are linked with others, and that they cannot succeed unless the others do (and vice versa). Individuals must believe that they sink or swim together. Positive interdependence may be structured through mutual goals, joint rewards, divided resources, complementary roles, and a shared identity.

Table 7-1. Understanding Cooperative Efforts

Types of Interdependence	Cooperative Learning	Essential Elements of Cooperation	Outcomes of Cooperation
Positive: Cooperation	Formal cooperative learning	Positive interdependence	Effort to achieve
Negative: Competition	Informal cooperative learning	Individual accountability	Positive relationships
None: Individualistic	Cooperative base groups	Promotive interaction	Psychological health
		Interpersonal and small group skills	
		Group processing	

Note: There are three types of interdependence, the most important of which is cooperation. The basic use of cooperation in schools is cooperative learning. There are three types of cooperative learning. Effective cooperation depends on five basic elements being structured into the situation. When the five elements are present, three types of outcomes tend to result.

- Second, each collaborator must be individually accountable to do his or her fair share of the work.
- Third, collaborators must have the opportunity to promote each other's success by helping, assisting, supporting, encouraging, and praising each other's efforts to achieve.
- Fourth, working together cooperatively requires interpersonal and small group skills, such as leadership, decisionmaking, building trust, communication, and conflict management skills.
- Finally, cooperative groups must engage in group processing, which exists when group members discuss how well they are achieving their goals and maintaining effective working relationships.

Figure 7-2. Outcomes of Cooperative Learning

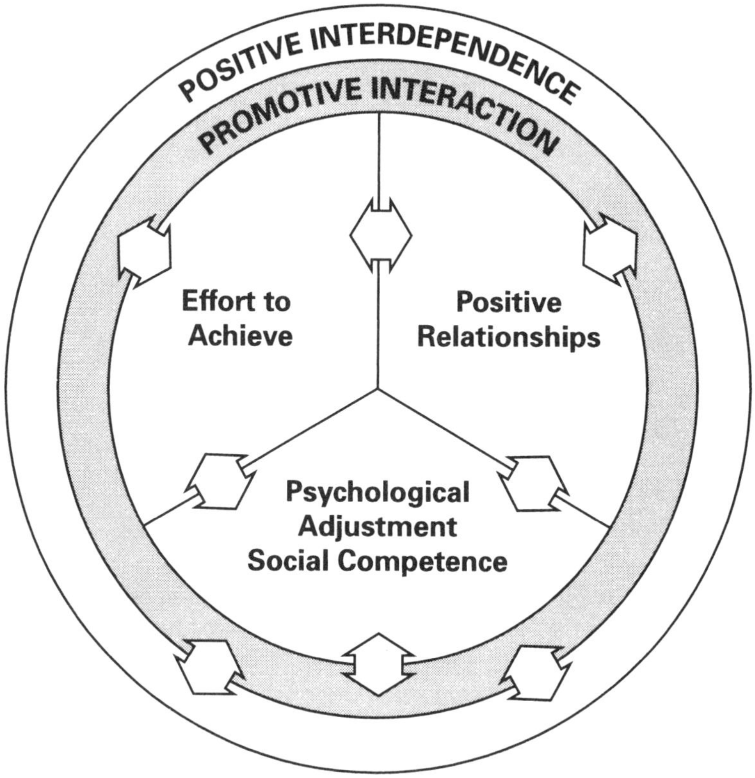

Cooperative Learning

> Two are better than one, because they have a good reward for toil. For if they fall, one will lift up his fellow; but woe to him who is alone when he falls and has not another to lift him up...And though a man might prevail against one who is alone, two will withstand him. A threefold cord is not quickly broken. [Ecclesiastics 4:9-12]

Positive development is enhanced by keeping students constructively engaged in learning from the moment they enter the classroom until the time they leave. The most effective way to do so is by using cooperative learning. Cooperative learning is the instructional use of small groups so that students work together to maximize their own and each other's learning [Johnson, Johnson, & Holubec, 1998a]. Within cooperative learning groups, students discuss the material to be learned, help and assist each other to understand it, and encourage each other to work hard. Any assignment in any curriculum for any age student can be done cooperatively. When you walk down the halls of a school, you should see signs of cooperative learning in every classroom. Desks should be clustered, group name placards should designate team work stations, posters should celebrate the benefits of teamwork, bulletin boards both inside and outside classrooms should display the products of students' cooperative efforts, and students should huddle in their groups and celebrate mutual accomplishments with high-fives, smiles, and handshakes. These signs are indicative of the use of the three types of cooperative learning (see Table 7-2) [Johnson, Johnson, & Holubec 1998a, 1998b].

Formal cooperative learning consists of students working together, for one class period to several weeks, to achieve shared learning goals and complete jointly specific tasks and assignments (such as decisionmaking or problem solving, completing a curriculum unit, writing a report, conducting a survey or experiment, or reading a chapter or reference book, learning vocabulary, or answering questions at the end of the chapter) [Johnson, Johnson, & Holubec 1998]. Any course requirement or assignment may be structured cooperatively. In formal cooperative learning groups, teachers may take several steps:

- **Make a number of preinstructional decisions.** Teachers specify the objectives for the lesson (both academic and social skills) and decide on the size of groups, the method of assigning students to groups, the roles students will be assigned, the materials needed to conduct the lesson, and the way the room will be arranged.

- **Explain the task and the positive interdependence.** A teacher clearly defines the assignment, teaches the required concepts and strategies, specifies the positive interdependence and individual accountability, gives the criteria for success, and explains the expected social skills to be used.

Table 7-2. Types of Cooperative Learning

Formal Cooperative Learning	Informal Cooperative Learning	Cooperative Base Groups
Completes assignment, lesson, unit, project to maximize own and groupmates' learning	Discusses assigned questions for few minutes to focus attention, organize knowledge, set expectations, create mood, ensure cognitive processing and rehearsal, summarize, precue next session, provide closure	Permanent, lasts for one semester, one year, or several years to ensure all members make academic progress and develop cognitively and socially in healthy ways
Teacher Procedure	**Teacher Procedure**	**Teacher Procedure**
Make pre-instructional decisions	Conduct introductory focused discussion	Structure opening class meeting to check homework, ensure members understand academic material, complete routine tasks such as attendance, and prepare members for the day
Explain task and cooperative structure	Conduct intermittent pair discussions every ten or 15 minutes	Structure ending class meeting to ensure all members understand the academic material, know what homework to do, and are making progress on long-term assignments
Monitor learning groups and intervene to improve taskwork and teamwork	Conduct closure-focused discussion	Members help and assist each other learn between classes
Assess learning and process group effectiveness		Conduct semester- or yearlong school or class service projects

- **Monitor students' learning and intervene within the groups to provide task assistance or to increase students' interpersonal and group skills.** A teacher systematically observes and collects data on each group as it works. When needed, the teacher intervenes to assist students in completing the task accurately and in working together effectively.
- **Assess students' learning and help students process how well their groups functioned.** Students' learning is carefully assessed and their performances evaluated. Members of the learning groups then discuss how effectively they worked together and how they can improve in the future.

Informal cooperative learning consists of having students work together to achieve a joint learning goal in temporary, ad-hoc groups that last from a few minutes to one class period [Johnson, Johnson, & Holubec 1998b; Johnson, Johnson, & Smith 1998]. During a lecture, demonstration, or film, informal cooperative learning can be used to focus student attention on the material to be learned, set a mood conducive to learning, help set expectations as to what will be covered in a class session, ensure that students cognitively process and rehearse the material being taught, summarize what was learned and precue the next session, and provide closure to an instructional session. During direct teaching, the instructional challenge for the teacher is to ensure that students do the intellectual work of organizing material, explaining it, summarizing it, and integrating it into existing conceptual structures. Informal cooperative learning groups are often organized so that students engage in three- to five-minute focused discussions before and after a lecture and two- to three-minute turn-to-your-partner discussions interspersed throughout a lecture.

Cooperative base groups are long-term, heterogeneous cooperative learning groups with stable membership [Johnson, Johnson, & Holubec 1998b; Johnson, Johnson, & Smith 1998]. Base groups give the support, help, encouragement, and assistance each member needs to make academic progress (attend class, complete all assignments, learn) and develop cognitively and socially in healthy ways. Base groups are permanent (lasting from one to several years) and provide the long-term, caring peer relationships necessary to influence members consistently to work hard in school. The use of base groups tends to improve attendance, personalize the work required and the school experience, and improve the quality and quantity of learning. Positive development is enhanced when base groups are given the responsibility for conducting a yearlong service project to improve the school.

Benefits Of Cooperative Learning

A focus on cooperative learning and persistence in implementing it in every classroom is instrumental in laying the foundation for a constructive learning environment [Johnson & Johnson 1989].

- First, cooperative learning ensures that all students are meaningfully and actively involved in learning. Active, involved students do not tend to engage in disruptive, off-task behavior.

- Second, cooperative learning ensures that students are achieving up to their potential and are experiencing psychological success so they are motivated to continue to invest energy and effort in learning. Those who experience academic failure are at risk for tuning out and acting up which often leads to physical or verbal aggression.

- Third, systematic use of cooperative learning promotes the development of caring and committed relationships for every student. Students who are isolated or alienated from their peers and who do not have friends are at-risk for violent and destructive behavior compared to students who experience social support and a sense of belonging.

- Fourth, cooperative groups provide an arena in which students develop the interpersonal and small group skills needed to work effectively with diverse schoolmates. Students learn how to communicate effectively, provide leadership, engage in effective decisionmaking, build trust, and understand others' perspectives.

- Fifth, the cooperative base groups provide the arena for discussions in which personal problems are shared and solved. As a result, students' resilience and ability to cope with adversity and stress tend to increase. Children who do not share their problems and who do not have caring, supportive help in solving them are at more risk for disruptive and destructive behavior.

- Sixth, cooperative groups promote a sense of meaning, pride, and esteem by academically helping and assisting classmates and contributing to their well-being and quality of life.
- Seventh, all the benefits of cooperation for students can also be found to result from the cooperation among faculty, between faculty and administrators, and among administrators.
- Finally, the systematic use of cooperative learning provides the context for resolving conflicts in constructive ways. To constructively resolve conflicts, students, faculty, and staff need a common set of procedures, which is why a schoolwide conflict resolution and peer mediation program is implemented.

Classroom Interdependence

Ways to extend the positive interdependence within the learning groups to the classroom as a whole include class goals (a criterion for each student, or a total class score as a specified criterion), class rewards or celebrations (academic and nonacademic rewards or a class party), class roles (establishing a classroom government, placing teams in charge of daily class cleanup, running a class bank or business), or dividing resources (having the class publish a newsletter in which each cooperative group contributes one article). Following is an example of divided resources:

> One class was studying geography. The ceiling was turned into a large grid giving latitude and longitude. The class was divided into eight cooperative groups. Each group was assigned a geographical location on which to do a report. The groups summarized the essential information about their location on a placard, located where on the ceiling it should be placed, and placed it there. The class then planned an itinerary for a trip to visit all eight places. Yarn

> was used to mark their journey. As they arrived at each spot, the appropriate group presented its report on the location, including its latitude and longitude.

Class meetings can be held as a forum for discussing how well the class is functioning and how the quality of classroom life may be improved. Finally, a common identity may be created by such things as a class name, slogan, flag, or song.

Interclass Interdependence

Cross-class cooperation can occur in many ways. An interdisciplinary team of three to six teachers may organize their classes into a "neighborhood" or a "school within a school," where classes work together and engage in joint projects for a number of years. Science and math, or English literature and social studies may be integrated and the classes combined. Students of different ages can be involved in cross-class "reading buddies" that meet weekly throughout the year so they can jointly share and explore literature. Several classes can do periodic projects on learning specific social skills and values so students from different classes can demonstrate the skills and values to each other and use them in the hallways, on the playground, and in the lunchroom. In these and many other ways, cross-class interdependence may be created.

School Interdependence

School level positive interdependence is established in numerous ways [Johnson & Johnson 1994]. First, the school mission statement may articulate the mutual goals shared by all members of the school and may be displayed on the school's walls and printed at the top of the agenda of every meeting involving faculty and staff. This "keeps the dream" in front of the faculty and staff and is a constant reminder of their commitment.

Second, just as students work in cooperative learning groups, ideally teachers will work in a variety of cooperative teams [Johnson & Johnson 1994]. All faculty and staff can meet weekly in teaching teams and/or study groups. Collegial teaching teams are formed to increase teachers' instructional expertise and success. They consist of two to five teachers who meet weekly and discuss how better to implement cooperative learning within their classrooms. The teaching teams plan lessons together, orchestrate their use of integrated curriculum units, schedule the times they will teach together and apart, and explore how best to promote each other's instructional success for the following week. Regular teaming among faculty promotes collegial relationships, ongoing professional growth, and induction of new faculty. Collegial study groups are formed to meet regularly to discuss a book about an instructional method (such as cooperative learning, block scheduling, or creating an integrated curriculum). Teaching teams and study groups remind faculty and staff about the important instructional procedures, involve the faculty in a continuously improvement process, and provide a procedure for socializing new teachers into the faculty. At one of the schools we work with, for example, a teacher stated:

> One challenge we face each year is bringing new faculty on board. We want them to become part of our school community as quickly as possible and that means training them in the components of our program. Study groups help accomplish this. We have one study group, for example, on the Nuts and Bolts of Cooperative Learning for new faculty who have not been trained in cooperative learning and another study group on Teaching Students to be Peacemakers for new faculty who have not been trained in conflict resolution. A trained, experienced teacher leads each study group. Each meeting we take a chapter in the book and go over it in detail. Then we plan how to implement it in our classrooms. We make sure we have those programs in every classroom in the school. This is how we keep the climate the way it is.

Third, in addition to the collegial teaching teams and study groups, teachers may be assigned to task forces to plan and implement solutions to schoolwide issues and problems such as curriculum adoptions and lunchroom behavior and ad hoc decisionmaking groups during faculty meetings to involve all staff members in important school decisions.

Finally, school interdependence may be highlighted in a variety of schoolwide activities, such as the weekly student-produced school news broadcast, special activities organized by the student council, all-school projects, and regular school assemblies.

School-Parent Interdependence

Cooperation is built between the school and the parents by involving parents in establishing mutual goals and the "strategic plan" to achieve the goals. Parents can produce a school weekly newsletter. Parents, with the help of students, can publish the school yearbook. Parents can volunteer in their children's classes and help conduct special projects. Parents may serve on all school committees and the site council. Parents can organize and conduct a variety of school activities, including a school carnival, a school gift-wrap sale, periodic parties in each classroom, and field trips. The PTA may raise money for additional supplies and technology. A faculty-parent task force may be formed to deal with serious discipline problems and ensure that parents are notified when a student misbehaves. The ideal goal is to have 100% of the parents participating in the school.

School-Neighborhood Interdependence

The school community may be extended into the neighborhood. Local merchants can support the school mission by giving a discount to students who achieve a "B" average or above. Members of the neighborhood could play in the school band. Classes could do neighborhood service projects, cleaning up a park or mowing the yards of elderly residents. There are many creative ways that the school and the neighborhood can join together to accomplish mutual goals.

The Second C: Constructive Conflict Resolution

Conflict is the moment of truth within any community. It is almost paradoxical that the more committed members are to the community's goals, and the more caring and committed the relationships among members, the more frequent and intense the conflicts. In addition, positive development requires that individuals learn how to manage conflicts constructively. When they are managed constructively, conflicts can result in such positive outcomes as (1) increasing energy, curiosity, and motivation; (2) increase achievement, retention, insight, creativity, problemsolving, and synthesis; (3) increase healthy cognitive and social development; (4) clarify own and others' identity, commitments, and values; and (5) strengthen relationships [Johnson & Johnson 1995a 1995c, 1996]: If the conflicts are managed destructively, they destroy relationships and tear the cooperative system apart.

Whether positive or negative outcomes result depends largely on disputants having clear procedures for managing conflicts, disputants being skilled in the use of the procedures and value using them, and whether the norms and values of the school encourage and support the use of the procedures. If one or more of these conditions are not met, then conflicts will tend to be managed destructively. Faculty and staff need to teach students (and learn themselves) three procedures for managing conflicts: academic controversy, problem-solving negotiation, and peer mediation procedures (see Table 7-3) [Johnson & Johnson 1995a, 1995c].

Academic Controversies

To promote healthy development, teachers can structure academic controversies frequently and teach students how to resolve them [Johnson & Johnson 1995c]. A controversy exists when one person's ideas, opinions, information, theories, or conclusions are incompatible with those of another and the two seek to reach an agreement. Controversies are resolved by engaging in what Aristotle called deliberate discourse (i.e., the discussion of the advantages and disadvantages of proposed actions), aimed at synthesizing novel solutions (i.e., creative problem solving). Teaching students how to engage in the controversy process begins with randomly assigning students to heterogeneous cooperative learning groups of four members [Johnson & Johnson 1979, 1989, 1995c]. The groups are given an issue on which to write a report and pass a test. Each cooperative group is divided into two pairs. One pair is given the con-position on the issue and the other pair is given the pro-position. Each pair is given the instructional materials needed to define their position and point them towards

Table 7-3. Types of Conflict

Academic Controversy	Conflicts of Interest
One person's ideas, information, theories, conclusions, and opinions are incompatible with those of another and the two seek to reach an agreement.	The actions of one person attempting to maximize benefits prevents, blocks, or interferes with another person maximizing their benefits.
Controversy Procedure	**Integrative (problemsolving) Negotiations**
Research and prepare positions	Describe wants
Present and advocate positions	Describe feelings
Refute opposing position and refute attacks on own position	Describe reasons for wants and feelings
Reverse perspectives	Take other's perspective
Synthesize and integrate best evidence and reasoning from all sides	Invent three optional agreements that maximize joint outcomes
	Choose one and formalize agreement

supporting information. The cooperative goal of reaching a consensus on the issue (by synthesizing the best reasoning from both sides) and writing a quality group report is highlighted. Students then go through the following process:

- **Research and prepare a position.** Each pair develops the position assigned, learns the relevant information, and plans how to present the best case possible to the other pair. Near the end of the period pairs are encouraged to compare notes with pairs from other groups who represent the same position.
- **Present and advocate their position.** Each pair makes their presentation to the opposing pair. Each member of the pair has to participate in the presentation. Students are to be as persuasive and convincing as possible. Members of the opposing pair are encouraged to take notes, listen carefully to learn the information being presented, and clarify anything they do not understand.

- **Refute opposing position and rebut attacks on their own.** Students argue forcefully and persuasively for their position, presenting as many facts as they can to support their point of view. Students analyze and critically evaluate the information, rationale, and inductive and deductive reasoning of the opposing pair, asking them for the facts that support their point of view. They refute the arguments of the opposing pair and rebut attacks on their position. They discuss the issue, following a set of rules to help them criticize ideas without criticizing people, differentiate the two positions, and assess the degree of evidence and logic supporting each position. They keep in mind that the issue is complex and they need to know both sides to write a good report.
- **Reverse perspectives.** The pairs reverse perspectives and present each other's positions. In arguing for the opposing position, students are forceful and persuasive. They add any new information that the opposing pair did not think to present. They strive to see the issue from both perspectives simultaneously.
- **Synthesize and integrate the best evidence and reasoning into a joint position.** The four group members drop all advocacy and synthesize and integrate what they know into a joint position to which all sides can agree. They (1) finalize the report (the teacher evaluates reports on the quality of the writing, the logical presentation of evidence, and the oral presentation of the report to the class), (2) present their conclusions to the class (all four members of the group are required to participate orally in the presentation), (3) individually take the test covering both sides of the issue (if every member of the group achieves up to criterion, they all receive bonus points), and (4) process how well they worked together and how they could be even more effective next time.

As Thomas Jefferson noted, "Difference of opinion leads to inquiry, and inquiry to truth." Over the past 30 years we have conducted more than 25 research studies on the impact of academic controversy and numerous other researchers have conducted studies directly on controversy and in related areas [Johnson & Johnson 1989, 1995c]. The considerable research available indicates that intellectual "disputed passages" create higher achievement (characterized by higher achievement, longer retention, more frequent use of higher level reasoning and metacognitive thought, more critical thinking, greater creativity, and continuing motivation to learn), more positive interpersonal relationships, and greater psychological health when they occur within cooperative learning groups and are carefully structured to ensure that students manage them constructively [Johnson & Johnson 1989, 1995c]. Engaging in a controversy can also be fun, enjoyable, and exciting. Two of the most important aspects for constructive learning environments, however, are the emphasis on viewing the issue from both perspectives and learning that conflicts can have positive outcomes when people listen to each other and work cooperatively to reach solutions.

Conflict Resolution Training

Conflict resolution and peer mediation programs have their roots in four sources [Johnson & Johnson 1995a]: Researchers in the field of conflict resolution, advocates of nonviolence, antinuclear war activists, and members of the legal profession. The research-based peer mediation programs began in the 1960s with the Teaching Students to Be Peacemakers Program [Johnson & R. Johnson 1995a, 1995b]. It was derived from social interdependence theory [Deutsch 1949; Lewin 1951]; Johnson & Johnson 1989] and focused on teaching all students in a school the nature of conflict, how to use an integrative negotiation procedure, and how to mediate peer conflicts. All students then take turns in being a class and school mediator. A similar program was initiated by Morton Deutsch in the 1990s [Deutsch 1993].

The nonviolence advocates, represented primarily by the Quaker Church, began a conflict resolution program in 1972 when Priscilla Prutzman directed a Quaker Educational project in New York City to teach nonviolence to children, known as the Children's Creative Response to Conflict.

They teach all students that the power of nonviolence lies in justice, caring, and personal integrity. The antinuclear war activists are represented by the Educators for Social Responsibility, who in 1985 began the Resolving Conflict Creatively Program. The program includes a 10-unit curriculum with lessons on intergroup relations, cooperative learning, and dispute resolution procedures, and 20 hours of training in how to be a peer mediator. Finally, the legal profession became involved in President Carter's Neighborhood Justice Centers and in the 1980s, Helena Davis wrote a conflict manager curriculum for training a cadre of peer mediators in elementary schools that was later extended and modified by Gail Sadalla. The training lasted for two days and focused on the role of mediator and basic communication skills. The program is known as the San Francisco Community Boards Conflict Managers Program.

Problem-Solving Negotiations

Intellectual conflicts are not the only conflicts that occur within a community and must be resolved constructively. There are conflicts based on individuals' differing interests within a situation. Conflict of interests exist when the actions of one person attempting to maximize his or her wants and benefits prevents, blocks, or interferes with another person maximizing his or her wants and benefits. Such conflicts are ideally resolved through problem-solving (integrative) negotiation. When negotiation does not work, then mediation is required.

All members of the school community need to know how to negotiate constructive resolutions to their conflicts. There are two types of negotiations: distributive or "win-lose" (where one person benefits only if the opponent agrees to make a concession), and integrative or problem solving (where disputants work together to create an agreement that benefits everyone involved). In ongoing relationships, only a problem-solving approach to negotiations is constructive. The steps in using problem solving negotiations are listed below [Johnson & Johnson 1995a, 1995b]:

- **Describe what you want.** "I want to use the book now." This includes using good communication skills and defining the conflict as a small and specific mutual problem.

- **Describe how you feel.** "I'm frustrated." Disputants must understand how they feel and communicate it openly and clearly.
- **Describe the reasons for your wants and feelings.** "You have been using the book for the past hour. If I don't get to use the book soon my report will not be done on time. It's frustrating to have to wait so long." This includes expressing cooperative intentions, listening carefully, separating interests from positions, and differentiating before trying to integrate the two sets of interests.
- **Take the other's perspective and summarize your understanding of what the other person wants, how the other person feels, and the reasons underlying both.** "My understanding of you is..." This includes understanding the perspective of the opposing disputant and being able to see the problem from both perspectives simultaneously.
- **Invent three optional plans to resolve the conflict that maximize joint benefits.** "Plan A is..., Plan B is..., Plan C is..." This includes inventing creative options to solve the problem.
- **Choose one and formalizing the agreement with a handshake.** "Let's agree on Plan B!" A wise agreement is fair to all disputants and is based on principles. It maximizes joint benefits and strengthens disputants' ability to work together cooperatively and resolve conflicts constructively in the future. It specifies how each disputant should act in the future and how the agreement will be reviewed and renegotiated if it does not work.

Peer Mediation

Once the problem-solving negotiation procedure is learned, all members of the school community need to learn how to mediate conflicts of interests [Johnson & Johnson 1995a, 1995b]. A mediator is a neutral person who helps two or more people resolve their conflict, usually by negotiating an integrative agreement. Mediation is not arbitration. Arbitration is the submission of a dispute to a disinterested third party (such as a teacher or principal) who makes a final and binding judgment as to how the conflict will be resolved. Mediation consists of four steps [Johnson & Johnson 1995a, 1995b]:

- **Ending hostilities.** Break up hostile encounters and cool off students.
- **Ensuring disputants are committed to the mediation process.** To ensure that disputants are committed to the mediation process and are ready to negotiate in good faith, the mediator introduces the process of mediation and sets the ground rules. The mediator first introduces him- or herself. The mediator asks students if they want to solve the problem and does not proceed until both answer "yes." Then the mediator explains:
    - "Mediation is voluntary. My role is to help you find a solution to your conflict that is acceptable to both of you."
    - "I am neutral. I will not take sides or attempt to decide who is right or wrong. I will help you decide how to solve the conflict."
    - "Each person will have the chance to state his or her view of the conflict without interruption."
    - "The rules you must agree to are (1) agree to solve the problem, (2) no name calling, (3) do not interrupt, (4) be as honest as you can, (5) if you agree to a solution, you must abide by it (you must do what you have agreed to do), and (6) anything said in mediation is confidential (you, the mediator, will not tell anyone what is said)."
- **Helping disputants successfully negotiate with each other.** The disputants are carefully taken through the negotiation sequence of (1) jointly defining the conflict by both persons stating what they want and how they feel, (2) exchanging reasons, (3) reversing perspectives so that each person is able to present the other's position and feelings to the other's satisfaction, (4) inventing at least three options for mutual benefit, and (5) reaching a wise agreement and shaking hands.

- **Formalizing the agreement.** The agreement is solidified into a contract. Disputants must agree to abide by their final decision and, in many ways, the mediator becomes "the keeper of the contract."

Once students understand how to negotiate and mediate, the peacemaker program is implemented. Each day the teacher selects two class members to serve as official mediators. Any conflicts students cannot resolve themselves are referred to the mediators. The mediators wear official T-shirts, patrol the playground and lunchroom, and are available to mediate any conflicts that occur in the classroom or school. An example is as follows.

> During lunch on the playground, a ball rolls out of bounds during a lively game of soccer. A cluster of students walking by laugh as one of them kicks the ball away from the player trying to retrieve it. An argument ensures. A pair of peer mediators with clipboards in hand quickly approach the two disputants. "Would you like some help resolving your conflict?" So begins the mediation process through which the disputants arrive at a mutually agreeable solution that makes both happy. They shake hands as friends and return to their activities while the peer mediators make a note of the resolution, then continue to be available for other schoolmates who may need help resolving conflicts.

The role of mediator is rotated so that all students in the class or school serve as mediators an equal amount of time. Initially, students mediate in pairs. This ensures that shy or nonverbal students get the same amount of experience as more extroverted and verbally fluent students. Mediating classmates' conflicts is perhaps the most effective way of teaching students the need for the skillful use of each step of the negotiation procedure.

If peer mediation fails, the teacher mediates the conflict. If teacher mediation fails, the teacher arbitrates by deciding who is right and who is wrong. If that fails, the principal mediates the conflict. If that fails, the principal arbitrates. Teaching all students to mediate properly results in a schoolwide discipline program where students are empowered to regulate and control their own and their classmates actions. Teachers and administrators are then freed to spend more of their energies on instruction.

Continuing Lessons to Refine and Upgrade Students' Skills

Additional lessons are needed to refine and upgrade students' skills in using the negotiation and mediation procedures. Gaining real expertise in resolving conflicts constructively takes years of training and practice. A few hours of training is clearly insufficient. Negotiation and mediation training may become part of the fabric of school life by integrating them into academic lessons. Literature, history, and science units typically involve conflict. Almost any lesson in these subject areas can be modified to include role-playing situations in which the negotiation and/or mediation procedures are used. In our recent research, for example, we have focused on integrating the peacemaker training into history units and English literature units involving the studying of a novel. Each of the major conflicts in the novel was used to teach the negotiation and/or mediation procedures and students participated in role playing how to use the procedures to resolve the conflicts in the novel constructively.

Spiral Curriculum from the First Through the Twelve Grades

The Teaching Students to be Peacemakers Program is a 12-year spiral program that is retaught each year in an increasingly sophisticated and complex way. It takes years to become competent in resolving conflicts. Twelve years of training and practice will result in a person with considerable expertise in resolving conflicts constructively.

Benefits of Conflict Resolution and Peer Mediation Programs

We have conducted fourteen studies on implementing the Peacemaker Program in schools involving students from kindergarten through the tenth-grade and several other researchers have conducted relevant studies [Johnson & Johnson 1995a, 1996]. The benefits of teaching students the problem-solving negotiation and the peer mediation procedures are as follows:

- First, students and faculty tended to develop a shared understanding of how conflicts should be managed and a common vocabulary to discuss conflicts.
- Second, students tended to learn the negotiation and mediation procedures, retain their knowledge throughout the school year and into

the following year, apply the procedures to their and other people's conflicts, transfer the procedures to nonclassroom settings such as the playground and lunchroom, transfer the procedures to nonschool settings such as the home, use the procedures similarly in family and school settings, and (when given the option) engage in problem-solving rather than win-lose negotiations.

- Third, students' attitudes toward conflict tended to became more positive. Students learned to view conflicts as potentially positive and faculty and parents viewed the conflict training as constructive and helpful.
- Fourth, students tended to resolve their conflicts without the involvement of faculty and administrators. A teacher states:

> It's so great to be able to say, "These people are having a conflict; is there someone who can help them resolve it?" Twenty hands go up and everybody wants to help them. And I choose someone and say, "All right, take these people back to the mediation table and solve the conflict and let me know how it goes." Sometimes it will take 2 minutes and sometimes it will take 15 minutes. As a teacher, I respect so much and appreciate immensely, that students can do that for themselves. It enables everybody in the class, including me, to focus on what we're learning.

Classroom management problems, in other words, tended to be significantly reduced. The number of discipline problems teachers have to deal with decreased by about 60% and referrals to administrators dropped about 90%. Faculty and administrators no longer had to arbitrate conflicts among students; instead they spend their time maintaining and supporting the peer mediation process. A teacher commented:

> Classroom management problems are nil as far as I'm concerned. We don't do a lot of disciplining per se. A lot of times, when a conflict occurs on the playground, they resolve it there and do not bring it back to the classroom. So there is a lot less I have to deal with in the classroom.

- Fifth, the conflict resolution procedures tended to enhance the basic values of the classroom and school. A teacher who emphasizes the value of "respect" states, "The procedures are a very respectful way to resolve conflicts. There's a calmness in the classroom because the students know the negotiation and mediation procedures."
- Sixth, students generally liked to engage in the procedures. A teacher states, "They never refuse to negotiate or mediate. When there's a conflict and you say it's time for conflict resolution, you never have either one say I won't do it. There are no refusals."
- Finally, when integrated into academic units, the conflict resolution training tended to increase academic achievement and long-term retention of the academic material. Academic units, especially in subject areas such as literature and history, provide a setting to understand conflicts, practice how to resolve them, and use them to gain insight into the material being studied.

The Third C: Civic Values

> Students are sitting in a circle on the carpet. A class meeting is in progress. Today the issue is respect. One of the students risked telling her classmates that she felt hurt during recess the day before because she was trying to tell kids the rules to a new game, but nobody would listen. So began a discussion on what it means to be respectful, why that is important, and the sharing of everyone's personal experiences of times they felt respected versus not respected.

Some historians claim that the decline and fall of Rome was set in motion by corruption from within, rather than by conquest from without. Rome fell, it can be argued, because Romans lost their civic virtue. Civic virtue exists when individuals meet both the letter and spirit of their public obligations. For a community to exist and be sustained, members must share common goals and values aimed at increasing the quality of life within the community. No one should be surprised that, in a community where competitive and individualistic values are taught, people will behave in accordance with such values. When that happens in a society, for example, people may stop obeying the law. Running stoplights may become a common occurrence as the individualist thinks it is rational to do so as he or she will arrive at the destination sooner. If someone is killed, it will be a pedestrian, not the driver. But each of us is at some time a pedestrian. Community cannot be maintained unless members value others and the community as a whole, as well as themselves.

There are a wide variety of programs to teach students values [Kohn 1997]. Some of these programs focus on listing values that should be taught and others on developing student character. Both approaches tend to be collections of exhortations and extrinsic inducements designed to make children work harder and do what they are told. Students are often drilled in specific behaviors rather than engaged in discussions that require reflection on how one should live. Kohn criticizes these approaches and concludes that a more generic approach is needed that (1) focuses on the overall organizational structure of the school, (2) assumes a positive view of human nature, (3) aims at developing individuals who are active advocates for democracy and social justice, (4) instills values (beyond selfishness) aimed at improving the quality of life for all societal members and the common good, and (5) utilizes cooperative learning as the primary means of instruction.

Positive development of students requires that all members of the school community adopt a set of civic values [Johnson & Johnson 1996b, in press). To create the common culture that defines a community, there must be common goals and shared values that help define appropriate behavior. A learning community cannot exist in schools dominated by competition, where students are taught to value striving for their personal success at the expense of others, or individualistic efforts, where students value only their own self-interests.

Rather, students need to internalize values underlying cooperation and integrative negotiations, such as commitment to the common good and to the well-being of other members, a sense of responsibility to contribute one's fair share of the work, respect for the efforts of others and for them as people, behaving with integrity, caring for other members, compassion when other members are in need, and appreciation of diversity. Such civic values both underlie and are promoted by the cooperation and constructive conflict resolution that take place in the school.

Membership in a community requires the adoption of the community's values. The community's values may be taught through direct instruction, modeling and identification, the enactment of assigned and voluntary roles, group influences, and the hidden curriculum existing in the pattern and flow of daily school life [Johnson & F. Johnson 1997]. First, the core values can be directly taught by placing them in the school's mission statement, posting them in every classroom, having lessons defining them and giving examples of how they may be expressed in interactions with other people, role playing how to put them into action, pointing out instances where a student demonstrated the values, pointing out models to be imitated, and integrating them into the curriculum. Children's literature may be used to teach values. *The Great Gilly Hopkins* by Katherine Paterson may be used to focus attention on compassion, and *The River* by Gary Paulsen may be used to help students focus on responsibility. Class meetings provide a safe forum for talking about the values and how they affect student and faculty lives. Being clear about what is valued enables aligned choice making throughout the curriculum—from instructional strategies, utilized to topics of study pursued, to instructional resources employed.

Second, faculty and administrators can teach students values through identification by building positive, caring, supportive relationships with the students and by consistently modeling the values in interactions with the students. In its simplest form, identification occurs when a student tries to be like someone (an adult, older student, or mythical figure) that the student admires—a person usually perceived as resourceful, powerful, or competent. A student can admire a teacher's scholarship, for example, and strive to become a scholar, or a student can see a teacher behaving honestly and decide to do likewise.

Third, values may be taught by assigning students social roles. A social role is a set of expectations (containing rights and responsibilities) aimed at structuring interactions within a reciprocal relationship. In school, students learn the roles of "student" as well as other roles such as "American," "citizen," "collaborator," and "mediator."

Fourth, individuals adopt the values of their reference groups. Reference groups are the groups to which individuals believe they belong or to which they aspire to belong [Johnson & F. Johnson 1997]. Individuals accept a system of values, attitudes, and behavioral patterns when they accept membership in a new group. The discussion and consensual validation that take place within a group result in personal commitments to adopt the values. Values are not inculcated by focusing on each individual separately, but rather by emphasizing membership in a group (or community) that holds the desired values. By adopting the school community as a reference group, students will adopt its civic values.

Fifth, the value systems underlying competitive, individualistic, and cooperative situations are a hidden curriculum beneath the surface of school life. Whenever students engage in *competitive* efforts, for example, they learn the following values:

- commitment to getting more than others (there is a built-in concern that one is smarter, faster, stronger, more competent, and more successful than others so that one will win and others will lose);
- success depends on beating, defeating, and getting more than other people (triumphing over others and being "Number One" are valued),
- what is important is winning, not mastery or excellence;
- opposing, obstructing, and sabotaging the success of others is a natural way of life (winning depends on a good offense—doing better than others—and a good defense—not letting anyone do better than you);
- feeling joy and pride in one's wins and others' losses (the pleasure of winning is associated with others' disappointment with losing);
- others are a threat to one's success;

- a person's worth (own and others) is conditional and contingent on his or her "wins" (a person's worth is never fixed, it depends on the latest victory);
- winning, not learning, is the goal of academic work; and
- people who are different are to be either feared (if they have an advantage) or held in contempt (if they have a handicap).

Listed below are the values inherently taught by *individualistic* experiences:

- commitment to one's own self-interest (only personal success is viewed as important, others' success is irrelevant),
- success depends on one's own efforts,
- the pleasure of succeeding is personal and relevant to only oneself,
- other people are irrelevant,
- self-worth is based on a unidimensional view that the characteristics that help the person succeed are valued (in school that is primarily reading and math ability),
- extrinsic motivation to gain rewards for achieving up to criteria is valued, and
- similar people are liked and dissimilar people are disliked.

The values inherently taught by *cooperative* efforts follow:

- commitment to own and others' success and well-being as well as to the common good,
- success depends on joint efforts to achieve mutual goals,
- facilitating, promoting, and encouraging the success of others is a natural way of life (a smart cooperator will always find ways to promote, facilitate, and encourage the efforts of others),
- the pleasure of succeeding is associated with others' happiness in their success,
- other people are potential contributors to one's success,

- own and other people's worth is unconditional (because there are so many diverse ways that a person may contribute to a joint effort, everyone has value all the time),
- intrinsic motivation based on striving to learn, grow, develop, and succeed is valued (learning is the goal, not winning), and
- people who are different from oneself are to be valued as they can make unique contributions to the joint effort.

Sixth, the value systems underlying problem-solving negotiations and mediation situations are a hidden curriculum beneath the surface of school life. Constructive conflict resolution promotes the values of subjecting one's conclusions to intellectual challenge, viewing issues from all perspectives, reaching agreements that are satisfying to all disputants, and maintaining effective and caring long-term relationships. In other words, constructive conflict resolution inherently teaches a set of civic values aimed at ensuring the fruitful continuation of the community.

Benefits Of Civic Values Program

There are too many developmental and personal benefits from learning civic values to detail all of them here. At the personal level, civic values provide the internal gyroscope each child and youth needs to guide his or her behavior. It ensures that each individual becomes inner-directed (as opposed to other-directed) and has the inner principles needed to regulate their behavior. At the school management level, teaching civic values takes the guesswork out of knowing what the school stands for. The values guide decision making about the curriculum, instruction, and resources. They provide a standard for making selections of curriculum materials. The values provide a structure for faculty and staff to talk to parents, students, visitors, and each other about what is important and why.

Evaluation Of Effectiveness

There are numerous articles reporting claims about the impact of programs aimed at providing a safe educational environment and enhancing the positive development of children and adolescents. The articles tend to provide purely descriptive, anecdotal accounts of the programs' impact on various dependents and descriptions of curriculum design and guidelines. Broad claims are presented but not supported by actual research data. Anecdotal reports are inspiring, but do not illuminate what programs are doing, how they are doing it, and how broadly their effects can be generalized. Most programs, furthermore, are atheoretical; they are based more on practical experience and brainstorming than on theory. The Three Cs Program is something of an exception. It is directly based on social interdependence and conflict theories. There is a great deal of research on cooperation [Johnson & Johnson 1989] and considerable research on the effectiveness of the controversy [Johnson & Johnson 1995c] and the peacemaker [Johnson & Johnson 1995a, 1997] programs. There is almost no valid or reliable evidence concerning the effectiveness of any values programs. The Three Cs Program is, therefore, the best researched and substantiated

Recommendations

For schools and communities trying to promote positive youth outcomes, there are recommendations that they may wish to follow:

- Structure the majority of learning activities cooperatively. This is the most significant influence on positive development.
- Minimize the use of competitive and individualistic situations.
- Hold regular class meetings in which students discuss issues, plan for improvements, decide on changes, and reflect on the quality of classroom life.
- Provide explicit opportunities for students to take each other's perspective and to practice "perspective-taking."
- Provide continuous opportunities for students to build positive, caring relationships with each other in which there are high levels of candor and personal interaction.
- Regularly engage all students in academic controversies.

- Teach all students how to engage in problem-solving negotiations and mediate their schoolmates' conflicts.
- Use academic subject matter (such as literature and history) to teach controversy and peacemaking (conflict resolution) skills and civic values. Role plays and discussions should be open ended rather than didactic.
- Provide opportunities for students to behave in ways that support the values being taught. Students, for example, should have the opportunity to tell the truth; opportunities to lie should be minimized.
- Structure cooperation at the class and school levels. Schools should be learning communities in which students care about each other and are committed to each other's success.
- Structure cooperation between the school and the parents and neighborhood. Students should have the opportunity to use their teamwork and conflict resolution skills and to express their values in settings beyond the school.
- Faculty and staff should model cooperation, constructive conflict resolution, and expression of civic values. In doing so, they make salient a concern for others illustrate their understanding of the effects of one's behavior on others, and show that they have the courage to face moral challenges.

Summary

Schools can create constructive learning environments that enhance positive development of children and youth based on a cooperative community, constructive conflict resolution, and civic values. To establish a learning community, cooperation must be carefully structured at all levels in the school. To maintain the learning community, constructive conflict resolution procedures must be taught to all members of the school. To guide and direct the cooperation and constructive conflict resolution, civic values must be inculcated in all school members. Together, the Three Cs are a complete program for creating effective and nurturing schools where children and youth develop in positive and healthy ways.

References

Deutsch, M. (1949). A theory of cooperation and competition. *Human Relations, 2*, 129-152.

Deutsch, M. (1973). The resolution of conflict. New Haven, CT: Yale University Press.

Deutsch, M. (1993). The effects of training in cooperative learning and conflict resolution in an alternative high school. *Cooperative Learning, 13*, 2-5.

Johnson D. W., & Johnson, F. (2000). *Joining together: Group theory and group skills* (7th ed.). Englewood Cliffs, NJ: Prentice-Hall.

Johnson, D. W., & Johnson, R. (1979). Conflict in the classroom: Controversy and learning. *Review of Educational Research, 49*, 51-61.

Johnson, D. W., & Johnson, R. (1989). *Cooperation and competition: Theory and research.* Edina, MN: Interaction Book Company.

Johnson, D. W., & Johnson, R. (1994). *Leading the cooperative school* (2nd ed.). Edina, MN: Interaction Book Company.

Johnson, D. W., & Johnson, R. (1995a). *Teaching students to be peacemakers* (3rd ed.). Edina, MN: Interaction Book Company.

Johnson, D. W., & Johnson, R. (1995b). *My mediation notebook* (3rd ed.). Edina, MN: Interaction Book Company.

Johnson, D. W., & Johnson, R. (1995c). *Creative controversy: Intellectual challenge in the classroom* (3rd ed.). Edina, MN: Interaction Book Company.

Johnson, D. W., & Johnson, R. (1995d). Teaching students to be peacemakers: Results of five years of research. *Peace and Conflict: Journal of Peace Psychology, 1*(4), 417-438.

Johnson, D. W., & Johnson, R. (1996a). Conflict resolution and peer mediation programs in elementary and secondary schools: A review of the research. *Review of Educational Research, 66*(4), 459-506.

Johnson, D. W., & Johnson, R. (1996b). Cooperative learning and traditional American values. *NASSP Bulletin, 80*(579), 11-18.

Johnson, D. W., & Johnson, R. (in press). Cooperative learning, values, and culturally plural classrooms. In Leicester, M., Modgill, C., & Modgil, S. (Eds.), *Values, the classroom, and cultural diversity*. London: Cassell PLC.

Johnson, D. W., Johnson, R., & Holubec, E. (1998a). *Cooperation in the classroom* (7th ed.). Edina, MN: Interaction Book Company.

Johnson, D. W., Johnson, R., & Holubec, E. (1998b). *Advanced cooperative learning* (2nd ed.). Edina, MN: Interaction Book Company.

Johnson, D. W., Johnson, R., & Smith, W. (1998). Active learning: Cooperation in the college classroom (4th ed.). Edina, MN: Interaction Book Co.

Kohn, A. (1997, February). How not to teach values. *Phi Delta Kappan*, 429-440.

Lewin, K. (1951). *Field theory and social science*. New York: Harper & Brothers.

Snow, M. (1997, March 6). Mindworks: Disbehavior. *Minneapolis Tribune*, Section E, 1-2, 14.

8 Preventing Drug Abuse

Gilbert J. Botvin and Kenneth W. Griffin

A great deal of research over the last two decades has focused on the etiology and prevention of drug use and abuse among children and adolescents. This research has increased our understanding of the multiple determinants of drug use among youth, as well as the developmental progression of drug use through adolescence. Furthermore, research findings have provided a firm conceptual foundation for the development of promising approaches to drug abuse prevention. Identifying effective prevention approaches, however, has been difficult, and there has been a great divide between what research tells us about how to prevent drug abuse and the approaches that have traditionally been used by prevention practitioners. Nevertheless, evidence of effective prevention approaches derived from sound empirical research has emerged over the past 15 years (reviewed in Botvin & Botvin [1992] and Goodstadt [1986]). Much of this research has been conducted in school settings and has tested the impact of drug abuse prevention programs designed to target the psychosocial factors associated with the initiation and early stages of drug use. While early studies focused largely on cigarette smoking, more recent studies have focused on the impact of preventive interventions on the use of multiple substances. These more recent evaluation studies have also been larger, better designed and more sophisticated, and have provided mounting empirical evidence that drug abuse prevention can work.

The goals of this chapter are to outline the scope of the problem of adolescent drug abuse and describe past and current prevention intervention approaches. This chapter will review the scientific evidence on the effectiveness of these approaches, including to what extent programs can be used with different populations, including minorities. One of the most extensively evaluated school-based drug abuse program, Life Skills Training, is reviewed. Finally, issues in disseminating successful programs for large-scale implementation are discussed. Our primary aim is to integrate findings from the growing drug abuse prevention literature, highlight some proven approaches to school-based prevention, and to provide some general principles that can help guide program developers, practitioners, and policymakers.

Adolescent Drug Abuse: Scope of the Problem

Prevalence and Trends

One of the factors responsible for the renewed interest in drug abuse is the fact that drug use among American youth has been on the rise. Results of national survey data indicate that drug use has increased consistently from the early- to mid-1990s. These increases have been observed for adolescents from different regions of the country, from different social classes, and for different age groups. Recent national survey data [Johnston et al. 1997] reports that 54% of eighth graders, 72% of tenth graders and 82% of twelfth graders have used alcohol; and that 47% of eighth graders, 60% of tenth graders, and 65% of twelfth graders have smoked cigarettes. Results from the same survey indicated that during the past 30 days, alcohol was used by 25% of eighth graders, 40% of tenth graders, and by 53% of twelfth graders. Cigarettes were used during the past 30 days by 19% of eighth graders, 30% of tenth graders, and 37% of twelfth graders. As shown in Figure 8-1, the use of one or more illicit drugs such as marijuana, stimulants, or hallucinogens has also been on the rise among adolescents since 1992, with up to 42% of high school seniors reporting having used an illicit drug in 1997 [Johnston et al. 1995, 1997].

Developmental Progression

In addition to showing that drug use in the United States is at an unacceptably high level, these statistics also suggest that for most substances there

Figure 8-1. Trends in Annual Prevalence of Illicit Drug Use Among Twelfth Graders

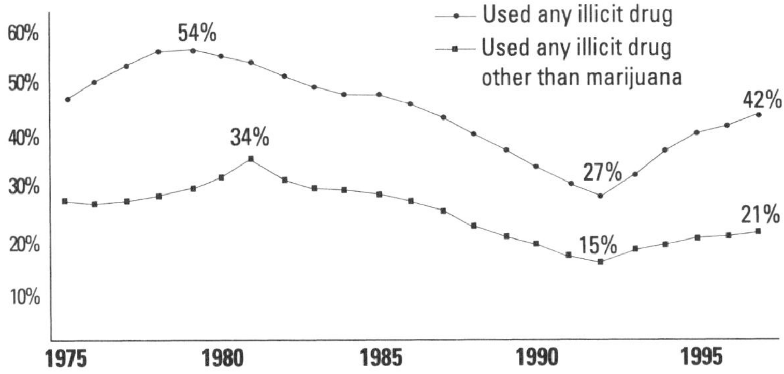

Source: Monitoring the Future [Johnson et al. 1997]

is a general developmental progression of use. Drug use is at its lowest during the beginning of adolescence, but rates of drug use generally increase with age and progress in a well-defined sequence [Millman & Botvin 1992]. This progression can be seen both in escalating use of a specific substance and in terms of the use of more substances over time. For a single substance, the progression occurs with respect to the amount and/or frequency of use: nonuse to initial use, to occasional (monthly) use, and to more frequent use (weekly and daily), as well as greater amounts used per episode. With certain dependency-producing drugs, this escalation in both the frequency and amount of use can lead to the development of tolerance in some individuals, where larger and/or more frequent administrations of the drug are needed to produce the same psychoactive effect. Individuals who reach these stages use run the risk of developing physical and/or psychological dependence on the substance.

The other way that drug use can progress during adolescence is in terms of the type or number of drugs used. For most adolescents, alcohol and tobacco are the first substances used. Inhalants also tend to be used early in the developmental progression because of their availability. Although there is obviously no fixed progression of drug use for all youth, using any substance that typically appears earlier in the progression increases the chances that an individual will eventually use substances later in the sequence. Thus, a proportion of individuals that use the "gateway" substances of alcohol, tobacco, and/or marijuana will eventually use stimulants, opiates, hallucinogens, cocaine, and other illicit substances.

Furthermore, low levels of drug use, including experimentation with drugs or occasional use, significantly increase the subsequent risk of serious drug use or drug-related problems, such as accidents or violence. For this reason, drug abuse prevention programs targeting youth should focus on preventing the early stages of drug involvement, with an emphasis on preventing the use of tobacco, alcohol, and marijuana. Since there is a direct relationship between early age of onset and the development of later serious drug-related problems, prevention programs are likely to be valuable even if they merely delay drug use initiation or prevent the transition from occasional use to more serious levels of drug involvement. In summary, our knowledge about the developmental progression of drug use among adolescents—combined with recent statistics showing that drug use among youth has increased in recent years—has contributed to a new sense of urgency regarding the identification and implementation of effective prevention approaches.

Approaches to Prevention

Approaches to prevention have become more sophisticated over the past two decades, and are increasingly based on sound theoretical models and supported by etiology studies. This is in contrast to earlier attempts at prevention, which were based largely on intuitive beliefs about what "should work." Thus, in recent years, there has been a shift towards the use of research-based prevention approaches.

Conventional Approaches to Prevention

Information-Only Approaches

Early school-based efforts to prevent drug abuse have taken the form of tobacco, alcohol, and drug education curricula. Of these, the most common form of drug education has traditionally consisted of didactic approaches that provide students with factual information about drugs and drug use, the pharmacological effects and adverse consequences of drug abuse, and other drug-related topics. In addition, health education approaches to drug abuse prevention have traditionally used fear-arousal techniques in many cases, in an attempt to scare students into not using drugs. For example, students may be provided with a graphic display or vivid description of various dangerous consequences of drug use. Despite their intuitive appeal, these educational approaches are based on several faulty assumptions, including: (1) drug use and abuse is a result of inadequate knowledge of the dangers of drugs, (2) drug abuse can be prevented by increasing students drug-related knowledge and/or fear levels, and (3) adolescents will make a rational decision to avoid drug use once they know the relevant facts. Studies have demonstrated that programs that only provide factual information (with or without arousing fear) have no effect on reducing drug use behavior [Goodstadt 1974; Kinder et al. 1980; Schaps et al. 1981]. In fact, there is some evidence that this approach may lead to increased drug use if it serves to stimulate curiosity [Swisher et al. 1971]. On the other hand, it should not be concluded that knowledge about drugs is irrelevant to drug abuse prevention efforts. Instead, it is important to provide personally relevant and age-appropriate health information about drugs as a part of a comprehensive drug abuse prevention program. In addition to increasing drug-related knowledge, such content may also lead to greater antidrug attitudes. However, it is clear that providing information about drugs by itself is not a viable approach to prevention. Lack of knowledge is only one of many factors that play a role in the etiology of drug abuse.

Affective Education Approaches

Some school-based prevention programs have focused primarily on affective factors and their relation to drug use. These approaches, referred to as affective education, have attempted to prevent drug abuse by promoting affective development. For example, these approaches attempt to increase self-understanding and improve the quality of interpersonal relationships through activities such as clarification of values, responsible decisionmaking, and by promoting effective communication and assertiveness. Despite their popularity during the 1960s and early 1970s, there has been little empirical support for the effectiveness of this approach. In fact, evaluations of the effectiveness of affective education approaches have generally been as discouraging as the knowledge-based approaches to drug abuse prevention. Like knowledge-based interventions, affective education approaches have not been shown to produce a measurable impact on drug use behavior, although in certain circumstances they may produce an impact on one or more correlates of drug use [Kearney & Hines 1980].

Social Influence Approaches

Beginning with research conducted in the late 1970s by Evans and his colleagues [Evans et al. 1978; Evans et al. 1979], there was a major paradigm shift in the field of drug abuse prevention—away from prevention efforts based largely on intuition and toward efforts grounded in theory and based on the findings of etiology research. As a pioneering prevention researcher, Evans was the first to publish scientifically rigorous studies on smoking prevention that were strongly grounded in social psychological theory. These studies demonstrated the utility of addressing the social influences that promote smoking among youth, and were among the first prevention research efforts that produced findings that were considerably stronger than earlier evaluation efforts. The recognition that social factors such as family, the media, and peers play a major role in the initiation and early stages of drug use led to the development of a new set of prevention approaches and new generation of studies that were a major departure from health education approaches thus far.

A central feature of the prevention approach developed and tested by Evans and his colleagues was the notion of psychological inoculation. This refers to a process in which adolescents are initially exposed to a weak form of the typical social influences promoting cigarette smoking, followed later by progressively stronger social influences to smoke. Through this gradual exposure, it was hoped that adolescents would build up resistance to the more virulent forms of these pro-smoking messages that they encounter in real world settings. Psychological inoculation has received considerably less emphasis in more recent prevention models, although other aspects of the social influence model originally developed by Evans have assumed greater emphasis in recent years in the work of other researchers.

Contemporary Approaches to Prevention

Two of the most important features of the contemporary social influence model include correcting normative expectations about drug use and teaching skills for resisting offers to use drugs. The prevalence of smoking, drinking, and illicit drug use is usually overestimated by adolescents [Fishbein 1977]. This overestimate leads to the formation of inaccurate normative expectations, or the forming of a set of normative beliefs that support drug use. To reduce pressure to use drugs, social influence approaches to prevention include a component designed to correct the misperception that many adults and most adolescents use drugs. Hansen and O'Malley [1996] have referred to this component as normative education. Teaching adolescents resistance skills to use in the face of peer pressure to smoke or use other substances also remains a central component of current social influence drug abuse prevention models. The primary focus of these prevention approaches has been on teaching adolescents a set of skills or tactics for resisting influences to smoke, drink, or use drugs—particularly influences coming from the media and from peers (see Table 8-1). With respect to the media, adolescence are taught how to identify and respond to pro-drug messages in advertisements, movies, rock videos, etc. Special attention is given to the persuasive appeals used by advertisers to promote the sale of tobacco and alcohol products. Students are taught how to identify specific advertising techniques, to analyze ads and their messages, and to formulate counterarguments to common advertising appeals. Teaching these skills is designed to provide adolescents with the tools for actively resisting advertisements promoting cigarette smoking and alcoholic beverages. This approach is particularly relevant given the

Table 8-1. Overview of Major Preventive Approaches

Approach	Focus	Methods
Information dissemination	Increase knowledge of drugs, the consequences of use; promote antidrug-use attitudes	Didactic instruction, discussion, audio/video presentations, displays of substances, posters, pamphlets, school assembly programs
Affective education	Increase self-esteem, responsible decisionmaking, interpersonal growth; generally includes little or no information about drugs	Didactic instruction, discussion, experiential activities, group problem-solving exercises
Resistance skills	Increase awareness of social influences to smoke, drink, or use drugs; develop skills for resisting substance use influences; increase knowledge of immediate negative consequences; establish non-substance use norms	Class discussion; resistance skills training; behavioral rehearsal; extended practice via behavioral "homework"; use of same-age or older peer leaders
Personal and social skills training	Increase decisionmaking, personal behavior change, anxiety-reduction, communication, social and assertive skills; application of generic skills to resist substance use influences	Class discussion; cognitive-behavioral skills training (instruction, demonstration, practice, feedback, reinforcement)

growing recognition that advertisers have developed sophisticated ad campaigns specifically targeting the youth market.

A central component of resistance skills training involves teaching adolescents a set of skills that they can use to resist offers from their peers to smoke, drink, or use drugs. Prevention programs that include resistance skills training emphasize verbal and nonverbal skills for resisting offers to use drugs, and specifically teach adolescents what to say when they are offered or pressured to engage in some form of drug use and how to say it most effectively. Adolescents are also taught how to identify "high-risk" situations where they are likely to experience peer pressure to use drugs, to avoid those situations where possible, and to develop "action plans" for handling peer pressure should those situations arise.

To be most effective, resistance skills training must provide adolescents with a general repertoire of verbal and nonverbal skills that they can call upon when confronted by peer pressure to use drugs in a variety of situations. Adolescents must not only develop these skills but also confidence in their ability to apply them when needed. To accomplish this, the best contemporary prevention programs teach students the specific skills and their applications and also provide opportunities for students to practice and master the use of these skills, both in and out of the classroom.

Competence Enhancement Approaches

New approaches to prevention have also been developed and tested during the past two decades. These approaches are designed to target a broader array of risk and protective factors compared to the social influence approaches. This competence enhancement approach to prevention has been evaluated in research conducted by our group at Cornell (e.g., Botvin & Eng [1982]; Botvin, Baker, Botvin, Filazzola & Millman [1984]; Botvin, Baker, Dusenbury, Tortu & Botvin [1990]; Botvin, Renick, & Baker [1983]; and by Schinke and his colleagues [Gilchrist & Schinke 1985; Schinke & Gilchrist 1983, 1984]). Although these intervention approaches typically have included elements of the social influence model, a distinguishing feature is that they also emphasize teaching a variety of personal self-management skills and general social skills to adolescents. These skills are taught to promote general competence and thus reduce vulnerability to pro-drug social influences and intrapsychic motivations to smoke, drink, or use illicit drugs. These approaches have included the teaching of generic skills such as general problem-solving and decisionmaking skills, cognitive skills for resisting interpersonal and media influences, skills for increasing self-control and self-esteem, skills for coping effectively with anxiety or stress, as well as assertiveness and general social skills.

Effectiveness of School-Based Prevention Programs

Over the past two decades there has been a gradual accumulation of empirical evidence supporting the effectiveness of school-based approaches to drug abuse prevention. This evidence provides strong empirical support for the short-term effectiveness of drug abuse prevention, together with evidence from a few studies demonstrating long-term effectiveness. Although evidence exists concerning the effectiveness of these prevention approaches on alcohol and marijuana use, most studies have focused on cigarette smoking. In addition, most studies have been conducted with white adolescent populations. Thus, less is known about the effectiveness of these approaches with substances other than tobacco, or for minority populations in general. Because the focus of this research has been on primary, universal prevention, these programs have been evaluated in terms of their ability to decrease or delay relatively low levels of drug involvement (e.g., occasional drug use or 30-day prevalence), rather than in terms of their impact on more serious levels of drug involvement. Still, the growing body of evidence in support of contemporary approaches to drug abuse prevention is impressive.

Short-Term Effects

The results of studies testing the effectiveness of social influence approaches to cigarette smoking have shown that they are typically able to reduce smoking rates by 30% to 50% after the initial intervention [Arkin et al. 1981; Hurd et al. 1980; McAlister et al. 1979; Luepker et al. 1983; Donaldson et al. 1994; Ellickson & Bell 1990; Sussman et al. 1993]. Studies testing prevention approaches that include both social influence and competence enhancement components have demonstrated that they can cut cigarette smoking by 40% to 75% [Botvin, Eng, & Williams 1980;

Botvin & Eng 1980, 1982; Botvin, Baker, Renick, Filazzola, & Botvin 1984; Botvin, Baker, Botvin, Filazzola, & Millman 1984; Botvin, Renick, & Baker 1983; Pentz 1983; Schinke & Gilchrist 1983; Schinke & Gilchrist 1984; Gilchrist & Schinke 1983; Schinke 1984]. Effects of roughly the same magnitude have been found for the social influences approaches with regard to their initial impact on alcohol and marijuana [Ellickson & Bell 1990; McAlister et al. 1980; Shope et al. 1992].

Similarly, evidence also exists for the efficacy of the competence enhancement approach for reducing alcohol use [Botvin, Baker, Renick, Filazzola, & Botvin 1984; Botvin, Baker, Botvin, Filazzola, & Millman 1984; Botvin, Dusenbury, Kerner, James-Ortiz, & Botvin 1990; Epstein et al. 1995; Pentz 1983] as well as marijuana use [Botvin, Baker, Botvin, Filazzola, & Millman 1984; Botvin, Baker, Dusenbury, Botvin, & Diaz 1990; Epstein et al. 1995]. Examination of the impact of these prevention approaches on tobacco, alcohol, and marijuana use indicates that the strongest effects have been found for cigarette smoking and marijuana use, while weaker and somewhat inconsistent effects have been found for alcohol use.

It is important to recognize that the social influence approaches and the competence enhancement approaches discussed here both include program components designed to increase drug resistance skills and promote antidrug norms. Thus, even the broader competence enhancement approaches include problem-specific material, along with generic skills training. The results from one study [Caplan et al. 1992] suggests that generic competence enhancement approaches may not be effective in reducing drug use unless they also include social resistance skills training content. The resistance skills training may be necessary because it helps students apply generic skills to drug-specific situations and also places emphasis on antidrug norms. Although approaches that combine the key elements of the problem-specific social influences model and the broader competence enhancement approach appear to be the most effective based on current evidence, additional research is necessary to better understand how and why effective prevention programs work.

Long-Term Effects

The results of longer term follow-up studies have gradually emerged in recent years. Although they present a somewhat mixed picture, evidence from several studies indicates that current prevention approaches have a reasonable degree of durability. For example, some studies have indicated that the social influence approach has produced reductions in cigarette smoking that last for up to four years [Luepker et al. 1983; Sussman et al. 1993; McAlister et al. 1980]. The results of one multicomponent study conducted by Perry and her colleagues found evidence of long-term prevention effects for cigarette smoking lasting up to seven years [Perry & Kelder 1992]. The results of other studies, however, indicate that the prevention effects produced by social influence approaches frequently erode over time, with effects being maintained for only one or two years [Murray et al. 1988; Flay et al. 1989; Ellickson et al. 1993].

Although it has been suggested that school-based prevention approaches may not be powerful enough to produce lasting prevention effects [Dryfoos 1993], this is likely to depend on the quality of the program. It is unreasonable to expect that a poorly designed prevention program would have the ability to produce lasting results. For example, long-term prevention effects may not be observed if (1) the length of the initial intervention is too short, (2) booster sessions are inadequate or not included, (3) the intervention is not implemented with sufficient fidelity, or (4) the intervention is based on faulty assumptions or is deficient in some other way [Resnicow & Botvin 1993]. Programs that address these limitations are much more likely to produce long-lasting effects.

Effectiveness with Minority Populations

A gap in the drug abuse prevention field has been the lack of high-quality research with racial/ethnic minority populations. Although several national, state, and local surveys have found that the prevalence of drug use is either the same or lower for ethnic minority youth than for white youth [Oetting & Beauvais 1990; Wallace et al. 1995], this may be changing. A recent report of the U.S. Surgeon General's office [U.S. Department of Health and Human Services 1998] found that smoking rates for African American and Hispanic youth have increased in the 1990s after several years of decline. Furthermore, ethnic minority youth have generally been found to be at disproportionately higher risk for a number of drug-related problems [Barnes & Welte, 1986; Newcomb et al. 1987]. While some studies (e.g., Ellickson & Bell [1990]) have included a subsample of minority youth in their populations, few studies have been conducted with a predominantly minority sample. This is beginning to change, however. Demonstration projects funded by CSAP (The Center for Substance Abuse Prevention) have included many projects designed to target minority populations.

Two general strategies have been followed in the development of new preventive interventions for minority adolescents. One strategy, common to many local prevention efforts, assumes that the etiology of drug abuse is different for different populations. Thus, many prevention providers have developed interventions designed to be population-specific (e.g., projects for African American youth with an Afrocentric cultural focus). A second strategy assumes that the etiology of drug abuse is more similar than different across populations. This approach involves the development of preventive interventions designed to be generalizable to a broad range of individuals from different populations. Although relatively little is known about the etiology of drug use among minority youth, several studies indicate that there is substantial overlap in the factors promoting and maintaining drug use among different populations [Bettes et al. 1990; Botvin, Baker, Botvin, Dusenbury, Cardwell, & Diaz 1993; Botvin, Epstein, Schinke, & Diaz 1994; Botvin, Goldberg, Botvin, & Dusenbury 1993; Epstein et al. 1994].

These studies suggest that prevention approaches may have application to a broad range of individuals from different populations. Beyond the commonality of etiological factors among different populations, there is a simple practical reason for pursuing this course. That is, most urban schools in the United Schools contain individuals from multiple racial/ethnic groups since schools are mandated by law to be integrated. Therefore, even if differences across populations warranted different interventions, it would be extremely difficult on a logistical and political level to implement separate interventions for different racial/ethnic groups. This raises serious questions about the feasibility and acceptability of prevention approaches designed to be specific to a particular racial/ethnic population.

Life Skills Training: A Competence Enhancement Program

In this section of the chapter, we describe our own work with a competence enhancement drug abuse prevention program called Life Skills Training (LST). The LST program is a primary prevention program intended to prevent the early stages of drug abuse by addressing risk factors associated with drug use, particularly occasional or experimental use. This approach is based upon the premise that preventing drug use with younger populations (e.g., junior high school students) will ultimately reduce the prevalence of drug abuse among these same individuals as they become older (e.g., seniors in high school). The LST approach was designed as a universal intervention that is appropriate for all individuals in a given setting, rather than as a selected intervention for individuals at "high risk" or an indicated intervention for youth already involved in drugs. In this section we discuss LST as it is implemented in middle-schools, although the program has been adapted successfully for other community settings (e.g., housing projects).

Overview of LST

The LST program is implemented over the course of 15 class periods for middle or junior high school students. A set of 10 booster sessions in the second year and five class periods in the third year can be used to reinforce the materials covered during the first year. Typically, the intervention is started with seventh graders and booster sessions (when included) are provided in the eighth and ninth grades. Curriculum materials have been developed to increase the standardization of implementing the LST program and increase its exportability, and these materials consist of a Teacher's Manual and Student Guide for each year of the program (published by Princeton Health Press).

The LST program was designed to promote the development of personal self-management skills and general social skills, while also influencing drug-related knowledge, attitudes and norms and teaching skills for resisting social influences to use drugs. The personal skills component of the LST program contains material to (1) foster the development of decisionmaking and problem solving, (2) provide students with self-control skills for coping with anxiety and anger/frustration, and (3) provide students with the basic principles of personal behavior change and self-improvement. The social skills component contains material designed to help students overcome shyness and improve general interpersonal skills. This material emphasizes the teaching of (1) communication skills; (2) general social skills, such as the ability to initiate social interactions, carry a conversation, and compliment others; (3) skills related to personal relationships, and (4) both verbal and nonverbal assertive skills.

The drug-related information and skills component is designed to impact on knowledge and attitudes concerning drug use, normative expectations, and skills for resisting drug use influences from the media and peers. The material contained in this component is similar to that contained in many psychosocial drug abuse prevention programs, which focus on the teaching of social resistance skills. Included is material concerning (1) the short- and long-term consequences of drug use; (2) knowledge about the actual levels of drug use among both adults and adolescents to correct normative expectations about drug use; (3) information about the declining social acceptability of cigarette smoking and other drug use; (4) information and class exercises demonstrating the immediate physiological effects of cigarette smoking; (5) material concerning media pressures to smoke, drink, or use drugs; (6) information concerning the techniques used by cigarette and alcoholic beverage advertisers to promote the use of these drugs and skills for resisting them; and (7) techniques for resisting direct peer pressure to smoke, drink, or use illicit drugs.

Prevention Methods

A variety of intervention methods have been used to teach the content of the LST program, including the use of traditional didactic teaching methods, facilitation/group discussion, classroom demonstrations, and cognitive-behavioral skills training. Although lecturing and conventional didactic teaching methods are appropriate for some of the material in the LST program, most of the material can best be taught by facilitating group discussion and through extensive skills training exercises. Since a major emphasis of the LST program is on the teaching of general personal self-management skills, social skills, and skills for resisting social influences to use drugs, the central role of intervention providers is that of a skills trainer or coach. The cognitive-behavioral skills taught in the LST program are taught using a combination of instruction, demonstration, behavioral rehearsal, feedback, social reinforcement (i.e., praise), and extended practice in the form of behavioral homework assignments:

- The first step in the skills training process involves **instruction and demonstration**. Instruction involves explaining a particular skill to students in a careful step-by-step fashion. Demonstration involves showing students how to perform a particular skill. This can be done by the program provider, by videotape, or even by a member of the class who has already learned the skill being taught.

- The next step in the process of skills training involves **behavioral rehearsal**. Once the skill has been explained and demonstrated, students are given the opportunity to practice the skill being taught. This can be done by having pairs of students participate in a brief role play in front of the class, or by dividing the class up into small groups to practice the skill under the supervision of the program provider.

- After students rehearse the skills being taught, they are provided with **feedback** concerning the strengths and weaknesses of their skills "performance." The provider conveys this information in a gentle and supportive manner so students understand what aspects of the skill they performed well, what needs improvement, and specific ways to improve future performance. The provider also provides verbal praise to reinforce specific positive elements of the student's performance of the skill. Since the primary objective of the LST program is to reduce risk for drug abuse, the goal of the skills training is to both improve the target skills and the student's self-efficacy for using the skill in the future. Therefore, students are assessed individually with respect to improvement over their own baseline levels, however low.

- The final step in the skills training process is **extended practice**, which provides opportunities for practicing and developing the target skills so that students can eventually use the skills as part of their everyday lives. This is accomplished through behavioral "homework" assignments, such as practicing a new technique for coping with anxiety once a day. An important goal of such assignments is to increase the likelihood that the newly learned skills will generalize to a variety of different situations.

Intervention Providers, Selection, and Training

A critical element of any effective intervention is the intervention provider. The LST program has been successfully implemented by several different types of intervention providers, including health professionals from outside the school [Botvin, Eng, & Williams 1980; Botvin, Schinke, Epstein, & Diaz 1994], older peer leaders [Botvin & Eng 1982; Botvin, Baker, Botvin, Filazzola, & Millman 1984], and regular classroom teachers [Botvin, Renick, & Baker 1983; Botvin, Baker, Renick, Filazzola, & Botvin 1984; Botvin, Baker, Dusenbury, Tortu, & Botvin 1990]. Of course, there are several advantages in being able to use a classroom teacher as program provider. Teachers are readily available and generally have more extensive classroom management skills and teaching experience compared to other potential providers. In selecting a provider, several factors should be considered. Providers should be enthusiastic about their involvement, as shown by their willingness to attend the training workshop, carefully implement the intervention according to protocol, and complete the necessary process evaluation forms. Providers should also be personally committed to drug abuse prevention; as such, they will serve as a positive role model

Provider training consists of a one- or two-day training workshop, the purpose of which is to familiarize providers with the prevention program, its rationale, and the results of prior studies. Training for providers must give teachers, peer leaders, and others directly involved in implementing the program an opportunity to learn and practice the relevant implementation skills [Tortu & Botvin 1989]. Teachers meet with peer leaders prior to each session to provide them with session-specific preparation for the upcoming session and debrief them regarding the last session. Other effective options for provider training include videotaped sessions [Botvin, Baker, Dusenbury, Tortu, & Botvin 1990].

Effectiveness of the LST Program

The results of our own work suggest that prevention effects from the LST program are relatively long-lasting. Results from a large-scale, randomized field trial involving nearly 6,000 seventh graders from 56 public schools in New York State found long-term reductions in smoking, alcohol, and marijuana use at the end of the twelfth grade [Botvin, Baker, Dusenbury, Botvin, & Diaz, 1995]. In this study schools were randomly assigned to prevention and control conditions. Participating students in the prevention condition received the LST program during the seventh grade (15 sessions) with booster sessions in the eighth grade (10 sessions) and ninth grade (five sessions). No intervention was provided during grades 10 through 12. According to the results, the prevalence of cigarette smoking, alcohol use, and marijuana use for the students in the prevention condition was as much as 44% lower than for controls. Significant reductions were also found with respect to the percentage of students who were using multiple substances one or more times per week, where the rate of multiple drug use was 66% lower for students who received the LST program relative to controls. These results suggest that to be effective, school-based prevention programs need to be more comprehensive and have a stronger initial dosage than most studies using the social influence approach. Another implication is that prevention programs also need to include at least two additional years of interventions (booster sessions) and must be implemented in a manner that is consistent with the underlying prevention model.

Tailoring LST to Minority Populations

The work that we have conducted in recent years at Cornell has largely followed the course of testing the same underlying prevention strategy with different populations to determine its potential effectiveness and generalizability. During the course of this work, some modifications were made, where warranted, to maximize generalizability, cultural sensitivity, relevance, and acceptability to predominantly African American and Hispanic inner-city youth. The initial focus of this research was on cigarette smoking, followed more recently by a focus on alcohol and marijuana use. This research has been conducted systematically through several different stages including (1) exploratory (qualitative) research consisting of focus group testing and key informant interviews, (2) expert review of prevention methods and materials, (3) consumer-based reviews of intervention materials and methods, (4) small-scale pilot studies, and (5) large-scale randomized field trials. Throughout this process, modifications in the prevention materials and methods were made as necessary. Still, none of the modifications in prevention materials and methods involved any fundamental changes to the underlying prevention strategy. Instead, these changes included such things as the reading level of the prevention materials, the inclusion of appropriate graphics (e.g., illustrations or pictures of minority youth), language, behavioral rehearsal scenarios, and other examples appropriate for the target population.

The results of these studies have consistently shown that the LST approach reduces cigarette smoking (relative to controls) for inner-city Hispanic youth [Botvin, Dusenbury, Baker, James-Ortiz, & Kerner 1989; Botvin, Dusenbury, Baker, James-Ortiz, Botvin, & Kerner 1992] and African American youth [Botvin, Batson, Witts-Vitale, Bess, Baker, & Dusenbury 1989]. (See Table 8-2.) Lower levels of cigarette smoking have also been found in at least one follow-up study involving a cohort of seventh graders who were followed up to the end of the ninth grade [Botvin, Schinke, Epstein, & Diaz 1994]. More recent studies have also shown that this prevention approach can reduce alcohol and marijuana use in minority populations [Botvin, et al. 1994; Botvin, Schinke, Epstein, Diaz, & Botvin 1995; Botvin, Epstein, Baker, Diaz, & Ifill-Williams 1997] and is also able to produce reductions in more serious levels of drug involvement such as the use of multiple drugs [Botvin, Epstein, Baker, Diaz, & Ifill-

Table 8-2. Selected Studies Testing Life Skills Training Approaches

Investigators	Subjects	Intervention Approach	Evaluation Design	Results
Life Skills Training [Botvin et al. 1989]	African American, urban	12 sessions in 7th grade	Pre- and post-test	Reduced tobacco use; increased knowledge of smoking consequences and normative expectations
Life Skills Training [Botvin et al. 1990b]	White, suburban	20 sessions in 7th grade; 10 boosters in 8th	Pre- and post-test; 1-year follow-up; compared peer vs. teacher-led, controls	Reduced tobacco, alcohol, and marijuana use in peer-led sessions with boosters and for females in teacher-lead condition; program effects on mediating variables
Life Skills Training [Botvin et al. 1990a]	White, suburban	15 sessions in 7th grade; 10 boosters in 8th; 5 boosters in 9th	Pre- and post-test; 3-year follow-up; compared training workshops vs. videotape, controls	Reduced cigarette, marijuana, and alcohol use; program effects on normative expectations, substance use knowledge, interpersonal and communication skills
Life Skills Training [Botvin et al. 1994]	Minority, urban	15 sessions in 7th grade	Pre- and post-test; 1-year follow-up; compared generic skills-training, culturally focused, controls	Both programs reduced intentions to drink alcohol; generic program reduced intentions to use illicit drugs; program effects on mediating variables

Table 8-2 continued

Investigators	Subjects	Intervention Approach	Evaluation Design	Results
Life Skills Training [Botvin et al. 1995b]	Minority, urban	15 sessions in 7th grade; 10 boosters in 8th	Pre- and post-test; 2-year follow-up	Reduced current alcohol use and intentions to drink alcohol; program effects on mediating variables
Life Skills Training [Botvin et al. 1995a]	White, suburban	15 sessions in 7th grade; 10 boosters in 8th; 5 boosters in 9th	Pre- and post-test; 6-year follow-up	Reduced drug and polydrug use; strongest effects for those receiving a more complete version of the program
Positive Youth Development Program [Caplan et al. 1992]	Urban and suburban	20 sessions in 6th and 7th grades	Pre- and post-test	Increased social adjustment and coping skills; intentions to use substances remained the same for program students, while control students reported increased intentions at postassessment; program effects on alcohol use, but no effects on reported drug use

Williams 1997]. Finally, one study indicated that tailoring the intervention to the culture of the target population can enhance its effectiveness [Botvin, Schinke et al. 1995]. Taken as a whole, these studies provide evidence that the same prevention approach with relatively modest modifications is effective with white, African American, and Hispanic youth. However, it also seems evident that for schools with a more homogeneous population than most inner-city schools, prevention effects may be increased by tailoring the intervention to the target population.

Moving from Research to Action

The challenge to prevention researchers and public health professionals has been to identify promising drug abuse prevention approaches, evaluate their efficacy, and provide evidence that they work in real world settings. Many of these challenges have been met, with recent advances in our knowledge about the causes of drug abuse and how to prevent it. Although we need to continue to refine existing approaches and develop even more effective ones, an important challenge facing us now concerns bridging the gap between research and practice. Recognizing this, efforts are underway to disseminate information concerning effective approaches to drug abuse prevention to move from research to action. Recent national conferences by the National Institute on Drug Abuse, the U.S. Department of Education, and the Justice Department's Office of Juvenile Justice and Delinquency Prevention have all focused on methods of communicating the results of research showing that some prevention approaches, such as the Life Skills Training program, have been demonstrated to work. Speakers at these conferences have exhorted practitioners to use research-based approaches.

In disseminating successful research-based prevention programs, one issue that will have to be addressed is cost. Although most prevention programs are inexpensive, schools and communities will have to be willing to allocate some of their resources to cover the cost of prevention materials and training. The Life Skills Training program cost approximately $5 to $10 per year per student including the cost of materials and training. To the extent several schools in a state or region can coordinate training and the purchase of curriculum materials, the costs can be closer to $5 per student due to cost efficiencies and volume discounts. While a formal economic analysis of cost-benefit and/or cost-effectiveness is planned for the Life Skills Training program, none has been conducted to date. However, compared to the expense of treatment or imprisonment, the cost of a prevention program like Life Skills Training is extremely inexpensive.

Conclusions

Substantial progress has been made over the past 20 years concerning the etiology of drug abuse and how to prevent it. We now have a greater understanding that drug abuse, like other types of human behavior, results from of a dynamic interaction of individual, social, and environmental factors. Social influences to use drugs (along with the availability of drugs) interact with individual vulnerability. Some individuals may be influenced to use drugs by the media, including television shows and movies that glamorize drug use and advertising efforts promoting the sale of alcohol and tobacco products. Other important social influences are family members who either use drugs or express pro-drug use attitudes, and/or by friends and acquaintances who use drugs or hold attitudes and beliefs supportive of drug use. Still others may succumb to peer pressure to use drugs because of intrapersonal factors such as low self-esteem, high anxiety, hopelessness, low personal control, or the need for excitement (sensation-seeking). The greater the number of risk factors that an individual has, the more likely it is that he/she will become a drug user and eventually a drug abuser, since the presence of multiple risk factors is associated with both initial drug use and with the severity of later drug involvement [Newcomb & Felix-Ortiz 1992].

Only recently have prevention approaches been based on the findings of etiology research. The best contemporary etiological models of drug use demonstrate several potential points of intervention for either preventing drug abuse or reducing drug abuse risk. Interventions can (and should) be developed to target individual, family, and community determinants of drug abuse. However, most prevention research has focused on testing the effectiveness of school-based interventions targeting individual-level factors. A school-based intervention is likely to effectively prevent drug abuse if it impacts on drug-related expectancies (knowledge, attitudes, and norms), drug-related resistance skills, and general competence (personal self-management skills and social skills). Increasing prevention-related drug knowledge and resistance skills can provide adolescents with the information and skills needed to develop antidrug attitudes and norms, as well as to resist peer and media pressure to use drugs. Teaching effective self-management skills and social skills offers the potential of reducing intrapersonal motivations to use drugs, as well as reducing vulnerability to pro-drug social influences.

The Life Skills Training program, the most extensively evaluated school-based prevention approach available, utilizes all of these approaches. Three types of self-management skills are taught in the LST Program: (1) self-appraisal, goal-setting, and self-directed behavior change; (2) decisionmaking and independent thinking; and (3) anxiety management skills. Adolescents are also taught a set of general social skills including communications skills, conversational skills, skills for asking someone out for a date, complimenting skills, and both verbal and nonverbal assertive skills. All of these skills are taught using a combination of instruction and demonstration, behavioral rehearsal (practice during class), feedback, reinforcement, and extended practice (outside of class) through behavioral homework assignments. Research with the Life Skills Training approach includes studies testing its short-term effectiveness as well as its long-term durability, studies testing different delivery methods and the effectiveness of booster sessions, studies testing its effectiveness when conducted by different program providers, and studies testing its effectiveness with different populations.

More than a decade and a half of research on the effectiveness of the LST program has demonstrated prevention effects with respect to tobacco, alcohol, and marijuana use, gateway polydrug use, and illicit drug use as well as on hypothesized mediating variables. These studies have ranged from small-scale pilot studies involving a few schools and a few hundred adolescents to large-scale, multisite, randomized field trials involving many schools and several thousand adolescents. The magnitude of reported effects of these approaches has typically been relatively large, with most studies demonstrating initial reductions in the rate of drug use (relative to controls) of 50% or more. These studies have generally produced reductions in both occasional (experimental) drug use as well as more serious levels of drug involvement.

While considerable progress has been made in the past two decades, further research is still needed in several areas. More studies are needed to better understand the mechanisms through which competence enhancement approaches prevent drug use and to understand its effectiveness with different populations, particularly minority youth. More research is also needed to determine the long-term effectiveness of current prevention approaches, including follow-up studies to determine the effectiveness of prevention approaches as individuals progress through college and into young adulthood. Additional prevention research is needed to develop additional (non-school-based) modalities for preventing drug abuse and different delivery channels such as family-based and community-based approaches, or preventive interventions conducted at community centers or as part of after-school programs. To bridge the gap between research and practice, research is needed concerning the dissemination, adoption, and institutionalization of effective prevention approaches by schools and communities. Finally, prevention scientists must do a better job of communicating their findings to policymakers, educators, parents, and community leaders. To address the problem of teen drug use, it is crucial that we actively disseminate the results of the best prevention research in order to help take what has been learned over the years and translate that into action.

References

Arkin, R.M., Roemhild, H.J., Johnson, C.A., Luepker, R.V., & Murray, D.M. (1981). The Minnesota smoking prevention program: A seventh grade health curriculum supplement. *Journal of School Health, 51*, 616-661.

Barnes, G.M., & Welte, J.W. (1986). Patterns and predictors of alcohol use among 7-12th grade students in New York State. *Journal of Studies on Alcohol, 47*, 53-62.

Bettes, B.A., Dusenbury, L., Kerner, J., James-Ortiz, S., & Botvin, G.J. (1990). Ethnicity and psychosocial factors in alcohol and tobacco use in adolescence. *Child Development, 61*, 557-565.

Botvin, G.J., Baker, E., Botvin, E. M., Dusenbury, L., Cardwell, J., & Diaz, T. (1993). Factors promoting cigarette smoking among black youth: A causal modeling approach. *Addictive Behaviors, 18,* 397-405.

Botvin, G.J., Baker, E., Botvin, E. M., Filazzola, A. D., & Millman, R. B. (1984). Alcohol abuse prevention through the development of personal and social competence: A pilot study. *Journal of Studies on Alcohol, 45*, 550-552.

Botvin, G.J., Baker, E., Dusenbury, L. D., Botvin, E. M., & Diaz, T. (1995). Long-term follow-up results of a randomized drug abuse prevention trial. *Journal of American Medical Association, 273*, 1106-1112.

Botvin, G.J., Baker, E., Dusenbury, L., Tortu, S., & Botvin, E. M. (1990). Preventing adolescent drug abuse through a multimodal cognitive-behavioral approach: Results of a 3-year study. *Journal of Consulting and Clinical Psychology, 58*, 437-446.

Botvin, G.J., Baker, E., Renick, N. L., Filazzola, A. D., & Botvin, E. M. (1984). A cognitive-behavioral approach to substance abuse prevention. *Addictive Behaviors, 9*, 137-147.

Botvin, G.J. & Botvin, E. M. (1992). Adolescent tobacco, alcohol, and drug abuse: Prevention strategies, empirical findings, and assessment issues. *Developmental and Behavioral Pediatrics, 13*, 290-301.

Botvin, G.J., Batson, H. W., Witts-Vitale, S., Bess, V., Baker, E., & Dusenbury, L. (1989). A psychosocial approach to smoking prevention for urban black youth. *Public Health Reports, 104*, 573-582.

Botvin, G. J., Dusenbury, L., Baker, E., James-Ortiz, S., Botvin, E. M., & Kerner, J. (1992). Smoking prevention among urban minority youth: Assessing effects on outcome and mediating variables. *Health Psychology, 11*, 290-299.

Botvin, G. J., Dusenbury, L., Baker, E., James-Ortiz, S., & Kerner, J. (1989). A skills training approach to smoking prevention among Hispanic youth. *Journal of Behavioral Medicine, 12*, 279-296.

Botvin, G. J., & Eng, A. (1980). A comprehensive school-based smoking prevention program. *Journal of School Health, 50*, 209-213.

Botvin, G. J. & Eng, A. (1982). The efficacy of a multicomponent approach to the prevention of cigarette smoking. *Preventive Medicine, 11*, 199-211.

Botvin, G. J., Eng, A., & Williams, C. L. (1980). Preventing the onset of cigarette smoking through Life Skills Training. *Preventive Medicine, 9*, 135-143.

Botvin, G. J., Epstein, J. A., Baker, E., Diaz, T., & Ifill-Williams, M. (1997). School-based drug abuse prevention with inner-city minority youth. *Journal of Child and Adolescent Substance Abuse, 6*, 5-20.

Botvin, G.J., Epstein, J. A., Schinke, S. P., & Diaz, T. (1994). Correlates and predictors of smoking among inner city youth. *Journal of Developmental and Behavioral Pediatrics, 15*, 67-73.

Botvin, G.J., Goldberg, C. J., Botvin, E. M., & Dusenbury, L. (1993). Smoking behavior of adolescents exposed to cigarette advertising. Public Health Reports, 108, 217-224.

Botvin, G.J., Renick, N., & Baker, E. (1983). The effects of scheduling format and booster sessions on a broad-spectrum psychosocial approach to smoking prevention. *Journal of Behavioral Medicine, 6*, 359-379.

Botvin, G.J., Schinke, S. P., Epstein, J. A., & Diaz, T. (1994). The effectiveness of culturally-focused & generic skills training approaches to alcohol and drug abuse prevention among minority youth. *Psychology of Addictive Behaviors, 8*, 116-127.

Botvin, G.J., Schinke, S. P., Epstein, J. A., Diaz, T., & Botvin, E. M. (1995). Effectiveness of culturally focused and generic skills training approaches to alcohol and drug abuse prevention among minority adolescents: Two-year follow-up results. *Psychology of Addictive Behaviors, 9*, 183-194.

Caplan, M., Weissberg, R. P., Grober, J. S., Sivo, P., Grady, K., & Jacoby, C. (1992). Social competence promotion with inner-city and suburban young adolescents: Effects of social adjustment and alcohol use. *Journal of Consulting & Clinical Psychology, 60*, 56-63.

Donaldson, S. I., Graham, J.W., & Hansen, W. B. (1994). Testing the generalizability of intervening mechanism theories: Understanding the effects of adolescent drug use prevention interventions. *Journal of Behavioral Medicine, 17*, 195-216.

Dryfoos, J. G. (1993). Common components of successful interventions with high-risk youth. In N. J. Bell & R. W. Bell (Eds.), *Adolescent Risk Taking* (pp. 131-147). Newbury Park, CA: Sage Publications

Ellickson, P. L., & Bell, R.M. (1990). Drug prevention in junior high: A multi-site longitudinal test. *Science, 247*, 1299-1305.

Ellickson, P. L., Bell, R.M., & McGuigan, K. (1993). Preventing adolescent drug use: Long term results of a junior high program. American *Journal of Public Health, 83*, 856-861.

Epstein, J. A., Botvin, G.J., Diaz, T., & Schinke, S. P. (1995). The role of social factors and individual characteristics in promoting alcohol among inner-city minority youth. *Journal of Studies on Alcohol, 56*, 39-46.

Epstein, J. A., Botvin, G.J., Diaz, T., Toth, V., & Schinke, S. P. (1995). Social and personal factors in marijuana use and intentions to use drugs among inner city minority youth. *Journal of Developmental and Behavioral Pediatrics, 16*, 14-20.

Epstein, J. A., Dusenbury, L., Botvin, G. J., & Diaz, T. (1994). Determinants of intentions of junior high school students to become sexually active and use condoms: Implications for reduction and prevention of AIDS risk. *Psychological Reports, 75*, 1043-1053.

Evans, R. I., Henderson, A. H., Hill, P. C. & Raines, B. E. (1979). Smoking in children and adolescents: Psychosocial determinants and prevention strategies. In U.S. Public Health Service (Ed.), *Smoking and Health: A Report of the Surgeon General.* Washington, DC: US Department of Health, Education and Welfare

Evans, R. I., Rozelle, R.M., Mittlemark, M. B., Hansen, W. B., Bane, A. L., & Havis, J. (1978). Deterring the onset of smoking in children: Knowledge of immediate physiological effects and coping with peer pressure, media pressure, and parent modeling. Journal of Applied Social Psychology, 8, 126-135.

Fishbein, M. (1977). Consumer beliefs and behavior with respect to cigarette smoking: A critical analysis of the public literature.. In Federal Trade Commission Report to Congress pursuant to the Public Health Cigarette Smoking Act of 1976. Washington, DC: U.S. Government Printing Office.

Flay, B. R., Keopke, D., Thomson, S. J., Santi, S., Best, J. A., & Brown, K. S. (1989). Long-term follow-up of the first Waterloo smoking prevention trial. American Journal of Public Health, 79, 1371-1376.

Gilchrist, L. D. & Schinke, S. P. (1983). Self-control skills for smoking prevention. In P. F. Engstrom, P. Anderson & L. E. Mortenson (Eds.). Advances in Cancer Control (pp. 125-130). New York: Alan R. Liss.

Goodstadt, M. S. (1974). Myths and methodology in drug education: A critical review of the research evidence. In M. Goodstadt (Ed.). Research on Methods and Programs of Drug Education.

Goodstadt, M. S. (1986). Drug education: The prevention issues. Journal of Drug Education, 19, 197-208.

Hansen, W. B., & O'Malley, P.M. (1996). Drug use. In R. J. DiClimente, W. B. Hansen, & L. E. Ponton (Eds.). Handbook of Adolescent Health Risk Behavior: Issues in Clinical Child Psychology, New York: Plenum Press.

Hurd, P., Johnson, C.A., Pechacek, T., Bast, C. P., Jacobs, D., & Luepker, R. (1980). Prevention of cigarette smoking in 7th grade students. Journal of Behavioral Medicine, 3, 15-28.

Johnston, L. D., O'Malley, P.M. & Bachman, J. G. (1995). National survey results on drug use from the Monitoring the Future Study, 1975-1994, Vol. I Secondary school students. Washington, DC: U.S. Department of Health and Human Services.

Johnston, L. D., O'Malley, P.M., & Bachman, J. G. (1997). *National press release on the continuing rise in illicit drug use among American teenagers.* Ann Arbor, MI: University of Michigan News and Information Services.

Kearney, A. L. & Hines, M. H. (1980). Evaluation of the effectiveness of a drug prevention education program. *Journal of Drug Education, 10,* 127-134.

Kinder, B. N., Pape, N. E., & Walfish, S. (1980). Drug and alcohol education programs: A review of outcome studies. *International Journal of the Addictions, 15,* 1035-1054.

Luepker, R.V., Johnson, C.A., Murray, D.M., & Pechacek, T. F. (1983). Prevention of cigarette smoking: Three year follow-up of educational programs for youth. *Journal of Behavioral Medicine, 6,* 53-61.

McAlister, A., Perry, C. L., Killen, J., Slinkard, L. A., & Maccoby, N. (1980). Pilot study of smoking, alcohol, and drug abuse prevention. *American Journal of Public Health, 70,* 719-721.

McAlister, A., Perry, C. L., & Maccoby, N. (1979). Adolescent smoking: Onset and prevention. *Pediatrics, 63,* 650-658.

Millman, R. B. & Botvin, G.J. (1992). Substance use, abuse, and dependence. In M. Levine, N. B. Carey, A. C. Crocker & R. T. Gross (Eds.). *Developmental-behavioral pediatrics* (2nd ed.) (pp. 451-467). New York: W. B. Saunders Company

Murray, D.M., Davis-Hearn, M., Goldman, A. I., Pirie, P., & Luepker, R.V. (1988). Four and five year follow-up results from four seventh-grade smoking prevention strategies. *Journal of Behavioral Medicine, 11,* 395-405.

Newcomb, M. D. & Felix-Ortiz, M. (1992). Multiple protective and risk factors for drug use and abuse: Cross-sectional and prospective findings. *Journal of Consulting and Clinical Psychology, 63,* 280-296.

Newcomb, M. D., Maddahian, E., Skager, R., & Bentler, P.M. (1987). Substance abuse and psychosocial risk factors among teenagers: Associations with sex, age, ethnicity, and type of school. *American Journal of Drug & Alcohol Abuse, 13,* 413-433.

Oetting, E. R. & Beauvais, F. (1990). Adolescent drug usc: Findings of national and local surveys. *Journal of Consulting and Clinical Psychology, 58*, 385-394.

Pentz, M. A. (1983). Prevention of adolescent substance abuse through social skill development. In T. J. Glynn, C. G. Leukefeld & J. B. Ludford (Eds.). Preventing Adolescent Drug Abuse: Intervention Strategies NIDA Research Monograph No. 47 (pp. 195-232). Washington, DC: U.S. Government Printing Office.

Perry, C. L. & Kelder, S. H. (1992). Models for effective prevention. Journal of Adolescent Health, 13, 355-363.

Resnicow, K. & Botvin, G.J. (1993). School-based substance use prevention programs: Why do effects decay? Preventive Medicine, 22, 484-490.

Schaps, E., Bartolo, R. D., Moskowitz, J., Palley, C. S., & Churgin, S. (1981). A review of 127 drug abuse prevention program evaluations. Journal of Drug Issues, 11,17-43.

Schinke, S. P. & Gilchrist, L. D. (1983). Primary prevention of tobacco smoking. Journal of School Health, 53, 416-419.

Schinke, S. P. & Gilchrist, L. D. (1984). Preventing cigarette smoking with youth. Journal of Primary Prevention, 5, 48-56.

Shope, J. T., Dielman, T. E., Butchart, A. T., & Campanelli, P.C. (1992). An elementary school-based alcohol misuse prevention program: A follow-up evaluation. Journal of Studies on Alcohol, 53, 106-121.

Sussman, S., Dent, C. W., Stacy, A. W., & Sun, P. (1993). Project Towards No Tobacco Use: 1-year behavior outcomes. American Journal of Public Health, 83, 1245-1250.

Swisher, J. D., Crawford, J. L., Goldstein, R., & Yura, M. (1971). Drug education: Pushing or preventing? Peabody Journal of Education, 49, 68-75.

Tortu, S. & Botvin, G.J. (1989). School-based smoking prevention: The teacher training process. Preventive Medicine, 18, 280-289.

U.S. Department of Health and Human Services. (1998). *Tobacco use among U.S. racial/ethnic minority groups: A report of the Surgeon General.* Washington, DC: Centers for Disease Control and Prevention, National Center for Chronic Disease Prevention and Health Promotion, Office of Smoking and Health.

Wallace, J. M., Jr., Bachman, J. G., O'Malley, P. M., & Johnston, L. D. (1995). Racial/ethnic differences in adolescent drug use: Exploring possible explanations. In G. J. Botvin, S. Schinke, & M. Orlandi (Eds.), *Drug abuse prevention with multi-ethnic youth* (pp. 59- 80). Thousand Oaks, CA: Sage.

9 Promoting Excellence in American Adolescents

Toni Falbo and Robert W. Glover

This chapter explains how every American youth can achieve excellence in high school. By excellence, we mean meeting high standards of academic skills which, for most students, will require years of sustained effort, as well as meeting high standards of social skills and self-discipline. While some teens in the United States meet these standards now, most do not. We are particularly interested in promoting in adolescence those qualities thought essential for success in the high performance workplaces of the 21st century. These skills have been identified and information about these skills have been disseminated to all 50 states [Secretary's Commission on Achieving Necessary Skills 1991]. In particular, these skills include strong English language and mathematics skills, problem-solving skills, and personal qualities, such as social skills. They also include a list of skills labeled as workplace competencies, such as skill at allocating resources, working effectively in teams, using technology to accomplish specific tasks, monitoring performance, and correcting mistakes. Altogether, these skills are important because the workplaces of the 21st century, specifically, those paying high wages, will require not only high academic skills, but also skills at self-management, self-correction, and working with others to solve problems [Marshall & Tucker 1992].

We argue that excellence for all can happen in the United States, because the school practices essential for achieving this excellence are already known and have been implemented in several high schools across the nation. Before the changes we recommend can become widespread, however, we need to change not only high schools, but also the communities that are served by these high schools. These communities include the current and future employers of high school students, as well as their parents and neighbors.

We do not regard excellence as something that only a small percentage of adolescents can attain. When people search for excellence, they are looking for something or someone who "surpasses a standard of quality," or is "very good of its kind." Excellence does not require exclusivity, but it does require the development of the habit of working hard every day for years.

Recently, American twelfth graders were found to score below the international average in mathematics and science, and among the lowest of the 21 nations participating in the Third International Mathematics and Science Study commonly referred to as TIMSS [Mullis 1998], despite the fact that our youth are scoring better in reading, math, and science than they did in the 70s and 80s. These results suggest that a higher percentage of adolescents in other countries are pursuing excellence. We are arguing that this is so because these other countries have structured their schools and communities so that the pursuit of excellence becomes the norm among adolescents.

Why Do Our Adolescents Score So Poorly in International Comparisons?

Tracking

Researchers working with these international data concluded that the American practice of providing different courses in science and mathematics to different kinds of students exaggerated differences in the students' achievement. This practice is called tracking, and in some schools it begins at kindergarten. None of the other countries that surpassed our performance used tracking in their elementary or middle schools. Furthermore, when the achievement of American students taking the most advanced mathematics courses were compared across countries, our students still performed below the international average. These findings are consistent with a large body of research indicating that tracking does not benefit the achievement of high school students—not even our best or brightest [Schmidt 1998].

Differences in Age of Students

The results of this international study (TIMSS) point to the fact many countries have significant percentages of their adolescents in secondary school for more years than the United States. The average age of the American students in the TIMSS study (18.1 years) was slightly lower than the international average (18.7 years). This age finding reflects the fact that some of the other nations included students in the thirteenth or fourteenth grade, their final year of secondary school. However, the older age and more years of schooling of some of the students in other countries cannot explain entirely the relatively poor showing of American high school seniors. The data from some countries included students in the tenth and twelfth grades, who outscored American twelfth graders.

Coursetaking and the Curriculum

In American schools today, most teenagers have little reason to take challenging courses and to strive for excellence, because hard work in high school does not pay off in either the short or the long term for most students [Bishop 1989]. At present, taking difficult courses throughout high school only benefits students who are eligible to enter prestigious universities. Other students can enter less prestigious postsecondary institutions or go straight to work after high school without having to take challenging courses in high school. While recent surveys of American high school students indicate that most express positive attitudes toward working hard and meeting high standards [Johnson & Farkas 1997], high schools are structured so that students can avoid hard work.

Furthermore, when students take math or science courses in high school, the content of these courses covers too many topics and does not give students the opportunity to think through and solve the problems. Other countries introduce a smaller number of topics and set up learning experiences in the classroom that require students to figure out the answer. American mathematics teachers commonly teach students by giving them formulas to apply to given problems or teaching them trick solutions to problems, thereby encouraging students not to think too deeply about mathematics or science.

Basic structural changes need to be made in our high schools and communities so that all students are guided toward excellence during this critical time in their lives. The following section discusses the essential components of the structural changes that must take place.

Structural Changes for Excellence

Excellence Must Be Expected from All Adolescents, Not Just a Few

Most Americans believe that only a few teens are able to pursue excellence. They typically define excellence in terms of scoring high on standardized tests, (e.g., what is needed to become a National Merit Scholar) or winning an athletic competition (e.g., what is needed to win a medal at the Olympics). Normal or average children are usually excluded from the pursuit of such forms of excellence, because the pursuit is defined in such a way that there can be only a few winners.

When one steps back from the traditional measures of excellence in high school to indicators of success in life, however, one finds that hard work, directed toward meeting specific goals, is key. In the 80s, when Tom Peters and John Waterman searched for excellence among American businesses, they found it among well-trained and motivated hotel clerks and snack delivery people—not research scientists or professional athletes [Peters & Waterman 1982]. What Americans should expect their high schools to produce are graduates who have developed the habit of working hard to meet specific goals, regardless of whether they are employed in agriculture, manufacturing, or university research.

John Bishop studied the problem of low motivation among high school students and found that, for most students, the courses they take and the grades they earn in high school have no bearing on their outcomes after high school [Bishop 1989]. For most students, there is little or no reward for taking hard courses. Unless a student plans to attend a prestigious university, there are few or no rewards for working hard in high school. Few employers consider high school grades or coursework when hiring new employees.

To promote excellence for all, high schools and youth labor markets need to be changed so that there are clear and immediate incentives for working hard, as well as clear and immediate disincentives for not working hard. To accomplish this, we need to do more than simply eliminate "dummy" courses and add Advanced Placement (AP) courses to the list of course offerings in every high school. We need to rethink the whole high school experience for all students.

Research about Catholic high schools suggests that one of the reasons that such schools are successful with a broad range of students is that all students are required to take the same, relatively high-level courses [Coleman et al. 1982]. Similarly, the TIMSS study found that in most other countries, once a student enrolls in a secondary program or school, the specific courses they take are fixed. The United States is unusual in the world for allowing high school students to avoid taking mathematics all four years of high school, for example.

The rationale for the current system of American high school coursetaking is based on the idea that students will be more motivated if they choose the courses they take. However, what has happened instead is that most students avoid difficult courses, substituting easier ones that require less effort, both inside and outside of the classroom [Johnson & Farkas 1997].

If we want all high school students to pursue excellence, then high schools must be changed so that hard work, directed toward meaningful goals, is an inescapable fact of life for all high school students. To make this happen, teachers, parents, and the community must demand that schools create learning environments that engage and challenge all students.

Teachers Must Expect Excellence from All

About 30 years ago, researchers began investigating the extent to which teacher expectancies influence student performance. The initial study that launched this area of research and debate focused on the effects of positive expectations on students' performance, the so-called Pygmalion effect [Rosenthal & Jacobson 1968]. The study reported that students who had been randomly selected and labeled as "bloomers" scored higher on IQ tests than students who had not been labeled as bloomers. The implication of the study was that if teachers expected improved school performance from students, then they would be likely to get it.

Critics of the original research argued that teacher expectancies are usually based on student performance, not vice versa [Dusek 1985]. They acknowledged that teachers have differential expectations of students, but argued that such expectations are appropriate and useful. Indeed, teachers are expected to use different teaching techniques to reach students with differing abilities and learning styles. Furthermore, in recent years, teachers have been encouraged to become more sensitive and responsive to the diverse, culturally based needs of students of differing ethnic and economic backgrounds.

While educators agree that students need to be treated differentially, many do not agree that all students can pursue excellence. If there is a major teacher expectancy effect operating in American high schools, it is the expectation that some students simply are unable to meet standards of excellence. School practices of testing, sorting, and tracking make it easy for teachers to identify "low-ability" students. Low-ability students are channeled into the same classrooms and typically labeled with such terms as "vocational" or "special education." Given the self-fulfilling nature of expectations, these negative expectations mean that teachers treat some students in such a way that their low performance is essentially inevitable.

If negative teacher expectancy effects are so powerful, one might wonder why they haven't been outlawed. The reason is that they are difficult to detect, let alone remedy. Most teachers do not admit to having negative expectations regarding specific students, sometimes not even to themselves [Rosenthal & Jacobson 1968]. Furthermore, the behavioral manifestation of teacher expectancies has been difficult to measure. Psychologists studying teachers have been able to distinguish such "biased" teachers largely via the discrepancies between what the teachers say in the classroom and the way they say it. For example, highly biased teachers may make neutral or even positive statements toward students, but at the same time, express these statements with hostile facial expressions, condescending voice tones, and tense body language. Such inconsistencies were labeled "leakage" by the authors [Babad et al. 1989].

Not surprisingly, students vary in terms of their susceptibility to these subtle cues. Students who are more sensitive to this "leakage" are more affected by it. This complicates the detection of negative teacher expectancies, because not all students within the same classroom are adversely affected by it [Babad et al. 1989].

If we cannot easily outlaw negative expectancies, how do we prevent them from harming student performance? Some advocate replacing "biased" teachers with computers and instructional software programmed to be free of bias. They argue that students who are especially sensitive to negative teacher expectations should be directed toward educational programs that deliver instruction via technology.

Another approach is to re-educate teachers. Teachers are susceptible to making negative expectancies when they lack confidence in their ability to motivate all students to work hard and acquire higher level skills. Many teachers do not know how to induce skill acquisition in all students. Rather than taking responsibility for their students' failure to meet standards, they blame the students' lack of ability or "unfortunate" background. Several researchers have concluded that teachers who avoid negative expectancy effects are those who have confidence in their own ability to help low-performing students master the material. Teachers who are "unbiased" have been found to be confident that the students who have had trouble meeting the standards in the past will be able to meet them in the future. Their beliefs are nested within a broader ideology that all students can and should be able to acquire the skills expected of them. In other words, they develop the strongly held view that skills and abilities are not fixed, but can be improved over time [Eccles & Wigfield 1985].

Parents Must Demand—and Support—Excellence for All Students

The pursuit of excellence for all adolescents will require strong parental support, in terms of their time and energy. At present, only some parents are willing to invest in this pursuit and, in general, their children are already involved in school and achieving as much as is possible there. Unfortunately, many parents do not expend the energy necessary to support their adolescent children's pursuit of excellence.

Although almost all parents say they want their children to get a good education, many parents do not engage in parenting practices that are essential to support their teens' pursuit of excellence. American parents typically become disengaged from the education of their children at about the time that their children become teenagers and enter secondary school.

A relatively large percentage of American parents are truly uninvolved in the lives of their adolescent children. According to Laurence Steinberg [1996], at least 25% of parents are disengaged from the lives of their adolescent children. Adolescents report that 25% of their parents are not involved in their decisions regarding what courses to take, 30% of their parents do not know what they are doing in school, and 33% of their parents do not know how they are spending their spare time. Steinberg [1996] reports that a recent survey of teens found between one-fourth and one-third of the teens said that they wished their parents were more involved in their schoolwork.

Teens with disengaged parents have difficulty pursuing excellence for two basic reasons. First, such teens are more likely to be attracted to risky behavior outside of school, such as alcohol and drug abuse, violence, and sexual precocity, and the fact that their parents are disengaged from their daily lives makes it easier for these teens to engage in such risky behavior. Unfortunately, the pursuit of risky behavior is incompatible with working hard in school. Second, such teens feel less committed to school and less motivated to do well in the classroom, because promoting hard work in school requires daily tending by concerned and involved parents [Crouter et al. 1990].

How do engaged parents promote their teens' success in school? According to research [Romo & Falbo 1996; Steinberg 1996], engaged parents do not regard their child's adolescence as a time when they should give up parental authority. Instead, they realize that they need to alter their relationship with their adolescent children, but this shift does not change the essential fact that they, as parents, are still in charge of their teenaged children. Engaged parents not only express warmth and concern for their teenaged children, but they also set limits and make sure that their children stay within these limits. Engaged parents don't just dictate the rules, they explain them, and sometimes change the rules when the teens come up with a good justification for this change. Such parents monitor daily the schoolwork, academic performance, and emotional life of their children. They encourage and motivate their teens to do their best, sometimes by acting like coaches or cheerleaders.

Certainly peers are extremely important to teens, but this does not mean that peers have to have an inhibiting effect on the school performance of all teens. Peer groups can have a facilitating effect on motivation to work hard in school, and successful students often have a group of friends who also are pursuing excellence in school [Arnold 1995]. Engaged parents know enough about their children's school experiences and friends to gauge whether their children's friends are facilitating or impairing their children's schoolwork. Engaged parents communicate to their children why they like the friends who facilitate schoolwork and why they don't like the friends who do not. Often such parents engineer a social network for their teenaged children by involving the teen in specific extracurricular, community, and/or religious organizations that the parents know contain other teens whose parents also closely monitor them [Romo & Falbo 1996; Steinberg 1996].

Engaged parents become involved in activities that draw them into the school physically, such as volunteering at the school, attending parent-teacher conferences, and otherwise supporting the activities of the school. Their presence within the school communicates to the teen that the parent values what goes on in the school and that if the student flunks a test or misbehaves in school, the parent will hear about it directly from teachers. Also, the parents' presence within the school sends an even more important message to the teachers and other school personnel. It signals to educators that the parents care about their children's education, and that if teachers do not treat the child properly, that the parent will find out about it and come to the school to negotiate for better treatment from the school. Engaged parents advocate for their children and work with the school so that the school can better serve their children's needs.

Why are so many American parents disengaged from their teens' high school experience? Part of the reason is that many secondary schools do not want parents to participate in their children's education. Although nearly all schools pay lip service to their desire to promote parental involvement, in practice many high schools only want parents to supervise their children when they are out of school and make sure that students show up and behave while in school. Schools have been unwilling to share with parents the management of the students' coursetaking or academic decisionmaking.

Yet for all students to pursue excellence in high school, schools and parents need to work as partners to create home and school environments that support and encourage the pursuit of excellence. Schools cannot succeed in motivating students without parental support; parents cannot succeed in motivating their children to pursue excellence in school without school support.

There are two major difficulties with establishing and maintaining this partnership. First, a substantial percentage of disengaged parents are unlikely to be effective partners with the high schools. To overcome this, teachers and the other parents will have to promote excellence in these students without the participation—perhaps even opposition—from the disengaged parents. This will be difficult, but if most of the other parents and all the teachers are working hard in pursuit of excellence, then the achievement norms will shift, the incentives for hard work and the disincentives for slacking off will be clear to all. In this way, even teens with little parental involvement can be drawn toward pursuing excellence in high school.

The second difficulty for parents is that although many American parents are critical of public education generally, they often express satisfaction with the schools their children attend [Stevenson & Stigler 1992]. Political and educational leaders will have to convince parents that their children can and should achieve more, and that it is in the best interest of their children to learn how to pursue excellence early in their lives.

Employers and the Whole Community Must Foster Excellence for All Students

The African proverb "It takes a whole village to raise a child" is exactly on target when it comes to promoting excellence among American adolescents. Unfortunately, after this proverb was appropriated by Hillary Clinton and incorporated into the title of her recent book [Clinton 1996], it was politicized by her critics. But the proverb's essential message is correct: raising children is a joint responsibility that involves families, schools, and the larger community in which each student lives.

By the term, "community," we include businesses, churches, youth-serving organizations, neighborhood groups, civic organizations, and governmental agencies. All of these types of community institutions must become part of the process of pursuing excellence for teens.

Churches, neighborhood groups, and other youth-serving organizations can establish homework centers, "safe havens," computer labs, and other facilities to encourage homework completion, the development of peer networks that promote the pursuit of excellence and other healthy activities. We need to make better use of out-of school time (especially after school and during summers) to extend "time on task" and reinforce learning. Community organizations can also provide services for youth that help them solve problems, such as peer conflict, personal problems, or health concerns, that might obstruct their pursuit of excellence.

Employers can have a powerful influence on youth behavior and motivation. If employers required school transcripts to take academic performance into account in hiring youth, students would have greater incentive to maintain their grades and school attendance. In making hiring and promotion decisions, employers have an important leverage over youth that has been largely unused. Employers also need to employ youth responsibly, for example, by avoiding scheduling them to work late hours on school nights.

Businesses can take other actions to promote incentives of youth to perform in school. For example, the Liberty Mutual Insurance Company offers a discount to young drivers who stay in school and maintain at least a B average, thereby promoting excellence by providing a clear reward for effort and achievement in school. Employers, labor unions, and community organizations can provide students with opportunities to explore a variety of possible careers, by disseminating information about the linkages between schooling and careers, by providing job shadowing opportunities, and mentoring youths who express interest in an industry or occupation.

There are numerous ways, both large and small, that employers can partner with schools to promote effort, achievement, and learning among high school students. The National Employer Leadership Council recently compiled and published a list of 56 actions that employers can use to encourage effort and achievement in school [National Employer Leadership Council 1996]. These include working with students and teachers, providing information needed to develop curriculum that will prepare students to work in their respective industries, and providing students and teachers with access to the technology they will need to use in their industries.

Success in high school is not sufficient to prepare our youth for many of the good jobs available in modern workplaces. Encouraging significant learning beyond high school needs greater emphasis for all students, not just those choosing to pursue bachelor's degree. We need to take a broader view of advanced learning that incorporates more options than obtaining a college baccalaureate degree.

Linking Schools, Families, and Communities to Foster Excellence

The third and final part of this chapter provides descriptions of school, family, and community environments that work together to promote excellence in adolescents. In general, these environments motivate students to pursue excellence by connecting teens more effectively with their communities.

High schools can be organized into "schools within schools" that are differentiated in terms of broad career clusters or other thematic topics. Rather than the "shopping mall high school" pattern common across America [Powell et al. 1985], we need to restructure high schools so that they provide a learning context for students that links what students are being taught with the kinds of paid and unpaid work they will be doing as adults. Students and their parents should select a career cluster "school" based on the students' interests, not abilities. The opportunity to choose a thematically organized "school within a school" should be available to every student, but no student should be compelled to participate. Students who cannot find a home in one of the clusters should be placed in a general cluster theme until he or she identifies a particular interest. Students should be part of such a thematic cluster school at least three of the four years of high school. Students should be able to change clusters, as their interests change, without suffering penalties. One way to assure this is to design the entire high school curriculum so that at least 75% of the core curriculum is shared across all the available clusters. In the ideal high school we envision, teams of teachers will be nested within each cluster to work with students on a continuous basis over a multiyear period in a personal rather than anonymous environment.

Feasible, effective alternatives to the shopping mall high school are available and in operation throughout the United States. The career academy model originally begun in Philadelphia in 1969 has been replicated in several hundred high schools across the country [Stern et al. 1992]. Career academies are "schools within schools" in which a group of students take several classes together with the same group of teachers over a multiyear period. Each academy focuses on a career theme, such as health care, electronics, or international business. Career academies enlist industry partners who provide adult mentors, internships, classroom speakers, and opportunities for students to make connections between schooling and their career aspirations. Careful evaluations of career academies have revealed that students enrolled in academies have recorded better attendance, failed fewer courses, earned more credits, obtained better grades, and enjoyed higher graduation rates than have students in comparison groups. In most cohorts, academy students were half as likely as their comparisons to drop out before completing high school [Stern et al. 1992].

A longitudinal evaluation of career academies in 10 sites undertaken by the Manpower Development and Research Corporation (MDRC) is showing promising results as a means of restructuring high schools to create more personalized, mutually supportive learning communities for students and their teachers [Kemple & Rock 1996; Kemple 1997]. In this evaluation, the students participating in the career academies were selected by a random assignment process. Their academic performance, persistence to graduation, enrollment rates in postsecondary education, and labor market outcomes beyond school are all being monitored.

Two other approaches to restructuring high schools that have received favorable reviews and produced tangible results are the "High Schools That Work" network, administered by the Southern Regional Education Board and the Coalition of Essential Schools network, administered by Brown University. Both of these efforts are grounded in a set of guiding principles (see Tables 9-1 and 9-2).

There is clearly no "one best way" or "single model" for restructuring high schools. As Ted Sizer concludes, "There is no such thing as a distinct, detailed blueprint for a fine school any more than there is for a successful family." Sizer explains:

> No two good schools are ever quite alike. No good school is exactly the same from one year to the next. Good schools sensitively reflect their communities—both the students and the teachers within the school building and the wider neighborhood it serves. [Sizer 1989, p. 1]

Several recurrent themes characterize these principles and guidelines. Found commonly among the programs' principles are solid and challenging curricular content, teacher collaboration, expectations of success for all students with special attention and assistance provided to those lag-

Table 9-1. The "High Schools That Work" Program: Site Development Guide Principles

1. Develop an upgraded academic core and a major for all students.
2. Have high expectations for all students.
3. Provide quality vocational studies.
4. Provide high-level academic studies.
5. Create interdisciplinary teams of teachers.
6. Provide ongoing guidance.
7. Give extra help and time to students who need it to meet standards.
8. Engage students as active learners.
9. Keep score to improve practice.

Source: Southern Regional Education Board. (not dated). *High Schools That Work Site Development Guide #1: Where Do You Begin?* Atlanta, GA: Author.

---

ging, good connections with families and community, incentives for performance, and systems to measure and report progress and to provide an empirical evidentiary base for diagnosing problems.

Another appealing approach recently has been promulgated by the New Urban High School Project. Announced in June 1998, the Project identified six essential design principles embodied in effective urban high schools [Big Picture Company and the U.S. Department of Education 1998, pp. 3-4]:

- **Personalization.** New Urban High Schools create settings where teachers and students can know each other well. Small enrollments (created either by establishing small high schools or by subdividing the enrollment of larger high schools into small "schools within schools") make it easier for positive relationships to develop and grow between teachers and students and among students.

- **Adult world immersion**. New Urban High Schools situate students directly into the world beyond school. These schools connect stu-

Table 9-2. Coalition of Essential Schools: Nine Essential Principles

1. An Essential School should focus on helping adolescents learn to use their minds well.
2. The school's goals should be simple: that each student master a limited number of essential skills and areas of knowledge.
3. The school's goals should apply to all students, although the means to these goals will vary as those students themselves vary. School practice should be tailored more to meet the needs to every group or class of adolescents.
4. Teaching and learning should be personalized to the maximum feasible extent.
5. The school's governing practical metaphor should be student-as-worker, rather than the more familiar metaphor of teacher-as-deliverer-of-instructional-services. Students should be coached to learn and teach themselves.
6. Students entering secondary school studies should be those who can show competence in language and elementary mathematics. Students of traditional high school age, but who have not yet achieved levels of competence to enter secondary school studies should be provided intensive remedial work to help them meet these standards. The diploma should be awarded upon a successful final demonstration for graduation—an "exhibition." The diploma is awarded when earned, so the school's program proceeds with no strict age grading and no system of credits collected by time spent in class.
7. The tone of the school should stress values of unanxious expectation, trust, and of decency (including the values of fairness, generosity, and tolerance). Incentives appropriate to the school's particular students should be emphasized, and parents should be treated as essential collaborators.
8. The principal and teachers should perceive themselves as generalists first (teachers and scholars in general education). Staff should expect to assume multiple obligations (as teachers, counselors, and managers), and demonstrate a sense of commitment to the entire school.

Table 9-2 continued

9. Ultimate administrative and budget targets should include, in addition to total student loads per teacher of 80 or fewer, substantial time for collective planning by teachers, competitive salaries for staff, and an ultimate per student cost not to exceed that at traditional schools by more than 10%. To accomplish this, administrative plans might include the phased reduction or elimination of some services not provided students in many traditional comprehensive secondary schools.

Source: Abstracted from T. R. Sizer. (1989). Diverse practice, shared ideas: The essential school. In H. J. Walberg & J. Lane (Eds.), *Organizing for learning: Toward the 21st century.* Reston, VA: National Association of Secondary School Principals.

---

dents with workplaces and the community through authentic projects involving active learning. The themes become contexts for learning. Not only do such linkages help students understand the relevance of what they are learning, but they also introduce students to adult worlds of work and learning, and open natural opportunities for meaningful connections to adult mentors.

- **Contexts for reflection.** The New Urban High Schools provide integrated, reflective contexts for students, including continuous opportunities to reflect upon their experiences in the world beyond school. Students are not just dumped in front of a cash register or into a community service project to pick up trash mindlessly. They are presented challenging opportunities, such as advising groups or academic courses that are connected to the worksite, to reflect their experiences with one other and with their teachers, and to compare their performance against specific adult standards.
- **Intellectual mission.** New Urban High Schools articulate a common intellectual mission for all students. They promote excellence by holding all students to high standards, while offering support so that

all students can meet these standards. All students are guided toward continuing their learning in tertiary settings.

- **Community partnership.** New Urban High Schools work closely with families and communities. Families are especially important partners in the promotion of excellence in teens. Parents can help guide their teens toward clusters that the parents and teens agree fit the teens' interests. Parents support their teens' schoolwork by monitoring their children's homework, school attendance, school participation, and academic performance. Parents support the school by helping teachers and employers create learning experiences for students outside the classroom, including worksite learning.

  Community leaders, particularly employers and elected officials, can be influential partners in the promotion of excellence in teens. Employers help by working with teachers and parents to create worksites that promote excellence. They collaborate with teachers to determine what the learning objectives should be, by monitoring progress against goals, by mentoring and guiding students, and by providing feedback to students in worksite learning.

- **Teacher as designer.** New Urban High Schools are good places for teachers, because they work jointly with other teachers as designers of the learning experiences of their students. Teachers work across disciplines in teams that meet regularly during the school day. The teachers design project-based learning and work-based learning experiences for students that cover the core curriculum while integrating this content into each thematic cluster of the school.

American High School Students Respond to the Challenge

Currently, American high school seniors spend fewer hours every day on homework (and studying) and more hours in paid employment than their counterparts around the world do [Mullis 1998]. The daily average for studying and doing homework among American students was found to be

1.7 hours, while the international average was 2.6 hours. Conversely, a little more than 50% of the American seniors reported they worked three or more hours per day. Only about 20% of international students worked as many hours a day. While too little homework and too much employment cannot totally account for the low scores of American seniors, these data on homework and employment do suggest that American students have time and energy available to be redirected toward meeting higher standards in high school.

Moreover, recent research suggests that many high school students would like to be challenged by their schoolwork. According to a recent survey, about 75% of American students said that they would pay more attention to their schoolwork and learn more if standards were raised and consistently enforced. Most students (65%) admitted that they could do much better in school if they tried harder [Johnson & Farkas 1997].

Summary and Implications for Policy

This chapter explains how to promote the pursuit of excellence among high school students. We reviewed the information indicating that, on average, our students have skill levels below the international average. The many causes of this underachievement were discussed, including flaws in our common educational practices. We explained that the United States is almost unique among industrialized nations in the use of tracking in elementary and middle schools, and the lack of challenging curriculum for all students in high school.

To promote the pursuit of excellence among all adolescents, we recommend that schools and communities restructure themselves to meet the following principles:

- excellence is expected from all adolescents,
- all teachers are trained in how to promote excellence in all students,
- parents demand and support excellence in their children, and
- excellence for all teenagers is fostered by all relevant community organizations, including employers.

We acknowledge that the amount of effort needed to make the fundamental changes we are recommending is comparable to the amount of effort needed to win a major war. This is true because any form of institutional change meets with resistance and the type of changes we are recommending have few, powerful advocates. Current educational practices in the United States benefit students whose parents are well-educated and involved in their children's lives. For the most part, these parents are satisfied with the education their children are receiving and perceive any change to educational practice as a threat to their children's chances of going to college. The students who will benefit most from the changes we are recommending are those teenagers who are not now pursuing excellence. At present, they have few powerful advocates.

Furthermore, fixing high schools alone will not solve the problem. Parents and community leaders will not only have to promote changes in educational practices, but they will also need to dedicate their own time and energy toward rewarding and supporting the pursuit of excellence among all high school students. Not only must high schools change, but also parents, teachers, employers, and many of the students themselves.

For the types of institutional changes we envision to have a chance for success, leaders in relevant institutions must work together to demand and promote them. A few vocal parents cannot make these changes alone, nor can a high school principal, nor the mayor, nor the CEO of the largest employer in town, nor the president of the local clergy organization, nor a labor leader, and certainly not a teachers' group. Only if all of these types of leaders come together to work out a consensus about what must be done to promote the pursuit of excellence among all high school students, will these changes occur. This will require enormous effort, but one that will pay off for America's communities, families, and youth.

References

Arnold, K. D. (1995). *Lives of promise*. San Francisco: Jossey-Bass.

Babad, E., Bernieri, F., & Rosenthal, R. (1989). Nonverbal communication and leakage in the behavior of biased and unbiased teachers. *Journal of Personality and Social Psychology, 56*, 89-94.

Big Picture Company and the U.S. Department of Education. (1998). *The new urban high school: A practitioner's guide*. Providence, RI: The Big Picture Company.

Bishop, J. (1989). Why the apathy in American high schools? *Educational Researcher, 18*(1), 6-10, 42.

Clinton, H. R. (1996). *It takes a village and other lessons children teach us*. New York: Simon & Schuster.

Coleman J. S. , Hoffer, T., & Kilgore, S. (1982). *High school achievement: Public, catholic, and private schools compared*. New York: Basic Books.

Crouter, A. C., MacDermid. S. M., McHale, S. M., & Jenkins, M. (1990). Parental monitoring and perceptions of children's school performance and conduct in dual- and single-earner families. *Developmental Psychology, 26*, 640-657.

Dusek, J. B. (1985). *Teacher expectancies*. Hillsdale, NJ: Lawrence Erlbaum Associates.

Eccles, J., & Wigfield, A. (1985). Teacher expectations and student motivation. In J. G. Dusek (Ed.), *Teacher expectancies* (pp. 185-228). Hillsdale, NJ: Lawrence Erlbaum Associates.

Johnson, J., & Farkas, S. (1997). *Getting by: What American teenagers really think about their schools*. New York: Public Agenda.

Kemple, J. J., & Rock, J. L. (1996). *Career academies: Early implementation lessons from a 10-site evaluation*. New York: Manpower Demonstration Research Corporation.

Kemple, J. J. (1997). *Career academies: Communities of support for students and teachers: emerging findings from a 10-site evaluation*. New York: Manpower Demonstration Research Corporation.

Marshall, R., & Tucker, M. (1992). *Thinking for a living: Education and the wealth of nations*. New York: Basic Books.

Mullis, I. (1998). *Mathematics and science achievement in the final year of secondary school: IEA's Third International Mathematics and Science Study*. Chestnut Hill, MA: Boston College.

Murname, R. J., & Levy, F. (1996). *Teaching the new basic skills: Principles for educating children to thrive in a changing economy.* New York: The Free Press.

National Employer Leadership Council. (1996). *The Employer Participation Model: Connecting learning and earning.* Washington, DC: National Employer Leadership Council.

Peters, T. J. & Waterman, R. H., Jr. (1982). *In search of excellence: Lessons from America's best-run companies.* New York: Harper and Row, Publishers.

Powell, A. G. , Farrar, E., & Cohen, D. K. (1985). *The shopping mall high school: Winners and losers in the educational marketplace.* Boston: Houghton Mifflin.

Romo, H. D., & Falbo, T. (1996). *Latino high school graduation: Defying the odds.* Austin: University of Texas Press.

Rosenthal, R., & Jacobson, L. (1968). *Pygmalion in the classroom.* New York: Holt, Rinehart, & Winston.

Schmidt, W. (1998). Press statement released at the American Association for the Advancement of Science Annual Meeting, Philadelphia, February 12-17.

Secretary's Commission on Achieving Necessary Skills (SCANS). (1991). *What work requires of schools: A SCANS report for America 2000.* Washington, DC: U.S. Department of Labor.

Sizer, T. R. (1989). Diverse practice, shared ideas: The essential school. In H. J. Walberg & J. Lane (Eds.), *Organizing for learning: Toward the 21st century* (pp. 1-8). Reston, VA: National Association of Secondary School Principals.

Southern Regional Education Board. (Not dated). *High schools that work. Site development guide #1: Where do you begin?* Atlanta, GA: Author.

Steinberg, L. (1996). *Beyond the classroom: Why school reform has failed and what parents need to do.* New York: Simon and Schuster.

Stern, D., Finkelstein, N., Stone, J. R. , Latting, J., & Dornstife. (1995). *Research on school-to-work transition programs in the United States*. Washington, DC: Bristol, Taylor & Francis, Inc.

Stern, D., Raby, M., & Dayton, C. (1992). *Career academies: Partnerships for reconstructing American high schools*. San Francisco: Jossey-Bass Publishers.

Stevenson, H. W., & Stigler, J. W. (1992). *The learning gap*. New York: Summit Books.

10 Promoting Literacy and the Concept of Possibility

Vivian L. Gadsden with Wanda Brooks and Jacqueline K. Jackson

> It seemed to me that if I could learn to read and write, this learning, might, nay, I really thought it would point out to me the way to freedom, influence and real secure happiness. (Thomas Jones, quoted in Anderson [1988, p. 16]).

Thomas Jones, in this quotation, captures the power that we as a nation have associated with literacy and the fascination that we have with both its acquisition and its potential to effect positive change in the lives of children and families. A North Carolina slave, Jones learned to read while hiding in the back of his master's store. However, rather than leading to publicly and socially recognized "influence and real secure happiness," Jones's secret attempt to educate himself resulted in pain and greater hardship—a brutal whipping by his owner—when it was discovered that he could read. In short, Jones did not share in the power of literacy and citizenship that he had imagined [Anderson 1988].

Like Jones, the slave owners understood the power of literacy and knowledge. Historian Thomas Holt writes that, "In a perverse way those beatings reinforced the slave's belief in the value of education. By the extraordinary efforts they made to keep blacks from learning, slave owners inadvertently acknowledged that learning was a powerful force in the world" [Holt 1990, p. 93]. Although neither knew exactly where literacy would lead Jones, each (Jones and the slave owner), through action and obstacle, acclaimed reading literacy and education as a source of access to rights and possibilities.

In ways that reflect Jones's image and vision of literacy, parents, children, and educators in current school and community settings associate literacy with positive outcomes. Holt [1990] recalls the ideologue perspective of literacy among African Americans in 1865 who referred to "knowledge as power" and reading and writing as the most basic and salient vestiges of knowledge. More recently, literacy has been highlighted in a range of public and national initiatives, such as Goals 2000 and America Reads. Two of the eight goals in Goals 2000, the conceptual framework for a school-ready population, specifically address literacy. In addition, literacy is a major area of focus for every achievement and assessment measure in the United States, including the National Assessment of Educational Progress (NAEP) and the National Adult Literacy Survey (NALS), which have received considerable attention from policymakers.

Introduction

Over the past 30 years of literacy research, two questions have persisted: (1) why do some children experience problems in developing literate abilities, particularly reading, and (2) what factors contribute to their learning to read? These two questions contribute to a larger, seemingly complex question of whether there is a literacy problem among children and adolescents. The assumptions about children's early reading are developed around an expectation by educators that parents hold certain ideas or beliefs about literacy, are or are not engaged in their children's school experiences, or have substantial influence on their children's literacy development. Discussions in emergent literacy indicate that literacy acquisition begins during the preschool years when children acquire concepts of literacy, learn about the conventions and functions of print, and develop an interest in reading and writing. How and when children engage in or practice specific literacy activities, current work in parent-child and family literacy suggests, depends in some measure on the kind, quality, and quantity of literacy events and activities within the home.

Particular features of the home environment have been found to be related positively to the emergence of literacy. Children's early experiences with books and reading are thought to contribute to their later success or failure in learning to read. Specifically, children may be socialized into the world of literacy through the presence of literacy artifacts (e.g., newspapers, children's books, paper, and pencils), experiences, (e.g., checking the schedule for television shows), events (e.g., watching adults as they read and write in different contexts and situations), and interactions (e.g., bedtime story reading) [Fitzgerald et al., 1991].

In my own work with low-income African American and Puerto Rican parents, I have found that the parents' perspectives on literacy converge around remarkably similar themes, irrespective of the parents' backgrounds:

- literacy creates opportunities and reduces poverty,
- literacy's power is reduced in the face of race,
- schools and classrooms are not necessarily viable places that engage children in literacy learning,
- literacy is "a way out,"
- literacy is family and community imbued,
- literacy encompasses public knowledge,
- [learning] literacy is a [metacognitive] act, and
- literacy should be communal in nature [Gadsden 1998].

In general, these parents link their ideas, beliefs, and perceptions about literacy to family-based views, cultural significance, and intergenerational impact of learning; the meaning of success; and the values of the family itself.

Despite a national history that lauds the virtues of literacy, not everyone agrees that there is a common good or honorable motive attached to national literacy efforts. There are divergent opinions within the research and general educational community about the significance of literacy and its relationships to the politics of education. More often than not, these stances are presented in private discussions or in verbal presentations. Others are part of written texts that, at the very least, challenge the field to interrogate its purposes and goals for supporting literacy education and to question its ability to understand the nature of difference and need within the population.

For example, Kathryn Flannery notes that recent historical and ethnographic studies of literacy make it difficult to argue that "learning to read and write will lead necessarily to socioeconomic advancement, political enlightenment, or more humanized behavior" [1990, p. 209]. In the same volume, C. H. Knoblauch describes literacy as "one of those mischievous concepts, like virtuousness and craftsmanship, that appear to denote capacities but that actually convey value judgments" [1990, p. 74]. Knoblauch's analysis is based upon seemingly antiquated dichotomies of "literate" and "illiterate," dichotomies that typified the field of literacy through the early 1980s. These references to literate and illiterate are less often used by researchers and educators today who study and who seek to understand better the social and cultural contexts, influences, and uses of literacy. The term "illiterate" is still part of the active public discourse, however.

Both Flannery and Knoblauch point to inherent problems in the meanings and expectations of literacy—meanings and expectations that often differ between those who provide literacy assistance and those who receive it. Both authors suggest that far too much emphasis is given to literacy in changing the course of individuals' options and possibilities. Jones himself might be said to have assigned too great significance to literacy and to have had expectations that were too high, colored by obstacles to opportunities and leading him to imagine rewards that fall outside the boundaries of what reading and writing literacies can promise. In their essays, Knoblauch and Flannery acknowledge that the concept of literacy is entrenched in the ideological dispositions of those who use the concept, those who profit from it, and those who have the standing and motivation to enforce it as a social requirement. Both might pose questions about what counts as positive outcomes, who decides, and for what purpose do we aim to ensure children's access to literacy and to experiences that can produce positive outcomes for children, their families, and their communities.

I mention the perspectives of researchers such as Flannery and Knoblauch because they remind us of the cycles of concern that are intended not to do harm, but do little good. They bring to the surface the sometimes separate (yet often shared) goals of those who advocate for literacy and those who are expected to be the recipients of this advocacy. Neither author probably would deny the need to hear the perspectives and concerns of parents and children, and both engage in respectful searches to determine what investments schools, parents, children, and society must make to increase the well-being of children.

Within the past ten years, I have observed children and adults learning to read in a number of different settings: elementary and secondary schools, adult literacy programs, and family and parenting community-based programs. In each setting, staff members have been deeply committed to the program's mission and typically have approached the problems facing the communities they serve with enormous energy and purpose. A goal that almost all share is to make families self-sufficient and ensure the success of children and families. Each begins with a decisive image of what the problems are and about the desire to help the families and the children and youth in them achieve positive outcomes.

Although these outcomes are defined differently by each program participant, more often than not, they resemble accepted Western-honored notions of financial security, respect, and support. Both parents and program staff alike agree that education is a necessity to such success and that to achieve these socially valued icons of success, children and youth must be able to read, write, and solve problems. Their past experiences with learning to read and write often are developed out of narrow definitions of knowledge and what counts as knowledge, however. Their expectations of literacy's power may be substantially greater than what society has been willing to ensure historically. Their sense of literacy is that it is more than reading and writing. Their observations of the world lead them both to acknowledge literacy as a viable pathway to improved life chances and to assign importance to obstacles around the race, culture, and class difference that persist. Not unlike Thomas Jones, the countless children and families who are not confined by obvious forms of slavery have ample reason and multiple opportunities to observe the power of literacy as both liberating and oppressing. Like Knoblauch and Flannery, they question how they will realize the opportunities.

It would be naive and unrealistic, but pleasantly optimistic, to suggest that literacy can cure all of the ills facing children and their families, that the investment in good teaching of literacy alone will result in children and adolescents learning literacy, or that achieving high levels of literacy will open all doors. However, a deep belief in what I have come to call "the reality of the ideal" suggests that although literacy, like the goals of justice itself, may not eliminate the personal hardships that children and adults face, it does promote positive outcomes, and it can begin the process of unlocking doors. Our vigilance in providing quality literacy teaching and schooling and opportunities to learn can open the doors entirely. The factors that determine whether and how these doors will open are likely not to be limited to one measurable outcome. Instead, they should be linked to an awakening of knowledge and the desire for learners to be able to pursue ideas, to question, and to participate fully in society. They are nested in perceptions of complex life issues and in the interpretation of scholarly and practical texts. They are defined not only by whether children can read, write, or even think critically but also by what children choose to read, write, and think, and how the society in which children live supports these activities.

In this chapter, I focus on the problems associated with literacy and on the possibilities that literacy can create for children and their families. I include families primarily because children rely upon their families in ways that we have yet to understand fully. Moreover, language and literacy are family matters as much as they are school-based issues. How children acquire, understand, value, and use literacy may not reflect patterns of family knowledge entirely, but these skills contribute knowledge to and reflect the "cultures of families"—what I have referred to as the cumulative effect of history, experiences, and beliefs with which families identify from one generation to another.

The chapter is divided into five short sections. In the first, I introduce the issues and discuss the scope of the problem. In the second, I describe the school and literacy experiences of child and adolescent learners who are vulnerable to what Lisbeth Schor refers as "rotten outcomes." In the third, I give examples of school- and community-based program efforts aimed at addressing problems through multiple approaches—efforts that show promise. In the fourth, I review the issues that the field continues to examine. In the last section, I offer closing considerations about the implications of child and adolescent literacy issues within and across practice, policy, and research.

Literacy for Children and Adolescents: Is There a Problem?

During the 1970s and 1980s, it was not uncommon for references to be made to the literacy problem. For people who interpreted the problem solely in terms of helping adults who could not read or who thought the problem was "illiteracy" (that the adults possessed "no" literacy), descriptions of literacy as a problem may have been baffling. By the "literacy problem," however, researchers and educators were referring to the scope of issues—from defining literacy, to determining what counts as literacy or "enough" literacy, to increasing rates of literacy in the general population, to improving the quality of literacy learning and teaching. In 1987, the NAEP Young Adult Survey provided an expansive definition of literacy as a range of reading, writing, numeracy, and problem-solving abilities. This new definition also suggested that the earlier, simplistic separation of individuals into literate and illiterate was probably inaccurate. It recognized that, even in the absence of reading and writing abilities, individuals may have developed several other cognitive abilities that enable them to survive and thrive in the world.

More than ten years later, it might be said that whether there is a literacy problem depends, in part, upon who is asking and who is being asked to respond. For example, some reports paint a relatively bleak picture and stress caution in overgeneralizing positive comparisons. Consider the

NAEP, one of the most recognized measures of the state of literacy. Since 1969, NAEP has provided data on literacy (reading, writing, and mathematical ability) and cross-sectional comparisons of student performance. In K-12 schools, NAEP is administered to 9-, 13-, and 17- year-olds (approximately grades 4, 8, and 12) every three years.

In the late 1980s, the broad pattern in NAEP reports showed that literacy rates among African American, Latino, and white students continued to increase, that reading proficiency improved with some age-group and time variation, and that the gap at each grade level had narrowed. In contrast, the 1992 NAEP report indicated that although most students at grades 4, 8, and 12 had mastered basic competencies, too few had reached levels likely to be required for an increasingly competitive workplace [Gorman 1993]. These results were reinforced by the 1993 NALS, in which large percentages of adults demonstrated limited reading literacy.

The NALS found that some 40 to 44 million of the 191 million adults in the United States demonstrated skills in the lowest level of prose, document, and quantitative proficiencies (e.g., able to locate an entry on a deposit slip, locate the time or place of a meeting on a form, and identify a piece of specific information in a brief news article). Another 25 to 28%, representing 50 million adults, demonstrated skills in the next higher level of proficiency (e.g., able to calculate the cost of a purchase or determine the difference in price between two items). Perhaps one of the most striking findings was that 66 to 75% of the adults in the lowest level and 93 to 97% in the second lowest level described themselves as being able to read or write English "well" or "very well" [Kirsch et al. 1993]. As the authors suggest, "it is possible that the adults' skills, while limited, allow them to meet some or most of their personal and occupational literacy needs" [Kirsch et al. 1993, p. xv].

More encouraging responses have been reported in the 1996 report, *Reading Literacy in the United States*, by the National Center for Education Statistics (NCES). NCES reported that the literacy performance of American children and youth was comparable to other Western nations, second only to Finland. Based upon a 32-nation IEA International Reading Literacy Survey, the report stated that American students outperformed the Organization for Economic Cooperation and Development (OECD) average and that even the most disadvantaged American students did not differ dramatically from the OECD average. Children who face the most difficult life circumstances as a function of race (e.g., African American students), income (e.g., poor students), and years of schooling (e.g.,less than a high school diploma), however, did not perform well using U.S. national standards, but did perform well compared to students in other countries with similar demographic and educational backgrounds [Binkley & Williams 1996].

It is not surprising that the recent NCES report has been quoted extensively and that many in the research and policy worlds took heart at the international comparisons. After all, Americans have harbored many fears about whether the young would demonstrate the competencies to participate in the global marketplace. On the one hand, the NCES report suggests that the picture is not so dismal. On the other, much of data in all of the reports raise concern: that is, the poor and minorities (African American and Latino students primarily) are not performing well and are experiencing high levels of poverty. In testimony to the Subcommittee on Education and the Workforce of the U. S. Congress, Richard Venezky in 1997 stated that these reports indicate "where America's reading problems reside [with minorities, particularly low-income minorities]" [Venezky 1997, p. 4], noting that income was a more significant variable than either race or ethnicity. By this, Venezky was referring, in part, to data from NAEP and NALS that point to a four-year gap between minority and white reading performance on both assessments.

How bleak is the outlook, and what is the urgency of improving outcomes for children and youth? Data from the national assessments show a substantial decline in literacy among minorities and a modest decline among whites; the effects related to income are more severe for minorities. The reading performance of African American and Latino students on NAEP increased from the 1970s to 1988 relative to white performance, but the gap began to widen again after 1988. These statistics and the underlying reasons for them merit investigation and close attention. As important as the statistics that denote the decline are the issues of why the performance continues to decline and the degree to which the decline reflects problems; e.g., structural barriers, poor schools, and family functioning.

For poor children and adults, the urgency lies in limited employment and schooling options and the potential for an intergenerational transfer of poverty and hardship. It is estimated that approximately one-half of African American children and more than one-third of Latino children will grow up in poverty [National Commission on Children 1991]. They will attend schools and live in neighborhoods with the greatest number of problems and with few financial and educational resources. Today, the obvious forms of exclusion and denial are less visible. Children of all races, ethnic groups, and cultures are free to enter school, learn to read and write, and achieve the literacy that will enable them to experience success. Yet, the disparity in opportunity and in the quality of schooling itself suggests that each child does not have equal access to opportunity and that some children are embattled by a range of familial, neighborhood, and school-related problems such that their talents are barely noticed or used. As increasing numbers of children and families become more vulnerable to hardship, and as the problems of low literacy among children and adults become entrenched, the issue of how to help children develop appropriate and necessary reading and writing abilities takes on a sense of urgency requiring intellectual strengths, social commitment, and political will to effect positive change.

The results of illiteracy for low-income children and low-income minority children are not simply difficult life circumstances but also low expectations that these children will experience positive outcomes. James Comer, in his recent volume *Waiting for a Miracle*, refers to the millions of children and families who, for whatever reasons, lack the resources and knowledge to translate desire into possibility. Disproportionate numbers of these children will not acquire the basic reading and writing abilities to enable them to use print effectively in everyday life or to achieve in adulthood. Their literacy and school experiences often mirror those of their parents who may have minimal reading and writing abilities. With each succeeding generation, the likelihood that these children will have access to opportunity or that their problems will be captured by the lens of helpful policies diminshes. Thus, all of us—the children, their families, and society in general—run the risk of constructing a future which reduces possibility.

William Damon [1990] suggests that the problems of literacy are not neatly packaged. He writes: "A republic that loses large portions of its citizenry to civic ignorance and disinterest is as troubled as a school system that loses large portions of its students to [low] literacy and early withdrawal. In contemporary America, we see warning signs of both" [p. 34]. Most would agree that there is a literacy problem, but that it differs in nature and scope from the problem as described just 20 years ago. Thus, the question that is most critical is not whether there is a problem, but what the nature of the problem is and what media are available to implement alternatives.

The Reality of Rotten Outcomes

In her 1988 book, *Within Our Reach*, Lisbeth Schor approaches the problem of outcomes for children in a straightforward way. She refers at the outset of the volume to a presentation by Harvard Professor Mary Jo Bane, in which Bane describes the continuum of "rotten outcomes" for children and adolescents. In their references to rotten outcomes, Bane and Schor describe problems that afflict adolescents, from having children too soon, to leaving school without the literate abilities to become employed or sustain employment, to committing illegal acts. Both Bane in her presentation and Schor in her book focused on prevention: Bane on learning more about who was destined for serious trouble before the trouble became serious and responding in appropriate ways and Schor on gathering what we already know and understanding better how to use what we already know to keep "'rotten outcomes' from happening" [Schor 1988, p. xviii].

Schor reviews a series of well-known programs and less well-known, but apparently successful, efforts. She highlights the problems faced by children and families in the most need and demonstrates the complexities of responding to the range of needs. As a result, she redirects attention away from our collective sense of helplessness and handwringing to a new sense of how we can build upon existing activities to develop appropriate alternatives—not only to avert the rotten outcomes but also to increase the opportunities to help children and families experience positive outcomes.

What was intriguing to me as I read Schor's description was the compelling notion of "rotten outcomes." At the time, I had recently completed my doctorate, had just landed my first academic appointment, and was sure that sheer commitment to improving the lives of children was enough. Schor's commentary, however, made the implicit messages of my graduate training explicit: We were not simply dealing with the possibilities for positive outcomes but had to struggle with the realities of rotten outcomes that defined and limited the experiences of children throughout the country. Schor refers to literacy and schooling throughout her work, focusing on the education of young children, the influence of parents and families, and the obstacles to adolescent children making sometimes abrupt transitions to adulthood, through dropping out, early parenting, physical or learning challenges, or a combination of these.

Low literacy has been linked to a range of problems, many of which may affect people who are low-literate at all levels of society. There is evidence that the problem is largely concentrated within low-income urban and rural communities. Two of the most debilitating effects are poverty and school dropout, both of which lead to more destructive experiences. Young adolescents living in poverty are more likely than other young people to lack grade-level literacy skills and are more likely to be tracked into less challenging classes, to be held back a grade, and to drop out of school [Davidson & Koppenhaver 1993].

Young children's futures are determined in the same way. In schools, young children are assigned to reading ability groups that dictate their placement well into high school where, absent of intervention, they are tracked, usually for their future. As Sean Walmsley and Richard Allington [1995] point out, these children's assignment to and placement in reading groups reflect their preschool familiarity with print rather than their reading ability. Walmsley and Allington assert that these placements ensure that the children fulfill the prophecies of failure, achieving low levels of reading competence with "alarming accuracy." The effects of low literacy may be felt in other ways also. Walmsley and Allington suggest that students who have poor reading and writing abilities often are retained in a grade and that being retained in one grade increases the risk of being a dropout later by 40 to 50%; being held back for two years increases the risk to 90%.

Many students make the decision to drop out while in middle school; in fact, the unwritten expectation of many urban schools is that if children stay in school through the middle (or junior high) school years, they may persist. While some drop out during this period, others wait until high school, frequently having been disengaged from learning in school or having left school mentally years earlier. Low literacy and the resulting dropout lead often to many dangerous and self-destructive youth behaviors, ranging from early sexual activity and teen pregnancy, to smoking, alcohol, and drug use, and juvenile delinquency. These are the fears that are strewn in our observations of Tommy, Ian, and Trudy.

Tommy

Tommy's School Life and Literacy Experiences

Tommy is a seventh grader who attends middle school in a low-income community in Philadelphia. His school is 95% African American and 5% Latino. The school has approximately 530 students in grades six through eight. All of the students are low-income, and the school has been designated a Title I School. The staff and faculty are African American and white, about 50% falling into each group. Both the principal and vice principal are African American men, and Tommy's teacher is an African American woman.

Although he is in seventh grade, Tommy has been assessed as reading at a third-grade level. This is particularly problematical because the content of most third-grade level passages is of little interest to Tommy. He gets frustrated with the third-grade reading passages and demonstrates his frustration in a number of ways, for example, misspelling words (such as "day," "his," and "its") that he knows well and forgetting to utilize basic rules of writing (such as capitalizing first words in sentences and ending them with punctuation). His seventh-grade reading and social studies books are too difficult for him to decode and to comprehend. As a result, Tommy completes almost none of his assigned classwork if it involves much reading and writing. Reading, language arts, social studies, and science are all subjects that "frighten him."

No one is quite sure how Tommy has managed first through sixth grades. Perhaps because he is extremely quiet and not a behavior problem, he has been passed on from grade to grade, despite his inability to read and write well. When he is sitting in class, there is a look on his face that indicates his discomfort with what is occurring. Several teachers have commented about his "black outs" or "aimless staring into space." Unlike many students, he does not act out his academic frustration aggressively by becoming disruptive in class. Instead, when he should be completing a writing assignment or reading pages from his assigned novel, he is writing rows of numbers over and over again on his paper. Tommy says this repetitive activity keeps him calm and helps him concentrate.

Tommy's teachers are unsure about how to help him. They indicate that he is far behind. The school, mired in inner-city academic failure and inadequate financial and personnel resources, is home to many children with problems similar to Tommy's. Like Tommy, these children are years behind in their literacy development. Teachers comment that "many children need so much more than is humanly possible to give in one school year, even for the best of teachers." Tommy's teachers try to provide him with as many opportunities as they can. For example, last year he attended tutoring one day a week after school, and this year for remedial help in reading, he is assigned to the schoolwide reading specialist for one period a day.

In one class, Tommy is one of three students identified as "special education" and is with other students identified as needing additional help with reading and writing. There are seven children in all who receive additional assistance. Tommy is performing at a level lower than the identified "special education" students. In his other seven classes, however, he is just one among 33 students hoping for a little individualized attention from his teachers. He is failing in every subject except math. His school achievement records do not reveal the reasons for this performance. There is no evidence that Tommy has ever been the subject of an Instructional Support Team's review.

Parent Involvement

Tommy comes from a single-parent home. His mother is his primary caregiver and is as active in his schooling as she can be. She has said that she knows that her son does not read as well as he should, and she reads to him at home frequently. The books she selects are between a second- and third-grade level. Although she hopes that she is mistaken, she wonders if her child has "dyslexia" or some other type of reading disorder, but has not had him tested. She blames herself, not the school, for his "poor" literacy development. According to her, when he first began school and demonstrated initial problems learning to read, she was incapable of providing adequate support because she was involved in her own "mess of problems." She says he has never recovered from this initial lack of neglect. A high school dropout herself, Tommy's mother is no stranger to academic failure. Currently, she is earning her General Education Diploma (GED) and attends classes several nights a week.

Tommy's mother has vowed to help her son as much as possible by going over his assignments, checking out library books, reading to him, discussing his social studies chapters, and checking his homework nightly. But even with this type of support at home, Tommy continually struggles in class each day.

Promoting Positive Literacy Outcomes for Tommy

Tommy's teacher was asked to comment on whether the school and Tommy's other teachers could promote positive outcomes for him. She indicated that, with the help at home and some increased attention to his literacy problems at school, Tommy will most likely make some progress. This progress may not be enough, however, at this late stage. The chances of his catching up before entering eighth grade are slim. In fact, the chances of his being passed on to eighth grade are even slimmer. Yet, simply retaining him for one year may not eliminate but further perpetuate a cycle of failure that began when he first entered school seven years ago.

Since Tommy is approximately five grades behind in his reading, he would need an extensive amount of classroom, in-school, and home support to develop his lagging literacy skills adequately. For instance, all of his teachers, not only his reading and language arts teachers, would need to become involved in this effort. Classes such as science and social studies both require extensive amounts of reading and writing in the middle school grades.

Once these teachers became aware of his problems, accommodations could be made in the classroom to have Tommy engage in partnered reading or to offer him time before or after school to read the class material with the help of a teacher or tutor. Other accommodations in his reading and language arts classes can be made for Tommy as well, such as providing him with specialized spelling or vocabulary lists that match his learning needs. Additionally, individualized reading and writing activities would be beneficial to enhancing his literacy skills. Outside of the classroom, Tommy should receive tutoring and continue to see the reading specialist. The time spent in tutoring and with the reading specialists must be substantial and consistent—neither of which may be guaranteed. Lastly, the continued support of his mother is going to be crucial. She can monitor his homework and offer him literacy opportunities, such as accompanying him to the library to select books of interest, checking his homework, reading to and with him, helping him study, and being in close contact with all of his teachers.

When asked what she might imagine for Tommy, his teacher responded:

> Considering how academically behind Tommy is, I hope he is able to complete high school successfully, without failing a grade or dropping out of school. He is completely disinterested in and overwhelmed by a school system that has essentially neglected many of his learning needs and devalued his potential as a human being. Tommy comes

> from a family where dropping out of school is not unusual and to end this cycle he will need to overcome a great deal of academic failure. At a minimum, I hope this is possible, and I hope that Tommy becomes a high school graduate rather than a statistic.
>
> My hopes for Tommy are not unlike the hopes and dreams his mother holds for him. She dreams for him, however, through the eyes of a parent and not a teacher. As his mother, she sees in Tommy much of herself. She knows how uninspired he is because she too felt the same way in school. On the other hand, she also knows how difficult her life has been because she did not graduate from high school and, subsequently, she desires so much more for her youngest son. Tommy's mother blames herself for his academic failure and is attempting to improve her life by going back to school while at the same time changing the downward academic spiral her son is on by giving him additional support at home. Indeed, our dreams for Tommy are similar, despite the fact that our understanding of who and/or what is to blame for his academic failure is, in some regards, quite different.

Ian

Ian is a second grader in a public elementary school, located in an affluent suburb outside of Philadelphia. He is one of approximately 20 children in his class, the only child of African descent in his class and grade, and one of a handful of children of African descent in his school. His parents are both African émigrés. Both are employed, and the family enjoys a modest middle-class lifestyle. His father works two jobs; his mother works and is completing studies toward a nursing degree. Both parents have verbal fluency in English. Ian has a younger brother.

Ian's parents decided to move to their current neighborhood because they wanted to ensure the safety of their children and expose them to "good" schools. The parents are consumed by the desire for Ian to be a good reader and a good student. They spend a considerable amount of time reading to him, buying books (particularly folk tales about Africa) for him, taking him to museums, and engaging him in educational activities. They participate fully in all of the parent-child interactions that have been associated with successful readers and school achievement.

Ian is highly verbal in English and well-read. He is a sensitive boy who is as comfortable talking about the history of his parents' homeland and the African continent as the events of his day at school. However, although Ian appears to have "bought into" the belief that literacy is important and performs well on literacy measures, it is not clear that his facility with literacy will result in positive outcomes. He was recently the focus of an Instructional Study Team review in response to his teacher's request. He tested average or above-average on every measure. Yet, throughout the review, every school person other than the psychologist reminded the group, the parents, and me of his problematic behavior, which includes responding with a blank stare rather than verbally responding, not following the rules, and not always following directions (rather remaking the assignment into something interesting for him). The teacher has interpreted Ian's failure to follow the directions as his not understanding the task, but provides little information about the dialogue between Ian and him when these moments of misunderstanding occur.

Despite Ian's love of reading and other literacy activities, his literacy future and continued school achievement are, at best, tenuous. Ian reports that he feels isolated and alone in his school. He does not appear to fit in; he is not like the other children, and the teachers are intolerant of his "defiant" behavior. Ian has reported that he is treated differently by his teachers and had by first grade assigned a range of negative characteristics to black boys, indicating his displeasure at being a black boy: "No one likes black boys." He is developing literate abilities, likes to read, write, solve puzzles, and learn about African culture. Despite these positive indicators, Ian's literacy may not be enough, and his parents fear that his literate abilities will decline because of his overwhelmingly negative attributions to black maleness in his school. If Ian is to achieve positive outcomes, he will need a range of other social supports, particularly if he continues in his current school.

What would it take to ensure positive outcomes for Ian? I recently began working with Ian, at the request of his parents, although I have been in conversation about him with his parents for the past year. They asked me to attend his Instructional Support Team review; they were unsure of what to expect. They were so unsure that they did not seem to understand fully until the day of the review that there were seemingly strong inclinations to label him as learning disabled. His scores on the tests extricated him from this future, and possibly the hard questions that the parents asked advantaged him and eliminated the possibility of his being labeled.

My interests are not simply around Ian's literacy but also connected to the reality that Ian, neatly located in a system with ostensible resources, may fail or feel so marginalized that he does not achieve the positive outcomes that are possible for him. Simple characteristics and demographics may become liabilities: Ian's status as the son of émigrés, as a boy of African descent, as a nonconformist in some ways, as a "strong personality," and as a child from a lower-middle income, Black immigrant family living in a upper-middle income community. Ian's problems currently do not revolve around literacy; however, his literacy seems to be among the first abilities to suffer in his current state of discomfort and unhappiness. Neither the range of needs nor the range of resources is yet clear to those of us who are working with him. It is clear that his current setting and the low expectations of those in it create a context of struggle for him that without intervention will diminish his possibilities.

Trudy: A Retrospective Account

Trudy grew up in a historically poor white neighborhood where she resides today. Her home is a brown row house in a narrow one-way block. There are no vacant houses, no visible graffiti, no abandoned houses on this street. There is a small porch area in the front of the house. A large air conditioner is in the first floor front window. On the day the teacher-researcher, an African American woman, visited to interview Trudy, the interviewer was met with long stares from the community people and family as she emerged from her car. Trudy's son answered the door and called for his "Ma." Trudy closed the door and talked to the interviewer on the porch.

Trudy's mother died when she was 12. Her father was a sheet metal worker. None of her five brothers and sisters completed high school. Although she had been enrolled in GED classes for three years, Trudy had not been able to earn a score of 225 required to pass the test. In her initial conversation with her teacher, Trudy admitted she had always been painfully shy and that she got so nervous when she went to take the test that she could not remember anything. "It was," she stated, "as if my mind went blank." In the next session, she talked about her schooling experiences. When asked whether she experienced anxiety and shyness in school, she responded, "Yes." In addition, she finally admitted she had been in "special classes" after her mother died. She stated, "I never told no one about being, in special classes... I was just too embarrassed." She could not recall ever being told why, however: "I guess I was just slow. I have to read and read it again. Everything takes me such a long time." Trudy was not able to gather school records to show why and when she had been placed in special education.

In search of a decent life, Trudy dropped out of school at 17 to marry a young man who went on to become a firefighter in this northeastern city. After 17 years of marriage, her husband left her, and in the ten years since, she has received welfare to support herself and four children.

The community in which she grew up was an industrial hub then. Seventeen years ago quitting school was not an end but a beginning. Employment at local mills, factories, and plants was plentiful, with many opportunities for overtime. Although this is no longer the case and there are few opportunities, none of Trudy's sons has completed high school. Her hopes for the future are pinned on her youngest daughter, now a high school student. In an earlier interview, Trudy states, "She's part of the reason I stuck it out. I wanted my kids to respect me. I wanted them to think highly of me." Since her sons no longer attend school, they are not on Trudy's welfare budget, although it still seems that they transitionally reside in the home and she continues to provide some support for them. Trudy maintains her aspirations for her daughter but appears to have accepted the lives of her sons.

Promoting Positive Outcomes

Over the past 30 years, we have seen the creation of many different programs focused on literacy assistance and support to children, adolescents, and adults. Several have been sustained over time and have been associated with positive outcomes for children and youth such as Tommy, Ian, and Trudy. Although their focuses may differ, these efforts share a goal of creating opportunities for children to achieve the literate abilities that will enable them to participate in society. Some programs work toward this goal by focusing on specific reading approaches for school-age children. Others provide assistance in school and community-based after-school and summer programs and in child, parent, and family literacy programs. As might be expected, many programs modify their original missions over time, but all offer ideas, innovations, and approaches from which we can learn.

School-Based Reading Programs

Reading Recovery

Reading Recovery, one of the most well-known efforts for poor children, was developed in New Zealand by Marie M. Clay, a clinical child psychologist. Reading Recovery is an early intervention program designed to reduce first-grade reading failure. The program enables the lowest achieving students of a first-grade classroom to catch up to the average readers in their own first grade and continue to learn with regular classroom instruction. Teachers are specially trained to teach students who have been making slow progress in how to become strategic, independent learners. Through weekly demonstration lessons, the students learn how to develop a sequence of reading and writing experiences. The teacher gradually diminishes his or her contributions while the students increase their contributions. Within the daily 30-minute lessons, students learn how to perform the same reading and writing tasks independently. The cumulative experience enables students to learn how to construct a repertoire of strategies that are used in a variety of ways [Stowall & Tierney 1995].

What is the potential contribution that Reading Recovery holds for promoting positive outcomes? When compared to four other methods used to correct reading difficulties among first graders, Reading Recovery was the only treatment for which there was a significant difference on measures such as Text Reading Level, Dictation Assessment Task, Woodcock Reading Mastery, and Gates MacGinite. It also was the only program indicating lasting effects [Pinnell, Lyons, DeFord, Bryk, & Seltzer 1994]. As Laura Stowall and Robert Tierney [1995] note, longitudinal program evaluation data demonstrate that Reading Recovery results in significant reductions in the number of first-grade students retained and placed in learning disability or remedial programs. Teachers' perceptions of what low-achieving students can do changes, and special education testing and diagnostic practices that lead to misclassification and placement of children in learning disabled programs are avoided.

"Success For All" and "Roots & Wings"

Success For All™ (SFA) and Roots & Wings™ are described as comprehensive school restructuring programs for students in prekindergarten to sixth grade. The programs were for several years based in the Center for Social Organization of Schools at Johns Hopkins University in Baltimore, but recently they became part of an independent foundation. The programs focus on prevention and early intervention to ensure "that virtually every student will succeed in reading throughout the elementary grades and no student will be allowed to 'fall between the cracks.'" The curriculum is developed around cooperative learning; i.e., students work together in partnerships and teams, helping one another to become strategic readers and writers. Emphasis is placed on individual accountability, common goals, and recognition of group success. The model is used currently in 750 schools in 37 states.

Literacy assistance in the programs is provided by specially trained, certified teachers working one-on-one with students in grades 1-3, with first-grade students having priority for tutoring. Students in grades 1-5 are assessed every eight weeks to determine whether they are making adequate progress in reading. Whenever possible, a half-day preschool program is provided for all 4-year-olds. The programs emphasize language development, readiness, and positive self-concept. A full-day kindergarten program continues the emphasis on language, using children's literature and big books, as well as oral and written composition activities promoting the development of concepts about print, alphabet games, and math concept development. Peabody Language Development Kits are used to provide additional experience in language.

At all levels, students read books of their choice for 20 minutes each evening as homework. Classroom libraries of books are developed for this purpose. For schools with Spanish bilingual programs, Success For All™ provides a Spanish reading curriculum, *Exito Para Todos*, in first through fifth grades. Writing is emphasized throughout the grades. Writing instruction uses a writing workshop format, in which students plan, draft, revise, edit, and publish compositions with feedback at each stage from teachers and peers.

According to Success For All™ reports, the program has been evaluated in ten school districts from all over the United States. In each, Success For All™ and control schools have been compared on individually administered reading scales and other measures, with the results consistently favoring Success For All™. The reports suggest that, in average grade equivalents, their students perform approximately three months ahead of comparison students by first grade, and more than a year ahead by fifth grade. Effects are particularly strong for students who are most at risk, those in the lowest 25% of their grades. The effects of the Spanish version of Success For AllTM, *Exito Para Todos*, also have been strong. Positive effects have also been found on district-administered standardized tests, and Success For All™ reportedly has produced substantial reductions in retentions and special education referrals and placements.

Structured Teaching in the Areas of Reading and Writing

The Structured Teaching in the Areas of Reading and Writing program (STAR) is an example of an innovative Chapter 1 program. Created by New York City's District 4, STAR aims to spark students' interest in reading and writing and to engage them in reading and writing tasks that will improve their literate abilities. The program was created by the district as a result of public and staff dissatisfaction with the district's first Chapter 1 Program in 1973-1978. STAR is no longer limited to District 4's Chapter 1 students, however. It was eventually used as a teaching method for classroom reading instruction in at least 11 of District 4's elementary and junior high schools. Davidson and Koppenhaver in 1993 reported that more than 63% of the students in the district were reading at grade level, with District 4 claiming the highest reading scores of New York City's school districts with high minority student populations [1993].

STAR focuses on teaching "strategies" and assists students by addressing the fundamental questions readers ask to help themselves decipher text. The program's approach stresses that strategies and comprehension are central to language and that literacy is only one part of the continuum of language learning. The program builds upon the language skills with which students enter the program, highlighting students' language strengths. The program promotes the idea that school-age children who have learned to speak one or more languages should be considered highly efficient and successful language learners with a wide repertoire of existing strategies for continuing their language learning. By emphasizing students' capabilities rather than their deficiencies, STAR is responsive to both the development and the instructional needs of students.

STAR advisors urge teachers to use methods and practices for remedial students, which in many schools are reserved exclusively for the highest achievers—for example, teaching students strategies as well as skills, having students make their own reading selections, conducting class activities that focus on reading extended texts rather than only words or sentences, and insisting on the importance of comprehension. Davidson and Koppenhaver [1993] report the responses of a 10-year-old who says her "STAR teacher [isn't] letting us down. She's forcing us to go on. She asks us—What is reading for? How does it help us?" Another student, Michelena, is reported to believe that she is going to be a more successful adult worker because of the skills she is learning in her class: "It's helping me. I want to graduate; this work helps so it won't be so hard in high school."

High Intensity Language Training

The High Intensity Language Training model (HILT) was founded in 1982 in the El Paso, Texas, Independent School District. Its primary purposes have been to ensure that students making the transition from Spanish-speaking environments to English-speaking classrooms and settings are comfortable and develop the skills they need to be successful in mainstream high school English classes and in other areas of their lives within and outside of school. As of 1993, HILT provided English language and literacy instruction in eight school sites to approximately 2,000 students in seventh through twelfth grades. HILT's primary goal has been to prepare students for a successful transition into the regular high school curriculum. HILT language lessons typically are provided in English; however, key concepts or specific directions occasionally are presented in Spanish. Students are free to use Spanish at any time, but teachers respond in the language that seems appropriate to the situation, students, and question. HILT is predicated on the belief that language lessons should and can be so interesting that the student is focused on the content and not on the language form.

The design of HILT is responsive to the cultural, academic, and developmental needs of young adolescents adjusting to a new country and school system and learning a new language. Beginning-level classes are kept small to facilitate the individual assistance many students need and to promote a feeling of security. Language experiences are typically used in reading and composition classes. Students are surrounded with the sights and sounds of written and spoken English. The program allows students to speak when they are ready, respond as they are able, and write according to their capabilities. Students who complete the program have low dropout rates, reportedly as low as 15% for those students who can persist in the program.

Comer School Development Program

The Comer School Development Program (SDP), also known as the Comer Process, is not a literacy program, but places literacy as one of its fundamental concerns. Created more than 25 years ago by child psychiatrist James Comer and his colleagues at the Yale Child Study Center, the initial intervention program was a two-year school project in two inner-city elementary schools in New Haven, Connecticut. Based upon his observations, Dr. Comer concluded that "children's experiences at home and in school deeply affect their psychosocial development, which in turn shapes their academic achievement." He asserted that poor academic performance is in large part a function of the failure to bridge the social and cultural gaps between home and school. The program has been implemented at more than 250 schools (elementary through high school) in 19 states.

The Comer Process is premised on three principles:

- schools must review problems in open discussion in a no-fault atmosphere;
- each school must develop collaborative working relationships among principals, parents, teachers, community leaders, superintendents, and health-care workers; and
- all decisions must be reached by consensus rather than by decree.

These principles are applied to a nine-part process to improve educators' understanding of child development and to foster healthier relations between school and home. The program is designed to create a school environment where children feel comfortable, valued, and secure. In this environment, children will form positive emotional bonds with school staff and parents and develop a positive attitude toward the school program, which promotes the children's overall development and, in turn, facilitates academic learning.

Program researchers have conducted numerous studies of student achievement in Comer schools over the past 15 years. Some studies have compared student achievement in Comer schools to student achievement in control schools. A 1985 study, for example, found that fourth- and fifth-grade students in Comer schools received significantly higher reading and math grades than students in control schools and that third- and fourth-grade students in Comer schools scored significantly higher on the California Achievement Test (CAT) for reading. Other studies have compared student achievement in Comer schools to student achievement for the district as a whole. In Prince George's County, Maryland, for example, average percentile gains on math, reading, and language arts CAT scores for the district's ten Comer schools were significantly higher than the average percentile gains for district schools as a whole. The program materials cite several studies that have found that student achievement improves more at schools that adhere strictly to the Comer Process than those that do not. Finally, a number of studies have documented improvements in behavior, attendance, self-concept, and school climate in Comer schools.

After-School and Summer Literacy Programs

After-school programs and summer programs are viable settings that contribute to positive outcomes for children and adolescents. Such programs may be offered in schools or through community-based organizations. Good after-school and summer programs serve as a connector before adolescence by linking the family, school, and community to a young child's future and providing continued support. In 1982, the Center for Early Adolescence conducted a search for successful after-school programs and identified 50 programs in 24 states. The Center's Project on Adolescent Literacy explored the impact of these programs on young adolescents. The Center identified three programs that were particularly noteworthy and that are still important: (1) the Friendly Place, (2) the Montgomery Ward-Cabrini Green Tutoring Program, and (3) the Highline Indian Tutoring Program [Davidson & Koppenhaver 1993].

The Friendly Place is a community literacy center that serves all ages and levels through a combination library-bookstore and special programming. Located in New York City's Harlem, the program emphasizes enrichment and achieves its goals by surrounding learners with "good books and good literacy experiences." Several mornings a week, a toddler-and-parent group meets. Children and adolescents mingle while enjoying literacy experiences. They explore a range of questions, from family relationships, to sexuality, to teen pregnancy through books and through peer interchanges. On Saturdays and during the summer, The Friendly Place sponsors clubs for young people in a variety of interest areas, from cooking to dance to drama. The Friendly Place is one of several literacy demonstration projects sponsored by the American Reading Council, founded in 1976. It affords children and adolescents an opportunity to mix in a world where everyone can exercise the right to read, where everyone has books, where preschool and school-aged children are read aloud to every day, and where young people can explore their future and past through written texts.

The **Montgomery Ward-Cabrini Green Tutoring Program** is one of the largest one-to-one scholastic tutoring organization working with young children. It serves approximately 500 children per week and has more than 400 volunteer tutors. It began as a partnership between business and the community. Established in 1965, the program was founded, is directed, and is staffed by volunteers. The program's tutors work with all neighborhood children on a first-come/first-serve basis, irrespective of reading level. The program is based in a low-income community with many children who have been placed at-risk and who need outside help if they are to achieve positive outcomes. One strength and source of appeal to the neighborhood is that the program does not consider itself a remedial program. Early descriptions of the program stated that the program met one evening a week, some Tuesdays and others on Wednesdays. Approximately 200 children from the nearby housing project and 200 tutors from Montgomery Ward, as well as other corporations, came to the old Ward's catalogue warehouse to learn, share, and grow. The purpose of the program is to build children's self-esteem so that they will be able to break out of the cycle of failure that so many children in Cabrini Green have experienced.

The **Highline Indian Tutoring Program** is a cross-age tutoring program that employs high school and college students to tutor young American Indians. The program serves American Indians in the Seattle, Washington area and works with students who are at high risk of failure in school. Davidson and Koppenhaver [1993] state that for many American Indian children in the Seattle area, the program may be the critical factor that weights the balance toward future success. The program recognizes that many of the problems experienced by American Indian children within classrooms may have less to do with their disadvantagement and more with their cultural backgrounds and learning styles that differ from those of white middle-class-focused classrooms. Staff are trained to appreciate these differences and to use teaching methods appropriate to the learner's style.

After-school programs have become a part of several school and community plans to provide students with additional literacy assistance. Although summer programs have been increasing, they have enjoyed less widespread implementation. When Entwisle and Alexander wrote in 1992 about the cognitive loss children experience during the summer, their article reiterated earlier discussions of educators who were aware of the loss in skills that children experience when they are not in school. Students from low-income backgrounds are affected most significantly.

Many summer programs were funded during the 1970s. There is relatively little concrete follow-up data that speak to their success, however. Little is known about the implementation of these programs. The well-known Kenosha, Wisconsin Model, for example, began as a summer program and is now a critical part of the school district's Title I effort. Another program about which there is little current information is the Growing Together program in Washington, DC. The program provided tutoring to approximately 100 students two or three days a week, either after school, on Saturdays, or during the summer. Community volunteers worked one-on-one with students with the support of an experienced teacher or tutor. Ninety percent of the students in the program reportedly gained one or more grade levels in reading as a result of participating in the program. Like Growing Together, after school and summer literacy programs often are sponsored by several agencies and could contribute to an expansive body of work that motivates children, resulting not simply in compensatory work but also stimulating participation in activities for advanced learners.

Parent-Child and Family Literacy Programs

Family literacy programs in the United States are developed generally around one of two assumptions about families and the purposes and uses of literacy, or they combine important features of both. In one, literacy is equated with performing school-like academic activities within the home.

The social and cultural characteristics of the family unit are seen as potential obstacles to overcome for learning to occur; parents are taught strategies and approaches to assist their children, using school-like models. In the second, the family is viewed as a source of information; literacy practices already used in the home or community serve as the basis for instruction. Family practices and interactions are examined to understand the functions, uses, and purposes of literacy within families.

Family literacy programs focus on a range of activities, such as parent involvement, after-school reading programs, and parent-child book reading projects in schools or in the home. Some programs describe themselves as intergenerational or multigenerational and aim to connect parents, grandparents, and grandchildren. In many programs, parents and children in one family work together or a child needing assistance is paired with a family member, other than the parent, who volunteers to assist the child through tutoring, book reading, or mentoring.

Four programs models are used widely in U.S. efforts: (1) the Kenan Model developed by the National Center for Family Literacy; (2) the Parents as Partners program, developed by Patricia Edwards and published by Children's Press; (3) the Missouri Parents as Teachers program, developed by Mildred Winter and her colleagues; and (4) the Home Instruction Program for Preschool Youngsters (HIPPY) (See Table 10-1). Programs typically use the models as introductory frameworks to "get started" or combine them with program-based or teacher-developed approaches. However, most programs and the practitioners in them recognize that the work of developing and implementing a good program requires a more integrated and intensive framework than is offered through any one model alone.

Perhaps the most successful family literacy effort in recent years is the federally funded Even Start Family Literacy Program, intended to improve the educational opportunities of children and adults by integrating early childhood education and adult education for parents into a unified program. In this program, parents are recognized as the first and most important teachers of their children. The program targets both the parent and

Table 10-1. Family Literacy Models

Name of Program/Mission	Focus of Program
Kenan Family Literacy Model/National Center for Family Literacy (four components) 1. Adult education that focuses on parents developing reading and math skills and setting goals; 2. Parenting that allows parents to discuss such issues as child development, health, social services, etc.; 3. Early childhood education classes that focus on specific literacy, organization, and social skills to prepare children for school; and 4. Parent-child interaction that includes parents and children together (PACT) time and allows parents and children to interact around various learning activities.	Parents and children learn in separate settings with short time periods set aside for parent-child activities.
Parents as Partners in Reading Designed to teach parents how to read effectively to their children and how to provide the language and reading readiness skills that children need to learn to read and write. (three phases) 1. Coaching in which a group leader models book reading behaviors and strategies, which are reinforced by videotapes (parents have opportunities to learn successful models of interactive book reading with their children); 2. Peer modeling that focuses on parents taking control of the book reading sessions to help each other to use appropriate strategies with their children (parents have the opportunity to model for the entire group how they would read a book to their children); and 3. Parent-child interaction in which parents bring their own children to sessions and practice their acquired strategies with them.	Parents learn in small peer sessions, practice concepts with other parents, and use strategies with children. Stresses community involvement.

Table 10-1. Family Literacy Models (continued)

Name of Program/Mission	Focus of Program
Parents as Teachers State-mandated program for economically or socially disadvantaged families with children from birth to 3 years of age. (three components) 1. An interactive component between home and school that begins with child's birth; 2. Personalized home visits by certified "Parent Educator," group meetings for parents, medical monitoring for developmental delays; and 3. A referral network that gives parents access to services beyond scope of program.	Parents are assisted by schools in the social and academic education of their children.
Home Instruction Program for Preschool Youngsters A home-based early childhood enrichment program with the following goals: 1. Prepare children for their future academic education, 2. Bolster children's self-esteem and confidence, and 3. Provide an environment where children explore their worlds through reading.	Parents are encouraged to become the primary educators in their child's life and become more sensitive to the needs of their child. Families learn to build on their strengths and use those strengths to enhance their community.

child but may involve other adult family members (e.g., grandparents). Even Start fosters a home-school-community partnership of sharing authority and responsibility for the educational development of the nation's children and adults.

The goals of the program are to help parents become full partners in the education of their children, assist children in reaching their full potential as learners, and provide literacy instruction for their parents. Even Start helps localities address three of the eight National Education Goals: (1) School Readiness, (2) Adult Literacy and Lifelong Learning, and (3) Parental Participation. Each Even Start project is required to target families in poverty who have educational needs. Specifically, projects must give priority to families living in areas of high concentration of poverty and ensure that a high percentage of those served have children who reside in a Title I school attendance area. Projects are also required to locate sites in areas designated as empowerment zones or enterprise communities. Considered by many to be among the most compelling components of Title I, Even Start can serve children from birth to age 7 and their parents.

Why Do These Programs Work?

The programs described here are but a few of hundreds throughout the country. What these programs demonstrate is that a considerable amount of work developed upon innovative ideas and unqualified commitment are leading to positive outcomes. It is difficult to ascertain exactly why each works specifically. However, it appears that there is combination of several features.

- The programs seem to have vision for the students and program staff.
- The programs have defined the parameters of their work, trying not to "bite off more than they can chew."
- The programs recognize the developmental needs of the students and their comfort levels in facing new and sometimes difficult learning experiences.
- The programs are mindful of the social needs of students and create situations in which literacy as a social and cognitive process can be developed.
- The programs maintain standards of success and excellence.
- The programs utilize relevant materials and are knowledgeable about new, effective, and appropriate approaches.
- The programs invest in staff recruitment and development.
- The programs involve parents and community organizations and members in ways that allow for and sustain mutual respect.

- The programs have high expectations that they articulate to program participants and to their families.
- The programs maintain that all children can be successful as learners and as future parents and workers.

In all programs, there is a deep understanding of the contextual and cultural embeddedness of literacy, of individuals' beliefs about literacy, of the real and perceived obstacles, and of the possibilities that exist when a program of sound instruction and support are provided.

Literacy Research and Practice

There is ample research that addresses the issues in children's learning, using, and benefiting from literacy [Gadsden 1998; Bloom & Greene 1982; Moll & Gonzalez 1994; Taylor & Dorsey-Gaines 1988], but there is considerably less focusing on adolescents. It appears, however, that from a life-course perspective, whether children and adolescents have successes in reading determines their relative accomplishments as adults, parents, workers, and citizens. Good schools with innovative and creative curricula, competent and committed teachers, and rich and stimulating classroom settings are essential.

In addition, there is an intergenerational transfer of literacy from parent to child, and this transfer affects not only whether children read but also whether literacy is valued, used, and understood. Intractable forms of poverty over multiple generations is both a cause and an effect of low literacy, and children whose parents have low literacy often experience the same problems as their parents. Moreover, schools are only one of many contexts that influence children's and adolescents' learning. There are several cultural and social contexts that contribute to children's and adolescents' literacy; families and communities are vital partners in their children's literacy development. Lastly, no isolated set of approaches will respond effectively to children's reading needs or provide a "quick fix." The educational and literacy problems facing children from diverse backgrounds are complex enough to warrant our undivided attention, more support for programs that examine the range of conditions affecting children and adolescents, and greater investments in multiple approaches.

In both my own work with low-income African American and Latino families in urban and rural communities and the work of several others, the roles of families, culture, and intergenerational learning are examined to determine how families and communities contribute to children's literacy through specific literacy events and acts, how children use literacy within these contexts, and the ways in which the tasks and opportunities presented in social and cultural contexts motivate children to read and to persist in school. Understanding the role of parents and supporting them in the work of preparing children for school and developing literacy are central to how we think about reading and promote access to literacy.

Through my review analysis of the status of reading and literacy research, I have found that the conceptual, empirical, and policy paradigms historically used to study, address, and understand the literacy needs and problems facing disproportionate numbers of children in urban and rural settings are *not* appropriate or intensive enough for contemporary problems. This is not to dismiss these long-established and venerable approaches, but rather to suggest that "one size does [not] fit all." Thus, the dilemma should not be over phonics or literature-based approaches, but over what individual or combined approaches enable children and adolescents to acquire, develop, and refine cognitive and social abilities associated with literacy and needed for life.

One focus that the field has continued is the connection between adult literacy, particularly reading, and children's literacy development. One argument is that adults with poor reading skills may be infrequent readers and also may read to their children infrequently. As a result, their offspring may receive less exposure to literacy activities than children whose parents are better readers. The inherent assumption in this argument is that, if offspring of poor readers are impeded in their acquisition of reading-related knowledge, such experiential differences may contribute to the well-established tendency for reading problems to aggregate in families [Fitzgerald et al. 1995]. A second, though not necessarily oppositional, stance is that children within homes in which parents have limited reading and writing abilities, in fact, may be exposed to a range of literate and other problem-solving activities, behaviors, and events that enable them to develop literate abilities, some of which are not measurable through traditional assessments.

This also is evident in my work on family cultures, which demonstrates the literacy continuity and variability within families intergenerationally [Gadsden 1998, 1993]. Family cultures connect the cumulative life experiences of an individual family member with the life goals of the family. They are built upon intergenerational practices and learning within families and are formed around several factors: accepted ethnic traditions, cultural rituals, sociopolitical histories, religious practices and beliefs, and negotiated roles within families over time. Talk and problems about race, discrimination, and culture are deeply embedded in family cultures, which are manipulated by societal events and affected by shifts in family mobility.

Family cultures often influence, if not dictate in many instances, the ways that individual family members think about, use, and pursue literacy and how they persist in educational programs. In most cases, family cultures seem to revolve around a premise that family members define and hold as central to their purpose. Families vary in their level of desire to reshape these cultures that may be fluid or static, depending upon the degree to which family members adapt or accommodate change. Family members construct traditions, practices, and behaviors that they believe are critical to survival and achievement and that are linked to a sense of their own family histories. In conceptualizing a framework for instruction, educators weigh family expectations and the social and cultural practices in which the family currently engages or hopes to develop.

The fathers and mothers whom we interviewed attach their ideas, beliefs, and perceptions about literacy to a range of other family-based views about the intergenerational impact of learning, the meaning of success, and the values of the family itself. If we were to examine the convergences and divergences in these parents' assumptions about, perspectives on, and expectations of literacy and schooling within a cultural difference analysis, we would argue for the importance of everyday experiences in relation to literacy. How these ideas are spoken about or shared and how they are used were part of the family portraits painted and the intergenerational hopes described. They were integrated into the family cultures that developed in different communities of parents, children, and families with whom we have worked.

How parents perceive their own literate ability and their children's literate behaviors and the literacies to which they assign value are critical issues in how they make meaning out of the developmental and literacy activities of their young children. For adolescent and young adult parents, particularly those with limited access to educational support and marginal school experiences, there may be few opportunities to explore their children's early literacies.

Closing Considerations and Recommendations

How do we respond to the literacy needs of children and adolescents, reduce the apparent intractability of low literacy, and increase positive outcomes?

How do we promote positive outcomes for children and youth? What are the investments that schools, parents, children, and society must make? I posed these questions to eight researchers and practitioners throughout the United States, and I have identified several themes that combine my own recommendations with those of my colleagues [Gadsden 1997].

- **A national effort to support young children and adolescents learning literacy.** This effort should ensure that young children and adolescents have access to committed and trained assistants and tutors who help them make the connections between and among literacy learning, their school life and home experiences, and the purposes and goals for the tasks of tutoring. Such efforts must be more than short-term agendas and must be implemented over time and with the knowledge that change for intergenerationally poor and educationally disadvantaged young children, adolescents, and families is not a short-term enterprise. Instead, it is intended to lead to self-sufficiency, self-efficacy, and the transfer of literacy knowledge, goals, and values from one generation to another.

- **A rejection of "one size fits all" philosophies that have a polarizing effect.** On the one hand, we must acknowledge the importance of phonemic awareness; on the other, we must utilize the strengths of whole language approaches and literature-based instruction. The field will need to act on behalf of young children and strive for informed and realistic approaches and balances.
- **A focus on the language and literacy needs with which young learners enter school and continue to have throughout schooling.** There is enormous variability in the knowledge with which young children enter school. What is needed is greater emphasis on language-related issues for bilingual learners, learners who speak African American vernacular or nonstandard dialects, and learners who have not received the necessary prereading and preschool experiences, without applying harmful stereotypes that contribute to their failure.
- **More thoughtful and creative ways to build and build upon communities and community resources.** Children learn in a variety of places and from a variety of human and material resources. Churches, libraries, and volunteer efforts in communities enhance the opportunities for children and youth in general to read and to receive support for literacy.
- **Investment in preservice and ongoing professional development.** There is variability in the undergraduate preparation of teachers. What is needed is more attention to preservice activities, including opportunities for prospective teachers to work with students as tutors and resources. In addition, a nationally recognized set of activities is needed that enables teachers to choose between and among the most strategic approaches. At present, teachers are often caught between the competing strategies of publishers, for example, who tend to pro-

duce work that highlights the most popular debate, rather than the most effective method for reaching diverse learners within classrooms and schools. Inherent in such initiatives as *America Reads* are opportunities to strengthen children's literacy experiences and contribute to a culture of cognitive support for and social investment in children.

- **Focus on families at-risk whose children are also at-risk and on the contributions of both fathers and mothers.** Poverty explains much of the variance in literacy, and the embeddedness of poverty in the lives of youth limits both their human and academic potential and ultimately their ability to contribute to society as good citizens.
- **Frameworks such as the National Institute for Literacy's *Equipped for the Future*, although focused on adults, are effective in connecting disparate concerns** and in helping to "develop a stronger, more effective literacy system focused on delivering results that really matter" [NIL 1998, p. 1].
- **The reality of culture, race, and diversity.** The relative absence of a critical discourse about diversity and culture, above and beyond the recognition of difference alone, requires a re-analysis of the approaches used to teach reading and writing, assessment of instructional tools and artifacts used to convey the meaning of literacy within different contexts, and a discussion of what counts as knowing and knowledge. Do the cultural and literate experiences of an African American boy from a low-income home in North Philadelphia count as much as the experiences of a white boy from a middle-class home in Bloomfield Hills, Michigan or an African American or Latino boy from a middle-class home in Los Angeles, California? What is the nature of each boy's prior knowledge, and when and how do we achieve access to this knowledge or use it on behalf of children's literacy development? These questions invite us to re-examine a range of concepts that have aided literacy learning and teaching over the past decade (e.g., collaboration and classroom interaction, relationships between home and school, and prior knowledge). Our responses

to them can serve as frames of reference to identify whether some sociocultural knowledge is more valued than others, who determines the value, and with what criteria.

From the outset of thinking about and writing this chapter, I have struggled with the concept of "positive outcomes." I have sought a balance between (1) radical objections to evaluations and assessments that denote whether and how well a learner is performing in relationship to another person or group, or some past behavior, and (2) responsible analyses of the needs of children and youth and effective responses to them. What I decided was that both seemingly opposite ends of the continuum share a common vision: the well-being of children and youth and a belief that in them lies extraordinary possibility.

The complexities around positive outcomes emanate from the reality that measures used to identify change in government-funded efforts for children and families do not capture necessarily or always the full range of positive outcomes and often pay little attention to adolescents. Apparent failure or limited growth may not reflect the incredible odds against which many children struggle and in fact seem to be winning. There is fear that evaluations may paint an unfinished portrait of potential in a child or adolescent aiming to "beat the odds" or a parent embattled to help herself and her children rise above the obstacles. In other words, there is a fear that the story may not be written and in its place, we will find numbers that add neither resources nor sound alternatives to limited opportunity. Despite considerable attention to children's literacy learning, we seemingly are caught between an apparent desire to improve children's literacy (because we think strong literate abilities will improve their life chances) and perplexity about how to translate what we know from research into effective learning experiences for children, particularly those who differ in income, ethnicity, and life experiences from each other and from us. The concept of possibility assumes that the story can be imagined and written—that the mechanisms and approaches needed, in fact, have been crafted but well may need to be refined and that ensuring the well-being of children and adolescents cannot be rendered untenable.

References

Anderson, J. E. (1988). *The education of blacks in the south, 1865-1930.* Chapel Hill, NC: University of North Carolina Press.

Binkley, M., & Williams, T. (1996). *Reading literacy in the United States: Findings from the IEA Reading Literacy Survey.* U. S. Department of Education, Office of Educational Research and Improvement (NCES 96-258). Washington, DC: U. S. Department of Education.

Bloome, D., & Golden, C. (1982). Literacy learning, classroom processes, and race: A microanalytic study of two desegregated classrooms. *Journal of Black Studies, 13*, 207-226.

Comer, J. R. (1998). *Waiting for a miracle: Why schools can't solve our problems and how we can.* New York: Dutton.

Damon, W. (1990). Reconciling the literacies of generation. *Daedulus, 119*, 33-53.

Davidson, J., & Koppenhaver, D. (1993). *Adolescent literacy: What works and why*. New York: Garland Publishing, Inc.

Entwisle, D. R., & Alexander, K. L. (1992). Summer setback: Race, poverty, school composition, and mathematics achievement in the first two years of school. *American Sociological Review, 57*, 27-84

Fitzgerald, J., Spiegel, D. L., & Cunningham, J. W. (1991). The relationship between parental literacy level and perceptions of emergent literacy. *Journal of Reading Behavior, 23*(2), 191-213.

Flannery, K. T. (1990). In praise of the local and transitory. In A.A. Lunsford, H. Moglen, and J. Slevin (Eds.), *The right to literacy* (pp. 208-214). New York: The Modern Language Association of America.

Gadsden, V. L. (1998). Family cultures and literacy learning. In J. Osborn & F. Lehr, (Eds.), *Literacy for all: Issues in teaching and learning* (pp. 32-50). New York: The Guilford Press.

Gadsden, V. L. (1997). *Learning to read.* Congressional hearing. Washington, DC: House Committee on Education and Labor, Senate Subcommittee on Education, Arts, and Humanities.

Gadsden, V. L. (1995). Representations of literacy: Parents' images in two cultural communities. In L.M. Morrow, (Ed.), *Family literacy: Connections in schools and communities* (pp. 287-303). New Brunswick, NJ: Rutgers.

Gadsden, V.L. (1993). Literacy, education, and identity among African Americans: The communal nature of learning. *Urban Education, 27*, 352-369.

Goals 2000: Educate America Act of 1994, H. R. 1804, 103d Cong., 2nd Sess.

Holt, T. (1990). Knowledge is power: The Black struggle for literacy. In A.A. Lunsford, H. Moglen, & J. Slevin (Eds.), *The right to literacy* (pp. 91-102). New York: The Modern Language Association of America.

Kirsch, I. S., Jungeblut, A., Jenkins, L., & Kolstad, A. (1993). *National adult literacy survey*. Washington, DC: U. S. Department of education, National Center for Education Statistics.

Knoblauch, C. H. (1990). Literacy and the politics of education. In A.A. Lunsford, H. Moglen, & J. Slevin (Eds.), *The right to literacy* (pp. 74-80). New York: The Modern Language Association of America.

Moll, L, & Gonzalez, N. (1994). Lessons from research with language-minority children. *Journal of Reading Behavior, 26*, 439-456.

Gorman, S. (1993). *NAEP 1992 reading report card summary*. Washington, DC: National Center for Education Statistics.

National Commission on Children. (1991). *Beyond rhetoric: A new American agenda for children and families*. Washington, DC: U.S. Government Printing Office.

National Institute for Literacy. (1998). *Equipped for the future: A framework for adult learning*. Washington, DC: Author.

Pinnell, G. S., Lyons, C. A., DeFord, D. E., Bryk, A. S., & Seltzer, M. (1994). Comparing instructional models for the literacy education of high-risk first graders. *Reading Research Quarterly, 29*(1), 9-38.

Schor, L. S. (1988). *Within our reach.* New York: Anchor Press/Doubleday

Stowell, L. P., & Tierney, R. J. (1995). Portfolios in the classroom: What happens when teachers and students negotiate assessment. In S. A. Walmsley & R. L. (Eds.), *No quick fix: rethinking literacy programs in America's elementary schools* (pp. 79-96). New York: Teachers College Press.

Taylor, D., & Dorsey-Gaines, C. (1988). *Growing up literate: Learning from inner city families.* Portsmouth, NH: Heinemann.

Venezky, R. (1997). Learning to read. Congressional hearing. Washington, DC: House Committee on Education and Labor, Senate Subcommittee on Education, Arts, and Humanities.

Walmsley, S. A., & Allington, R. L. (1995) Redefining and reforming instructional support programs for at-risk students. In S. A. Walmsley & R. L. Allington (Eds.), *No quick fix: Rethinking literacy programs in America's elementary schools* (pp. 19- 44). New York: Teachers College Press.

11 Preparing Youth for the Work Force

Stephen F. Hamilton

In simpler societies, rites of passage initiate all the males and all the females from an age cohort into the transition to adulthood. High school graduation is the closest approximation the United States has to a rite of passage, but it divides rather than unifies. Nineteen-year-olds can be placed in four major groupings, each accounting for about one quarter of the population. In October 1996, 28% were enrolled in postsecondary education and not employed. Twenty-six percent were simultaneously enrolled and employed. Employment without enrollment engaged 27%. Seventeen percent were neither employed nor enrolled. Two percent were in the military and 1% were institutionalized [U.S. Bureau of the Census 1996].

Further divisions occur as high school graduates enroll full-time or part-time in two-year and four-year institutions, move into and out of school, and either complete or fail to complete a degree. Forty-two percent of students in postsecondary institutions were enrolled part-time in the fall of 1995. Forty-five percent of students enrolled in institutions of higher education were in two-year institutions [Barbett & Korb 1997]. Among 25- to 29-year-olds, 13% have failed to graduate from high school or earn a GED, and 26% have completed a bachelor's degree [U.S. Department of Education 1997].

The nature of youth employment further complicates the picture of what happens after high school graduation. A high school diploma no longer opens the doors to adult careers. Recent high school graduates who seek regular full-time employment discover that they are mostly limited to part-time, low-wage jobs like those they held while in high school; sometimes the best they can do is increase their hours at the very same jobs [Hamilton & Levine-Powers 1990]. The reason is that most employers in the United States with career entry jobs—jobs that pay more than minimum wage, offer reasonable security and benefits, and are a step on a career ladder—do not hire recent high school graduates [Osterman 1980]. They search instead for entry-level career workers with more work experience and more maturity. It is not lack of education that is the problem; the same applicants can qualify for those jobs four or five years later without additional education.

As a result, rather than ushering in the next set of communal experiences, high school graduation fragments an age cohort into several subgroups. The most privileged are those enrolling (and remaining) in four-year residential colleges and universities. The least are those who are neither employed nor enrolled. Among young women, this status is most often associated with motherhood. Fluctuation in status is common at this age, especially among those not enrolled full-time, who tend to flounder in a labor market that offers little reward and few opportunities.

This picture of what happens after high school graduation does not arouse universal concern. Many labor economists consider the "floundering" or "churning" that Osterman [1980] diagnosed a matching process by which young people try out a series of jobs to find which ones match their needs, skills, and preferences (e.g., Klerman & Karoly [1995]). However, this line of argument does not make clear why such a sequence is functional now, when it was once possible for high school graduates (and even dropouts) to move directly into well-paid jobs, notably in manufacturing, and to establish independent households in their late teens and early twenties. Nor does it account for quite different transition patterns in other countries, notably Germany, where apprenticeship provides a relatively direct route into the "primary labor market."

The term, "primary labor market," reflects a conception of the labor market as having at least two distinct segments, one containing jobs that offer reasonable earnings and benefits, some security, and prospects for upward mobility, the other (the secondary labor market) containing minimum wage jobs with no benefits or security and no career ladder. Economists do not agree on this conception, but some of the controversy is based on unrealistically pure definitions. While it is possible to make a career in the fast food industry, the vast majority of employees do not. The presence of a secondary segment in the labor market is a helpful way of explaining why poverty coexists with low levels of unemployment and why simply having a job is not the same as being economically self-sufficient. Minorities, women, and teenagers are most often found in the secondary labor market.

Employment in the secondary labor market is not necessarily bad. Teenagers whose primary commitment is to education and mothers who are primarily committed to child care may welcome the opportunity to work part-time in a situation where regularity and longevity are not critical. Teenagers and welfare recipients can learn valuable lessons about punctuality, reliability, responsiveness to supervision, and customer relations in jobs where mistakes are recoverable. The main problem with the secondary labor market is that too many people remain in it for too long.

As with high school graduation, the key question about youth employment in the secondary labor market is, "What happens next?" Teenagers who continue their education and move into career-entry positions use the secondary labor market as a stepping stone, while earning spending money. Others fail to make it out of the secondary labor market, remaining behind while their age-mates begin more rewarding careers. Sadly, that group has been growing, as indicated by a growing disparity in income between workers with college degrees and those without. In 1970, young adult men (ages 25-34) with a bachelor's degree earned 25% more than those with no more than a high school diploma. By 1995, that difference had climbed above 50%. For women of the same age, the difference in earnings started out higher, at 70% in 1970, and rose to 90% in 1995 [U.S. Department of Education 1997].

Much of this difference results from serious declines in the real earnings of the least educated workers. In 1979, a 30-year-old man with a high school diploma earned on average $27,000 (in 1993 dollars). Four years later, that average had dropped to $23,000, and by 1993 it was $20,000. This decline in earnings of more than 25% is hardly trivial in view of the fact that in 1993, half of all 30-year-old men had not gone beyond high school [Murnane & Levy 1996, p. 3]. It is equivalent to the average decline in purchasing power suffered by Americans in the Great Depression. (A comparable account of women's earnings is impeded by their greater propensity to leave the labor force altogether for child care.)

Employers are willing to pay a larger premium for education because more jobs pay well and require a combination of knowledge, communication, problem solving, and technical skill. This is not true of all jobs. Many jobs require less than a high school education—notably in retail sales and food service—but they do not pay enough to make young people independent, much less able to support a family.

Murnane and Levy [1996] closely examined hiring by three firms, two auto manufacturers and an insurance company, to illustrate this trend and illuminate some of the complexities of matching people with jobs. All three firms select among applicants with great care, seeking evidence that they have mastered "the new basic skills," which Murnane and Levy describe as:

- The ability to read at the ninth-grade level or higher
- The ability to do math at the ninth-grade level or higher
- The ability to solve semistructured problems where hypotheses must be formed and tested
- The ability to work in groups with persons of various backgrounds
- The ability to use personal computers to carry out simple tasks like word processing [1996, p. 32].

These three firms used formal tests to assess applicants' "hard skills," i.e., their ability to read and do math, and they set thresholds or standards that applicants must meet. In one firm, Diamond Star Motors, a formal study validated their academic standards, demonstrating that test scores correlated with job performance. But Mundane and Levy's s most interesting finding was that it was *achieving* the threshold that mattered, not the absolute score. That is, people who scored below the threshold were unlikely to succeed, but once they had surpassed the threshold, workers' scores were not correlated with job performance. Above the threshold, job performance is correlated with the last three skills listed above, called "soft skills," because they are harder to measure [1996, pp. 36-37].

The challenge facing educators is to enable students who were formerly tracked into academically weak general and vocational programs to achieve at the level of students preparing for enrollment in selective colleges. How can this goal be met when some students are neither highly motivated nor terribly adept at academic work? Setting high standards is part of the answer, but not sufficient. Students need effective motivation and teaching. High school students hoping to make rewarding careers without graduating from four-year colleges must enroll in courses previously considered appropriate only for those bound for selective colleges.

School-to-Work

The School-to-Work Opportunities Act of 1994 engages this challenge. It provides seed money to states and communities to create systems incorporating school-based learning pitched to high academic standards, work-based learning leading to industry-recognized certification, and connections between school-based and work-based learning (such as advising). It also calls for the integration of academic and vocational education and of secondary with postsecondary education. FY 1997 appropriation for the initiative was $400 million. By October 1998, all 50 states plus the District of Columbia had received implementation grants (ranging from $1.3 million to almost $20 million) that were then distributed within the states to leverage other resources. In addition, 109 direct federal grants were made to low-income communities. The notion of seed money or investment capital was built into the legislation from the beginning. Recognizing the absence of political support for large-scale federal spending, the Clinton administration adopted a strategy of using modest federal funds to stimulate changes in practice and funding at the state and local levels. The legislation has a sunset clause terminating funded activity (except for the completion of grants in progress) by October 2001. (An excellent review of research related to School-to-Work has been written by Urquiola, Stern Horn, Dornsife, Chi, Williams, Merritt, Hughes, and Bailey [1997]. For an overview of evaluation related to the legislation, see U.S. Department of Labor [1997].)

Work-based learning encompasses a range of intentional experiential learning opportunities that occur in locations where the primary activity is producing goods or services. Examples include youth apprenticeship, co-operative education, job shadowing, and field trips to workplaces. When properly designed, service learning, subsidized employment training (e.g., through the Job Training Partnership Act [JTPA] and the Job Corps), youth-run enterprises, and even conventional youth jobs also provide opportunities for work-based learning. To qualify as work-based learning, the context must be one in which work is primary, but the purpose must include learning. Thus, pupils listening to a guest speaker talking about her career in an elementary school classroom are not engaged in work-based learning, but those in a school class that is designing, constructing, and operating a commercial fish farm are. A student hired to help out in the school cafeteria is not engaged in work-based learning, but a food preparation class that runs the faculty cafeteria is. A high school student working part-time after school in a drug store is not doing work-based learning, unless part of the experience explicitly involves learning about the retail business and gaining skills beyond those required to perform the specific job.

The line separating work-based learning from either work on one side or school-based learning on the other cannot always be drawn sharply. Ambiguity is inevitable. The point of defining the term is to avoid labeling all work experience education or predominantly school-based activities work. If a school-to-work system is designed to provide multiple work-based learning opportunities to each student, then the ambiguity is inconsequential.

The term, "work-based learning," represents a broadening of concepts based in apprenticeship, a derivation visible in both the frequency of reference to apprenticeship in the legislation and in the bill's history, which includes legislation proposed during the Bush administration specifically in support of youth apprenticeship. The bill's authors proposed a more differentiated approach than strictly youth apprenticeship, one that would be equally suitable for all students, regardless of their post-high school plans. Although concern about the troubled transition from school-to-work arose in relation to the "forgotten half" [1988]—young people who did not enroll in college—it broadened in recognition that only a quarter to a third of young people eventually earn a bachelor's degree. A political and pedagogical perception also guided this broadening, namely that provisions for students experiencing difficulty are always prone to be experienced as second-class treatment and dismissed by voters as "not for my kids." Thus youth apprenticeship was initially presented as "a mainstream reform with a hidden agenda," [Lerman & Pouncy 1990], that is, as potentially involving all youth (mainstream), but being especially critical for those at the greatest risk of failing to make a successful transition (the hidden agenda).

School-based learning, the second key component, is hardly novel, but the provisions of the act are challenging. Conventional high schools require different levels of achievement of students with different trajectories. They commonly separate students into three or more tracks: college preparatory, general, and vocational (and just as commonly deny tracking). The strongest consensus growing out of the secondary school reform movement that was stimulated by the publication of *A Nation at Risk* [National Commission on Excellence in Education 1983] is that this distinction has been damaging, particularly for those in the residual "general" track, which is defined by being neither college preparatory nor vocational. Since *A Nation at Risk*, support has gathered around the idea of setting high expectations for all students. Goals 2000 and a multitude of statewide reform efforts have aimed at this target, with predictably varied definitions of what constitutes high standards or expectations.

The School-to-Work Opportunities Act requires that high academic standards apply to all youth, especially those who were formerly relegated to the vocational and general tracks. It also calls for "career majors" for all students. This provision is consistent with others in the Act that link academic learning with vocational interests. It suggests the influence of career academies, small schools, or schools-within-schools organized around career themes, that have demonstrated positive effects on students.

The third key component, connecting activities, is the most poorly defined by the legislation, which provides a diffuse list of such practices as mentoring, student selection, and technical assistance (Section 104). More helpful examples of connecting activities include student advising from parents, teachers, worksite mentors, counselors, and others; projects planned and executed by students as individuals or in groups that link school learning with workplace and community issues; and communication among adults in school, family, and workplace in support of young people's learning.

The two most ambitious and distinctive components of the legislation are its call for serious work-based learning and its goal of creating systems rather than programs. Both of these components emerged from international comparisons revealing the uniqueness of the United States in not providing any systematic, institutional connection between education and employment for youth other than higher education [National Center on Education and the Economy 1990; Hamilton 1990]. The comparison invoked most frequently was with Germany's apprenticeship system.

The German Apprenticeship System

German apprenticeship epitomizes a system that relies on work-based learning. It is a massive institution, involving at least half of older teenagers (ages approximately 16 to 19) in a combination of schooling and formal on-the-job training, typically for three years. The knowledge and skills associated with each of about 360 different occupations are spelled out in great detail, as is the employer's training obligation. Work-based learning predominates, accounting for about 80% of the total time (usually four days per week). It is systematic both in its formality and in the strength of the connections it makes between education and employment. Apprentices are tested on both academic and applied topics and must pass rigorous examinations before they are allowed to enter their chosen field. In most apprenticeable occupations, employers are required by law and collective bargaining agreements to hire only applicants who have qualified by virtue of serving their apprenticeship and passing the appropriate examinations—unless no applicants who meet these qualifications can be found. For example, banks must give preference to applicants for teller positions who have served an apprenticeship, even over an applicant with a university degree in banking and finance, because the university graduate has not been formally trained and is, therefore, not qualified to do the work of a teller.

While this strikes many Americans as overly rigid, and probably requires some loosening to serve the German economy well in an increasingly dynamic world, the legal preference for certified apprentices has some real advantages in clarifying for young people what their career prospects are and how to prepare themselves to take advantage of them. One difficulty with the relative lack of formal training and credentials in the middle levels of the American occupational hierarchy is that young people who have decided they are not going to follow the long road through higher education into the professions have no clear guidelines about what they should do instead. Too many of them end up doing the least amount of work required to earn a high school diploma, and that severely restricts their chances for rising above the secondary labor market [Hamilton 1994].

Building a system is simultaneously ambitious and ambiguous. Several qualities differentiate German apprenticeship and other systems from programs that are the more typical embodiment of educational policy and legislation:

- **A system has a place for everyone who belongs in it**; a program often has to select among eligible applicants.
- **A system is linked with other systems**, in the case of German apprenticeship and the optimal school-to-work opportunities system, the links are with the school system on one side and the labor market on the other. One test of linkages is to ask what accomplishment in one system means in another. By this test, American secondary schools are much more closely linked with higher education than with the labor market.

- **A system is comprehensive and coherent.** It is whole and it can be understood by people involved in it. German youth and the adults who advise them understand how apprenticeship works, what it takes to succeed in it, and what the implications are for future employment. Few Americans can describe how the middle ranks of the labor market are filled, much less give useful advice to a teenager about how to become, say, an insurance adjuster, a machinist, or a computer support technician.
- **A system endures.** It does not rely on special funding that is unpredictable from year to year. From an American perspective, one of the most impressive features of German apprenticeship is the level and extent of employer commitment to it and the combination of government, employers, and labor that governs all aspects of it. Although participation in the system has fallen in recent years as the German economy has been racked by global competition, especially from the United States, it remains the largest form of upper-secondary education. Some Germans have forecast its demise, but such forecasts have always proved false in the past [Lempert 1995].

The German system has been transformed twice already in this century; it will certainly be transformed again, but is unlikely to disappear.

Indicators of the Impact of School-to-Work

After the legislation was signed in the spring of 1994, a small School-to-Work Office was established as a joint entity of the Departments of Labor and of Education. The first implementation grants to states were made a year later, which means that the oldest efforts are now just four years old. Most of the money allocated to states was immediately passed on to communities on a competitive basis, requiring yet another round of proposal writing and grant making. Therefore, no mature school-to-work initiatives can be found that were stimulated primarily by school-to-work funding. The best evidence for the impact of school-to-work comes from initiatives that predated the legislation. That evidence is more illuminating about the impact of parts of the initiative than about what the creation of comprehensive systems is likely to accomplish. We can, however, look both to research on German apprenticeship and to studies of some of those early efforts in the mode that Rose [1991] called "prospective evaluation." A review of German research on the impact of German apprenticeship on adolescent development found them to be predominantly positive on career development, political socialization, and personality development [Hamilton & Lempert 1997].

German Apprenticeship

German apprenticeship provides a solid foundation for careers. The vast majority of those who complete apprenticeship training either remain in the skilled occupation for which they were trained, move laterally into another, or move up the occupational hierarchy, often with additional education and training. One survey found that only 11% of apprenticeship completers lost occupational status. Moreover, formal apprenticeship provides even greater flexibility and mobility than school-based vocational education. A few occupations may be entered via either route, and those workers who are trained as apprentices are more likely to gain status than those who are trained in school. The generally high reputation of the system among employers and the universal recognition of the apprenticeship credential surely explain at least part of this advantage.

The system is not without flaws; indeed, it is a favorite target of criticism among Germans, especially now as the German economy is beset by persistent high unemployment and slow growth. Many German firms have reduced the numbers of apprentices they train and some have even stopped training altogether, something that would have been unthinkable just a few years ago. Furthermore, apprenticeship helps perpetuate Germany's class system and gender inequity. The children of university graduates are far more likely to attend universities than the children of blue-collar workers. Young women must contend with a labor market that remains stratified by gender. The most desirable and best paid jobs are predominantly male. This poses daunting barriers to mature women. It is even more daunting when specific vocational training is done on the job and begins during the teenage years. It takes great courage for a young woman to accept and retain an apprenticeship in a masculine occupation. Some large firms have successfully integrated groups of young women into such occupations, but most firms lack the scale to train more than one or a few at a time.

The potential impact of youth apprenticeship on adolescents' political socialization has not been a topic of debate in the United States, with the exception of a few skeptical voices warning that the practice could be misused by employers to indoctrinate young people to passive roles as subordinates in the corporate hierarchy. In contrast, it was the focus of several large-scale German studies in the early 1980s funded by the Social Democratic government then in office (equivalent to the Labour party in the United Kingdom). Results assuaged those fears, but also gave scant support for the hope that apprentices would gain commitment to participation in democratic institutions in the workplace and in the society.

Research on the impact of German apprenticeship on personality development has examined moral development and "control consciousness" or locus of control. Both have been found to vary depending on the authority structures within firms. That is, the impact is not dependent on the institution of apprenticeship itself, but rather on the ways in which power and authority are wielded within the work organization. Apprentices who have opportunities to participate in decisions become more reflective. Those in repressive, authoritarian circumstances do not.

The results of German research emphasize the importance of quality. It is not enough to create work-based learning opportunities for youth. Those opportunities must be good ones in the sense that they provide real knowledge and skills that are transferable to other settings, and opportunities for the exercise and development of young people's decisionmaking faculties. Both the social and the technical aspects of the experience require attention.

In Germany and the United States the prospects for employer support of high-quality training defined in these terms appear to be growing as the nature of work is transformed by technology and by global competition.

To the extent that workers need to be able to apply multiple skills in self-managed teams, they must be trained well but also educated as responsible decisionmakers.

These lessons seem perfectly transferable. However, the utility of the German comparison is limited by the systemic nature of the effort in both countries. We can neither import the German system whole nor predict based on its effects as a system how a necessarily different system would function in the United States. Moreover, because the aim of the School-to-Work Opportunities Act is to create an American-style system, simply examining the parts of the system that have been created to date can only be suggestive of how a full-scale system would operate. Nevertheless, indicators of potential impact may usefully be sought among initial efforts to build such a system.

Youth Apprenticeship Demonstration Projects

The first demonstration projects inspired by German apprenticeship began in 1990. Reports on those projects have been more descriptive than evaluative. Some impact indicators have been reported, however. It should be noted that the most direct effects of youth apprenticeship are taken for granted: young people who are apprenticed in adult work roles almost always learn to perform those roles effectively. This result is quite important in view of the differences between the primary and secondary labor markets and the predominant practice of confining youth to the secondary labor market. It means that teenagers are capable of functioning at adult levels in the labor market if given opportunity and support, an implication also supported by German apprenticeship.

Other outcome indicators are less direct, but they are also important because they bear on more generalizable effects. For example, if participants' educational aspirations and attainment rise, then they are better able to qualify for more productive employment in the future.

Several youth apprenticeship demonstration projects reported that large proportions of participants enrolled in postsecondary education after graduating from high school [Kopp & Kazis, with Churchill, no date], a surprising result because the target group was "non-college" youth. Some school-to-work sites have also reported this result, along with higher grades and improved postgraduate employment. (For examples, see the report on the National School-to-Work Office website: www.stw.ed.gov/ research/ evidence.htm.) Although these results must be treated with caution because they are usually based on high school seniors' reports of their postgraduation intentions rather than follow-up surveys, and because they seldom employ control groups or comparison groups, they should allay concerns that youth apprenticeship and other approaches to school-to-work would, like vocational education, reduce the likelihood of high school graduates enrolling in postsecondary education. One report based on postgraduation interviews with youth apprentices indicated that three-fourths of graduates remained enrolled in postsecondary education in the first year after graduation and more than two-thirds remained enrolled two years later. It also found rather high levels of career directedness one and two years after graduation, suggesting that youth apprenticeship can counteract the tendency of youth without college degrees to "flounder" during their first few years in the labor market [Hamilton & Hamilton 1997].

One of the most carefully designed studies examined Wisconsin youth apprentices in printing. Using as a comparison group students enrolled in printing courses in conventional vocational education, including a few with cooperative education placements, as well as youth apprentices' classmates who were enrolled in the general course of study (i.e., neither college preparatory nor vocational), Orr [unpublished] found that youth apprentices achieved higher grades, had relatively fewer absences, reported clearer career goals, and reported more hours of employment and higher earnings six to eight months after graduation. In contrast to reports on other youth apprenticeship programs, Wisconsin printing graduates were less likely than comparison graduates to enroll in higher education, largely because nearly all were employed in printing, and in the same firm where they received their training.

Cooperative Education

Youth apprenticeship shares some features with cooperative education, a well-established practice associated with secondary vocational education and with postsecondary education as well, especially in engineering. Both provide paid work experience that is related to a student's course of study, planned jointly by workplace and school representatives, formally supervised and evaluated, and given academic credit. Apprenticeships usually last two years or more, while cooperative education placements are typically for a school year or a semester. Apprenticeships are "standardized" in the sense that they are designed to achieve certain common standards, whereas cooperative education placements are usually "customized," that is, each is tailored to match an individual student's interests and needs with an employer's options. This makes cooperative education more flexible, but it also means that cooperative education does not yield a transferable credential as apprenticeship does.

Because apprentices are certified as having achieved a specified level of competence in a recognized occupation, other employers recognize their achievements and accept their credentials. In contrast, high school graduates who have had cooperative education and then go to work for the same employer earn more than comparable classmates without cooperative education, but those who go to work for a different employer are indistinguishable from their classmates [Stern & Stevens 1992].

Career Academies

Career academies are small high schools, usually schools-within-schools, enrolling perhaps 100-200 students who share an interest in a career area such as health care, aviation, transportation, or banking and finance. In addition to one or more courses specifically about the career focus, academies offer basic academic courses—English, math, science, and social studies—that are also related. History classes in a health academy might pay special attention to the effects of epidemics, for example, and English assignments might include literature and writing about illness and dying. In these aspects, career academies are like magnet or theme schools. Their size makes them different and is given credit for a measure of their success. By working closely together over two or three years, a group of students comes to feel a strong sense of identity with each other and with the academy. They also get to know and are known well by a small cadre of teachers. And they often engage in classroom and other projects together, further strengthening their social bonds.

Career academies also draw on outside resources. Guest speakers inform students about the career area, addressing topics ranging from educational requirements to dress codes. Field trips and job shadowing are common. Some add paid and unpaid internships as well, both during the school year and over the summer. The addition of work-based learning and its connections with school-based learning makes career academies school-to-work institutions.

Research on career academies has been encouraging. Many of the original academies were designed for students seen as likely to drop out. As they have grown they have attracted students from the entire spectrum. Students' attitudes, attendance rates, grades, and postsecondary enrollment rates have shown substantial improvement in carefully designed studies [Stern et al. 1992; Kemple 1997].

Career academies demonstrate the use of careers as foci for secondary education, not only as specific preparation for the focal occupational area, but more generally as a means of stimulating engagement with and success in schooling. A student who learns biology because it is critical to health care may subsequently change career directions, but will have acquired the academic background that will enable her or him to succeed, as well as such less tangible assets as discipline and self-confidence.

One especially appealing aspect of career academies is that they often attract students with a wide range of family backgrounds, achievement levels, and career plans. Because occupational areas are defined broadly to include careers with varied educational requirements, future physicians, radiologists, and medical records clerks attend classes together, something that is not likely to happen in typical high school classes, which are stratified by difficulty level.

Vocational Education Reform

Another approach to educational reform takes whole schools as its primary unit and emphasizes the integration of high-quality vocational education with demanding academic standards. The Southern Regional Education Board's High Schools That Work program has identified several schools that have succeeded in substantially improving students' academic performance and postsecondary enrollments by attending closely to specific indicators of effectiveness as they infuse academic courses with a career orientation and vocational courses with academic learning [Bottoms & Sharpe, no date]. Like career academies, High Schools That Work demonstrate the efficacy of focusing secondary education more sharply on careers. However, they encompass whole schools and, more than career academies, they stress achieving higher academic standards and measuring that achievement using standardized tests.

Large-Scale Implementation

The perennial question since youth apprenticeship and related initiatives were first proposed has been, "Is it possible to achieve large scale with high quality?" Education reforms are especially prone to the "boutique" constraint; that is, innovative practices that thrive in small settings led by creative and committed visionaries often fail when tried on a large scale with ordinary people in charge. The two most distinctive aspects of the school-to-work initiative are especially susceptible to this constraint: reliance on work-based learning, and emphasis on system building.

Work-Based Learning

Employers who criticize the public schools for failing to educate young people to the standards required by contemporary work may be willing to advocate for more effective schools, even higher taxes to pay for them, but not necessarily to participate directly in the educational process by providing work-based learning opportunities for youth. The costs can be considerable. Paying young workers is one cost, but that has not proved the most serious. In most workplaces, youth apprentices quickly learn enough to earn their pay. More costly is the time of regular adult workers who teach and supervise youth, including the time required for planning, evaluating work performance, and communicating with educators, parents, and other employer partners. Less obvious costs may also be counted. Employers must be exceptionally vigilant to assure that they do not violate child labor laws. Even if they are careful, they realize that a work-related injury to a teenager is likely to be regarded as more serious than one to an adult worker. Resentment and suspicion from adult workers is another potential cost. In a time when job security cannot be taken for granted, some workers may view youth as competitors, potentially replacing them. This is more likely if the youth are given the broad training they deserve, which qualifies them for a wider range of jobs than typical employees.

If work-based learning is of high quality, many of these concerns recede. Adult supervisors of youth make an investment of time in their apprentices or interns, then as the youth become increasingly competent, that investment pays off in enhanced productivity by the youth-adult team. Moreover, adult coaches and mentors who learn to work well with youth necessarily acquire many of the skills needed by good managers. Taking responsibility for teaching apprentices is an excellent form of staff development, providing on-the-job supervisory training to future managers. In addition, the same reaction to perceived threat that can make some adult employees resistant to youth apprentices can, if interpreted just a little differently, lead those adults to seek out opportunities for skill training to make themselves more competitive. The optimal setting for work-based learning for youth is in a learning organization that takes seriously the need for all employees to learn continuously. One critically important lesson this imparts to youth is that, wherever their program may end, work-based learning continues throughout life. Learning this lesson and learning how to learn well at work are ultimately far more useful than learning specific knowledge and skills that will soon be outmoded.

The German example is instructive but not decisive on the issue of employers' benefits from teaching youth. In sharp contrast to employers in the United States who typically resist hiring teenagers for career entry jobs regardless of the match with educational achievement, German employers prefer to take responsibility themselves for teaching youth how to work while they are still at an impressionable age. This is one reason why they willingly pay most of the costs of apprentice training. However, some costs are shared through an elaborate mechanism of chambers, which are quasi-public nongovernmental organizations that all businesses must join, and through tax-supported components of the system, including vocational schools, curriculum development, and test construction. A national process of collective bargaining keeps wages uniformly high, which encourages most German firms to rely on highly skilled frontline employees. Moreover, so long as apprenticeship training is widespread, skilled worker are less likely to be poached by employers who do not train. Indeed, failing to train apprentices means having to hire on the open market skilled workers who were let go by their training firms, which is risky.

System Building

The need to create systems rather than programs is equally daunting. The typical American response to a perceived problem is to invent new programs. Sometimes they are effective programs, but their fragmented nature may ultimately undercut their effectiveness. As noted above, a system, unlike a program, accommodates everyone who needs it. Compare a school system with a Head Start program. If an unexpectedly large cohort of first-graders appears in September, a school system is required by law to expand to hold them all. Head Start serves less than half of the children who qualify.

A system is connected with other relevant systems. There are explicit, visible connections from one to the other. Medical school, for example, is connected to the practice of medicine. Medical school is the only route to becoming a physician. It prepares students for the professional examinations they must pass to be licensed as practitioners. Some other occupations have such strong links, especially in the professions, but they are mostly absent in the middle levels of the occupational hierarchy in the United States. Some people become auto mechanics by taking vocational school courses, others by tinkering in their back yard.

A system provides clear guidance for people moving through it. One of the disadvantages of the United States' "non-system" is that it provides no information to young people about how to get from where they are now to where they would like to be in the future. Those aiming for the professions have that guidance. Anyone can tell a future physician, at least in outline form, what they need to do to achieve their career goal. But students who have decided they will not spend years in higher education tend to proceed in a negative fashion, not taking college preparatory courses, not believing they have to get good grades, because they have no positive goal. In contrast, almost any German 14-year-old knows that to become, say, a bookkeeper or an electronics technician, she or he needs to get good grades to qualify for an apprenticeship in a prestigious firm. Then they must successfully complete their apprenticeship, do well in the accompanying part-time vocational school, and obtain a high score on the qualifying examination. As the example of physicians illustrates, credentials serve as a unifying feature in a system, linking education with employment and providing understandable information about how people move within the system.

Finally, a system endures. Its financial base is stronger than year-to-year. Programs funded on a short-term basis cannot do what systems do. Neither the people the program is designed to serve (students in this case), nor those who work in it can count on them lasting. Nor can representatives of other systems assume that time they spend building connections will be repaid if the initiative may disappear within a few years.

Systems of this kind normally evolve over time. They are not created from nothing. Building a system from the ground up is difficult because the components need to be tried out and refined before they be adopted with confidence and before substantial financial support can be arranged. Yet the components cannot function the same way initially as they will when part of a system.

By definition, a system must incorporate existing programs and link them with new system components, and other systems. Thus, a school-to-work system should incorporate relevant programs like cooperative education and other aspects of vocational education, career academies, and career counseling and tie them more closely to postsecondary education and to the labor market. While necessary, this charge carries serious risks.

People who are dedicated to an existing approach may understandably resent being told that what they are doing is inadequate and what they need to become part of a larger system. Vocational educators, for example, frequently respond to school-to-work by saying they have been doing it for years, and indeed they have been doing some important parts of it. But the separation of vocational education from academic education and its generally low status are indicators of the need for system building, for conceiving of vocational education as a part of a larger system and simultaneously strengthening it and strengthening its connections to both postsecondary education and the new labor market.

Another risk is simply that system building is such a vague, amorphous task that many people have difficulty understanding what it means in practice. If existing programs should be part of an emerging system, an effort that merely channels new money into existing programs may seem legitimate. Indeed, because of the dominance of programmatic rather than systematic approaches, a likely outcome of any new funding is that it is divided up among existing programs. Although it may be used for good purposes, nothing is left behind when the new funding disappears, as School-to-Work funding will by design in the fall of 2001.

Systems must ultimately extend over a substantial geographical area. A national system is ideal, but difficult to achieve in a large diverse nation that values state and local autonomy. State systems are the next best, but regional systems related to regional labor markets are also possible. Individual schools and school districts can act systemically, but they are limited in the extent to which they can produce portable occupational credentials—major constituents in a school-to-work system.

Several states have made progress toward developing systems. Wisconsin, for example, was a pioneer in the development of youth apprenticeship and built its demonstration efforts on the foundation of special legislation that added to the state's apprenticeship statute a new provision defining youth apprenticeship and its place in the law. Next, officials in Wisconsin worked with employers, unions, and educators to devise occupational skill standards and apprenticeship programs to meet them. This framework of explicit objectives and curricula for apprentices made it easier for regional school-to-work partnerships to create apprenticeships. Employers' associations and unions had already endorsed the effort and there was no need to reinvent work-based learning curricula in each location. As a result, Wisconsin boasts several thousand formal youth apprenticeships in strategic areas such as printing and metalworking—still not enough to accommodate a substantial proportion of the youth population, but more than can be found in most areas.

School reform has been a central systemic element in several states' efforts. Oregon was an early leader in this realm, passing six major pieces of legislation directed at meshing education with employment training and improving both. At the core of the Oregon system is the "Certificate of Initial Mastery," a statewide standard or benchmark for academic achievement in 12 subject areas that all students are expected to reach by grade 10 or earlier. Thereafter, high school students may choose a career focus for the remainder of their secondary education and for postsecondary education as well. Achieving the standards in one of these career areas results in the award of a "Certificate of Advanced Mastery," which is intended to serve as an occupational credential. (This framework was first proposed by the National Center on Education and Employment [1990].) A Workforce Quality Council with representatives from business, labor, government, education, and the public, has a legal mandate to plan a statewide workforce development strategy and to supervise its implementation. Fifteen regional workforce quality committees under its umbrella design and implement local plans that support the overall state policy.

Boston's ProTech is an example of system building in a large city school district. ProTech grew out of a 1982 initiative called the Boston Compact, in which business leaders agreed to increase their support for education if educators would accept the challenge of reaching higher achievement goals with students. The first round of the Compact was disappointing. Boosting student achievement in the Boston schools proved more daunting than had been anticipated. In the second round, which included the initiation of ProTech in 1990, employers agreed to play a more active role, most dramatically by guaranteeing jobs to any graduates of the Boston Public Schools who achieved a C average or better and maintained a good attendance record without severe discipline problems.

The health care industry went even farther, agreeing to work closely with the schools to prepare young people for health care careers. Youth apprenticeship was the vehicle chosen for this collaboration. ProTech engaged high school juniors and seniors in planned and supervised work-based learning experiences that were tied to their academic programs. Its goal was to motivate higher academic achievement, as well as to provide an introduction to health care occupations. Recognizing that most health care occupations require at least an associate's degree, ProTech emphasized postsecondary education and enrolled some students in community college courses while they were still in high school. After the passage of the School-to-Work Opportunities Act and related state legislation, Boston's school system made an even stronger commitment to higher academic standards and career-focused education, including career academies. ProTech then began to expand into other industries. Follow-up studies of ProTech graduates indicate marginally higher rates of college enrollment and persistence than a comparison group, combined with higher levels of employment and earnings [Jobs for the Future 1998].

Early Evaluation Results

Two studies have examined early results of school-to-work implementation. Pedraza, Pauly, and Kopp [1997] selected 16 school-to-work efforts that preceded the passage of the School-to-Work Opportunities Act in 1994. They included youth apprenticeships, career academies, tech-prep programs, restructured vocational education programs, and occupational academic cluster programs (multiple course sequences in a high school related to clusters of occupations). Perhaps the most important finding was that all 16 programs had not only survived but grown, some not only in size but also in scope, adding new components as well as larger numbers of youth. In addition, they tended to compensate for initial weaknesses: those originally emphasizing work-based learning strengthened the school-based side and vice versa. Scale with quality was an issue in all the sites. In general, those that provided intensive work-based learning remained smaller than those emphasizing school-based activities, which made fewer changes in students' learning experiences. Career academies remained small as a matter of principle, but in several cases the original academies served as pilots stimulating the formation of new academies in other occupational areas. Contrary to concerns that school-to-work would become another stigmatized program, these sites reported attracting increasing proportions of high-achieving students.

In a study of the implementation of the School-to-Work Opportunities Act for the U.S. Department of Education, Hershey, Hudis, Silverberg, and Haimson [1997] examined eight states and 39 local partnerships in depth, including student surveys and transcript analyses. They found substantial progress toward the legislation's goals, notably in establishing collaborative relationships between educators and employers and in beginning to put in place elements of a system infrastructure. However, they also cautioned that the greatest achievements to date have been in the least demanding arenas. Career awareness has received more attention than the creation of coherent career paths. School curricula have not yet been seriously affected. Work-based learning activities are predominantly short-term, such as field trips and job shadowing, in contrast to more intensive activities such as cooperative education and apprenticeship. Student surveys and transcript analyses indicate the magnitude of the task still to come. While 63% of students had engaged in comprehensive career development activities, 16% had participated in a work-based learning activity that was linked to the school, and 12% had a career major, only 2% experienced all three of these components.

School-to-work implementation to date is relatively wide but not comprehensive and it is rather shallow. Exemplary sites and programs can be found that demonstrate the promise and the value of improving the transition from school to career. But building a new system and realigning both schools and workplaces simultaneously is an exceedingly ambitious goal. In the absence of a new groundswell of support and enthusiasm, many states and communities are likely to abandon current efforts after federal funding is withdrawn. The principles behind the legislation have taken deep enough root in some places to survive without continued federal money, however.

Implications for Other Initiatives

Although the aims of the School-to-Work Opportunities Act to expand work-based learning and to build systems are unique, the challenge of trying to achieve large scale with high quality is not. Several strategies being employed in this initiative are equally appropriate to others. The first, a common strategy, is the use of demonstration projects that illustrate what can be done, how to do it, and what the effects are likely to be. Another is an emphasis on communicating basic principles, purposes, and definitions of terms and working toward consensus on them. Networking among individuals and organizations has aided in that process, as did the creation of the National School-to-Work Office and of a Learning and Information Center within it to coordinate training and technical assistance. Third is prescribing principles, but encouraging different ways of putting them into practice. A fourth strategy has been building partnerships among stakeholders, especially educators, employers, parents, community organizations, and labor. These and others are represented at every level: national, state, and local. Finally, there has been a constructive use of "best practices," the effort to identify and describe effective approaches taken in some locations so that others can learn from and adapt them.

Conclusion

The United States has created the world's preeminent system of higher education, which does an excellent job of preparing youth for work. Its diversity is one of its strengths. We loosely refer to as "colleges" institutions that include huge state universities and small church-related universities, prestigious private universities and small liberal arts colleges. Included are two-year community colleges and for-profit business colleges. However, the nation's commitment to higher education has left a gap for the majority who never obtain a postsecondary degree. In an industrial economy, high school graduates, even dropouts, especially white males, could find skilled and semiskilled jobs that paid middle-class wages and provided ample security and benefits. As factories have shrunk, closed, and moved overseas, an increasing number of jobs has either paid at or near the minimum wage or required the kind of communication and problem-solving skills associated with postsecondary education.

The most obvious way to prepare youth for higher paying jobs is to improve secondary education and make postsecondary education more accessible. However, this process assumes a level of motivation on the part of students and a quality of instruction that are often in short supply. School-to-Work was conceived as a means of connecting education more closely to employment, especially by exploiting workplaces as learning environments for youth. Research on German apprenticeship, one of the key inspirations for this approach, and on such previously implemented components as career academies, cooperative education, youth apprenticeship, and reformed vocational education have all affirmed the value of the approach. It is impossible, however, to test in advance how a comprehensive system would function and creating such a system is extraordinarily challenging.

Federal funding specifically for School-to-Work will be phased out far too soon to establish systems unless conditions are right in states and localities. Those conditions include strong employer demand and long-term commitment to thorough school reform. When employers have jointly identified a need for better educated workers and have agreed to work with each other and with educators to meet that need and when they have committed themselves to school reform emphasizing universal attainment of high academic standards as a means of meeting that need, the prospects are good for sustaining work-based learning that is closely connected to school-based learning. The best hope for continued progress in implementing such systems is that the places that meet these conditions will prove so vital and successful that they will become nodes from which effective practices spread.

References

Barbett, S. F., & Korb, R. A. (1997). *Enrollment in higher education: Fall 1995*. Washington, DC: U.S. Department of Education, Office of Educational Research and Improvement, National Center for Educational Statistics (97-440).

Bottoms, G., & Sharpe, D. (no date). *Teaching for understanding and integration of academic and technical education*. Atlanta: Southern Regional Education Board.

Hamilton, S. F. (1990). *Apprenticeship for adulthood: Preparing youth for the future*. New York: Free Press.

Hamilton, S. F. (1994). Employment prospects as motivation for school achievement: Links and gaps between school and work in seven countries. In F. K. Silbereisen & E. Todt (Eds.), *Adolescence in context: The interplay of family, school, peers, and work in adjustment* (pp. 267-283). New York: Springer.

Hamilton, M. A., & Hamilton, S. F. (1997). *Learning well at work: Choices for quality*. Washington, DC: National School-to-Work Office.

Hamilton, S. F., & Lempert, W. (1997). The impact of apprenticeship on youth: A prospective analysis. *Journal of Research on Adolescence, 6*, 427-455.

Hamilton, S. F. & Levine-Powers, J. (1990). Failed expectations: Working-class girls' transition from school to work. *Youth and Society, 22*, 241-262.

Hershey, A. M., Hudis, P., Silverberg, M., & Haimson, J. (1997). *Partners in progress: Early steps in creating school-to-work programs*. Princeton, NJ: Mathematica Policy Research, Inc.

Jobs for the Future. (1998). *School-to-career initiative demonstrates significant impact on young people*. Boston: Author.

Kemple, J. J. (1997). *Career academies: Communities of support for students and teachers. Emerging findings from a 10-site evaluation*. New York: Manpower Demonstration Research Corporation.

Klerman, J. A., & Karoly, L. A. (1995). *The transition to stable employment: The experience of US youth in their early labor market career.* Santa Monica, CA: Rand.

Kopp, H., & Kazis, R., with Churchill, A. (no date). *Promising practices: A study of ten school-to-career programs.* Boston: Jobs for the Future.

Lempert, W. (1995). Das Märchen vom unaufhaltsam Niedergang des "dualen Systems" (The fairy tale of the perpetual decline of the dual system). *Zeitschrift für Berufs- und Wirtschaftspädagogik, 91*, 225-231.

Lerman, R. I. & Pouncy, H. (1990). The compelling case for youth apprenticeships. *The Public Interest, 90*, 62-77.

Murnane, R. J., & Levy, F. (1996). *Teaching the new basic skills: Principles for educating children to thrive in a changing economy.* New York: Free Press.

National Center on Education and the Economy. (1990). *America's choice: High skills or low wages!* Rochester, NY: Author.

National Commission on Excellence in Education. (1983). *A nation at risk: The imperative for educational reform.* Washington, DC: U.S. Government Printing Office.

Orr, M. T. (unpublished). *Youth apprenticeship program: Delivering on a promise.* New York: Teachers College, Columbia University.

Osterman, P. (1980). *Getting started: The youth labor market.* Cambridge, MA: MIT Press.

Pedraza, R. A., Pauly, E., & Kopp, H. (1997). *Home-grown progress: The evolution of innovative school-to-work programs.* New York: Manpower Demonstration Research Corporation.

Rose, R. (1991). Prospective evaluation through comparative analysis: Youth training in a time-space perspective. In P. Ryan (Ed.), *International comparisons of vocational education and training for intermediate skills* (pp. 68-92). London: Falmer Press.

Stern, D., Raby, M., & Dayton, C. (1992). *Career academies: Partnerships for reconstructing American high schools.* San Francisco: Jossey-Bass.

Stern, D., & Stevens, D. (1992). Analysis of unemployment insurance data on the relationship between high school cooperative education and subsequent employment. Paper prepared for the National Assessment of Vocational Education. Berkeley, CA: University of California at Berkeley, School of Education.

Urquiola, M., Stern, D., Horn, I., Dornsife, C., Chi, B., Williams, L., Merritt, D., Hughes, K., & Bailey, T. (1997). *School to work, college and career: A review of policy, practice, and results*, 1993-1997. Berkeley, CA: University of California, National Center for Research in Vocational Education.

U.S. Bureau of the Census. (1996, October). *Current Population Survey, School Enrollment Supplement for October 1996, and National Estimates.* Washington, DC: Author.

U.S. Department of Education. (1997). *The condition of education.* Washington, DC: U.S. Government Printing Office.

U.S. Department of Labor. (1997). *Evaluating the net impact of school-to-work: Proceedings of a roundtable.* Washington, DC: U.S. Government Printing Office

Youth and America's Future: The William T. Grant Commission on Work, Family and Citizenship. (1988). *The forgotten half: Pathways to success for America's youth and young families.* Washington, DC: Author.

Part III
Integration of Research, Programs, and Policies

12 Psychological and Educational Resilience

*Margaret C. Wang, Geneva D. Haertel, & Herbert J. Walberg**

The idea of resilience among humans originated among psychologists investigating the development of children and families faced with a multitude of co-occurring adversities. Garmezy [1974] first used the term in describing children's successful coping with developmental risk and adversity. Observing that some psychopathic children responded well to treatment, he hypothesized they had resources that could be tapped through therapy to enable recovery. Because many childhood psychoses have poor prognoses, their success defied the odds. This idea of resilience grew to dominate the field of developmental psychopathology.

Recent study has broadened the application of resilience research to include education; it focuses on children and youth, the institutions that serve them, and the communities in which they live. As Wang and Gordon noted [Wang & Gordon 1994a; Taylor & Wang, in press], the resilience research reflects a possible paradigm shift—a search for alterable conditions that enhance learning and life chances of the many children and youth faced with adversity and risks. This paper provides an overview of the emerging idea of educational resilience, discusses its theoretical and research bases, and draws implication for improvement of educational prac-

* The research reported herein is supported in part by the Office of Educational Research and Improvement of the U.S. Department of Education through a grant to the National Center on Education in the Inner Cities at the Temple University Center for Research in Human Development and Education. The opinions expressed do not necessarily reflect the position of the supporting agencies, and no official endorsement should be inferred.

tice. It identifies the conditions in homes, classrooms, schools, and communities that appear to contribute to educational resilience.

Resilience: A Psychological Construct

Various definitions of resilience have emerged over the past two decades. Rutter [1990] refers to it as "the positive pole of the ubiquitous phenomenon of individual differences in people's response to stress and adversity" [p. 181]. Masten, Best, and Garmezy [1991] define it as "the capacity for or outcome of successful adaptation despite challenging or threatening circumstances" [p. 425]. Other definitions focus on the ability of individuals to exploit positive features of their environment [Hogman 1983]. Thus, resilience can be characterized as emanating from sources within both the individual and environment.

Since the 1970s, developmental psychopathology has grown rapidly as a scientific and professional discipline. It provides an integrative framework for understanding maladaptation among children and adolescents, as well as the roles of risk and protective factors. Clinical psychologists and psychiatrists have documented the phenomenon of psychosocial resilience in diverse populations at risk of educational failure [Rolf et al. 1990]. They studied children exposed to divorce, maternal stress, family violence, early parental death, poverty, and medical and mental illness. Their retrospective and prospective studies of these populations uncovered evidence of resilience and protective or enabling factors that allow children and youth to overcome adversity. Although some children in these high-risk circumstances develop psychopathologies, a larger percentage avoid maladaptation and become healthy, competent adults [Garmezy 1991]. Research on resilience suggests, for example, that only one out of four children born to alcoholic parents will become alcoholic [Benard 1991].

The first decade of resilience studies catalogued the attributes and environmental conditions of children, youth, and adults who thrived despite their at-risk circumstances, and identified characteristics of such individuals and environments. The most commonly cited attributes of resilient children include social competence, cognitive problem-solving skills, independence, resourcefulness, self-determination, and purposiveness. Individuals with such attributes are referred to as "invincible," "hardy," and "invulnerable." Rutter [1990] identified high activity levels as an important characteristic of resilient individuals. Children who are proactive and engage in a variety of activities increase their likelihood of achieving success. Another key characteristic of resilient children is a well-developed "self-system," including an internal locus of control, high self-esteem, high self-efficacy, and autonomy [Garmezy 1974].

Rutter [1990] found that families who promoted resilience provided an orderly, organized home environment where at least one caring adult was available to provide support, attention, direction, and resources to children, and where economic and social stability prevailed. Nonresilient children exhibited sloppiness, eating and sleeping irregularities, low malleability, and moodiness, which reduced their likelihood of receiving positive attention from adults. In contrast, even temperament, high malleability, predictable behavior, mild-to-moderate emotional reactions, and a sense of humor protected resilient children and attracted affection and support from adults. Some resilient children, however, achieved success by resisting family circumstances. Chess [1989], for example, describes "adaptive distancing," which allows resilient children to stand apart from their disordered families and accomplish constructive goals. Such distancing may allow resilient children to interact with peers and adults outside the family in constructive ways that contribute to their healthy development.

Using the National Educational Longitudinal Study [NELS:88] data, Peng et al. [1992] found confirming evidence of resilient children's psy chosocial, cognitive, and familial assets. They identified educationally resilient students as those of low socioeconomic status from economically depressed urban communities, whose combined reading and mathematics test scores were in the top quartile of achievement norms. These students achieved academic performance despite their family's economic status and despite attending schools with a high percentage of students from economically disadvantaged and high-risk neighborhoods. They had higher self-concepts and educational aspirations and felt more internally controlled than nonresilient students; they also interacted more often with their parents and were more often encouraged to do their best. Thus, both intensive observational studies and a large national survey suggest that children and youth can thrive psychologically and educationally despite adverse circumstances.

During the 1970s and 1980s, Garmezy, Masten, and Tellegen [1984] conducted a longitudinal study, Project Competence, which examined stress, competence, and protective factors among children at risk of psychopathology. This project, one of the few early resilience studies investigating school performance, focused on the impact of stressful life events on children's functional competence. Regression models showed the relation among measures of competence, stress, personal attributes, and contextual features of the home and school. The "challenge model" presents stress as a potential enhancer of competence. In this model, the relationship between stress and competence is curvilinear: at low to moderate levels of stress, competence increases, but at higher levels of stress, competence begins to decrease. The "immunity-versus-vulnerability model" shows how attributes modulate the impact of stress on competence. It demonstrates how personal and contextual attributes serve as protective factors to help children meet the challenges of stress-producing adversities.

Educational resilience is the product not of a single precipitating event, but of continuous interaction between a child's attributes and alterable features of the environment. Wang, Haertel, and Walberg [1994] defined educational resilience as success in school despite personal vulnerabilities and adversities brought about by environmental conditions and early experiences. Thus, based on this definition, educational resilience is fostered through interventions that develop children's coping abilities, establish protective factors, and buffer children against adversities.

Results from research on psychological resilience show that psychologically resilient children often further their own healthy development and actively select environments and people that facilitate their growth. Analogously, educationally resilient children may select academic people, programs, and activities that enhance their skills, extend their experiences, and increase their academic opportunities. Educationally resilient students may elicit their teachers' and peers' support and receive attention even in challenging circumstances.

An Ecological Framework for Fostering Educational Resilience

In accord with an ecological perspective [Bronfenbrenner 1986], research on educational resilience recognizes the overlapping and multiple contexts that affect development and learning. Four contexts in particular are pervasive and powerful: family, school, peer, and community. Vulnerabilities and adversities may place children at risk, but their negative impact may be mitigated by the presence of protective factors within these contexts that safeguard children. Discussion in the following sections focuses on how these four contexts can be altered by including protective factors that promote educational resilience.

The ecological framework holds that the educational success of children and youth, as well as later life accomplishments, depends upon family, school, peer, and community contexts. The interdependency of these contexts affects the likelihood of successful adaptation. For example, attendance in preschool accompanied by family support for schooling may increase the likelihood of high school graduation among children from impoverished communities.

The learning influences of variables within the four contexts are keys for understanding educational resilience and for designing educational conditions and programs to raise the achievement of children. Many protective factors have emerged from developmental psychopathology studies. More recently, educational researchers have explored how educational experiences promote resilience [Wang & Gordon 1994a]. These education studies have identified protective factors that lead to enhanced learning and buffer children against the effects of adversities by increasing their knowledge, skills, and constructive behaviors and positive attitudes toward school and learning.

In the following sections, influences on learning are briefly discussed based on findings from a mega-research synthesis of 91 meta-analyses,

179 authoritative review articles, and a survey of 61 educational researchers [Wang et al. 1993]. This synthesis identified six characteristics of the individual learner and 22 features of the family, school, peer, and community contexts that influence student learning and are likely to promote educational resilience (see Figure 12-1). Scores representing the magnitude of each of the influences on learning were calculated by combining statistical results (effect sizes and correlations) from the meta-analyses, review articles, and survey results. To make the 28 scores comparable, they were transformed into T-scores (standard scores with a mean of 50 and a standard deviation of 10). Figure 12-1 depicts the magnitude of the 28 influences on learning categorized by learner characteristics, and family, school, peer, and community contexts. The following sections discuss those learner characteristics and contextual features that influence student learning and promote educational resilience.

Learner Characteristics

Findings from psychological studies and studies of behavioral characteristics of students in school settings are congruent with research results noted earlier (cf. Masten [1994]; Teddlie & Stringfield [1993]). Characteristics of resilient children have included both positive social and intellectual attributes. Among these attributes are proaction, strong interpersonal skills, an even temperament, high malleability, predictable behavior, and a sense of humor. Using their intellectual resources, resilient children set goals, change their environment, and alter their lives in successful ways. Many of these children exhibit above-average intelligence, high verbal skills, divergent thinking, and a capacity for successful reflection on their problems. These protective factors increase the likelihood that children will receive support from caregivers, adults, and peers, and facilitate children's intellectual and social endeavors.

The research synthesis results [Wang et al. 1993] depicted in Figure 12-1 corroborate these findings. As Figure 12-1 shows, characteristics of learners are among the most salient influences on learning. For example, metacognitive and cognitive processes are among the most powerful

Figure 12-1. Magnitude of Influence

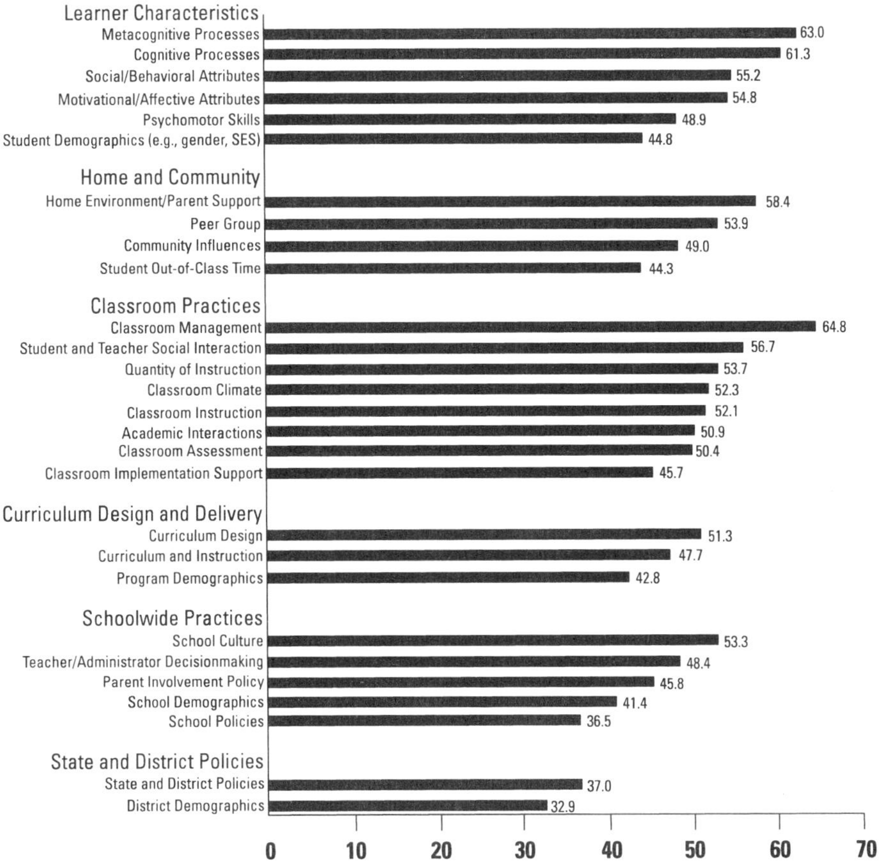

influences on learning. These processes include students' use of learning strategies, self-monitoring, and self-evaluation, as well as students' general intelligence and prior knowledge, including competencies in reading and mathematics. Given the social nature of schooling, children's social and behavioral attributes also strongly influence learning. Children that are socially skillful and exhibit constructive behaviors are more likely to be engaged in their schoolwork and perform well academically. High motivation and positive learning attitudes determine effort and perseverance.

Motivation and positive attitudes toward school have long been recognized as constituents of academic success. Recent research results suggest they are fundamental to the development of self-controlled, self-regulated learning [Blumenfeld 1992].

Like the attributes of resilient children identified in developmental psychopathology, Figure 12-1 illustrates the relative importance of students' cognitive, social, behavioral, and motivational attributes as protective factors that support academic learning. These psychological attributes confer academic benefits and contribute to the development of educational resilience. The following sections discuss protective factors that have been identified within the family, school, peer, and community contexts.

The Family Context

Since families are the child's first protective agents, they are a logical starting point for analyzing resilience. Masten et al. [1991] noted that parents

> nurture mastery motivation and self-esteem as well as physical growth. Parents provide information, learning opportunities, behavioral models, and connections to other resources. When these transactional protective processes are absent or are severely limited for prolonged periods, a child may be significantly handicapped in subsequent adaptation by low self-esteem, inadequate information or social know-how, a disinclination to learn or interact with the world, and a distrust of people as resources. [p. 438]

Table 12-1 presents a sample of risk factors that occur within the family context and place children at risk of school failure. It also provides an illustrative list of protective factors in the family context that buffer children against educational failure and promote resilience. As shown in Table 12-1, three types of protective factors promote educational resilience in family contexts: resource availability; nurturance of children's motivation, expectations, and skills; and a stable and orderly family environment.

Among parent characteristics that promote resilience development are (1) being structured and caring; (2) holding high academic, moral, and social expectations for children's behavior; and (3) encouraging participa-

Table 12-1. An Illustrative List of Risk and Protective Factors Within the Family Context

Risk Factors That Contribute to Educational Failure	Protective Factors That Mitigate Against Educational Failure
Resource Availability	
• Poverty • Toxic environment • Limited transportation • Malnutrition • Inadequate housing • Inadequate health care • Substance abuse • Teen pregnancy and parenting	• Family provides food, shelter, and basic needs • Family provides connections to other resources • Family provides transportation • Family nurtures physical growth • Family provides information • Family provides learning opportunities • Family provides behavioral models
Nurturance of Motivation, Expectations, and Skills	
• Poor parenting skills • Poor communication skills • Limited parental education	• Family nurtures self-esteem, self-efficacy • Family nurtures mastery motivation • Family holds high academic expectations • Family involvement in programs and courses that advance their skills
Stable and Orderly Family Environment	
• Child maltreatment • Family discord • Divorce/family dissolution • Frequent relocations • Chronic family illnesses • Unemployment	• Strong relationship with adult (not always a parent) • Absence of serious family discord • Family warmth • Family cohesion • Children perform chores to help family • Orderly household environment

tion in the life of the family. Most resilient children appear to have at least one strong, enduring relationship with an adult (though not always a parent). Receiving care and affection appears critical throughout childhood and adolescence, but particularly during the first year of life [Werner & Smith 1982].

Rutter [1990] documented the importance of positive parent-child relationships in a review of short-term observational studies, intergenerational analyses of high-risk populations, and studies of adult recall. His research suggests that secure childhood attachments protect against adversity in later life. Positive, intimate relationships appear to enhance the individual's self-concept and sense of social worth. In their review of studies of competence under stress, Masten et al. [1991] showed that children whose families had histories of marital instability and frequent moves were more often rated as disruptive by peers and teachers.

Migration is a serious and pervasive risk factor for student learning among poor and minority children, as revealed by large national surveys [Straits 1987]. When children move from a community of lower socioeconomic status to one of higher socioeconomic status, they often suffer grade retardation. Early grade retardation forecasts further retardation, poor achievement, and school dropout.

Lee, Winfield, and Wilson [1991] found family characteristics to be an important differentiating factor between low- and high-achieving African American students. Using the National Assessment of Educational Progress (NAEP) data, they found that higher achieving African American students tend to come from higher social classes and have working mothers. In addition, these students are twice as likely as their low-achieving counterparts to attend Catholic schools and to reside in urban areas.

Research findings show the importance of family cohesion, family warmth, and an absence of discord. In addition to holding high expectations of children (i.e., expectations that children will succeed in school and become good citizens in their community), families that employ consistent discipline, rules, and regulations produce better outcomes among children from at-risk families [Bennett et al. 1988]. In contrast, household disorder is related to disruptiveness in school [Masten et al. 1990].

Intervention research suggests that problems students experience cannot be fully addressed without the direct involvement of the family. Werner and Smith [1982] emphasized the value of assigned chores, caring for brothers and sisters, and the contribution of part-time work in supporting the family. These helping behaviors show children that they can improve their circumstances, which leads to enhanced self-esteem and fosters resilience.

Family involvement in children's education also enhances children's school performance. Of the 28 influences on learning depicted in Figure 12-1, home environment and parental support were the fourth most influential. The active participation of family members in children's educational experiences has improved their achievement, and attendance, and decreased dropout, delinquency, and pregnancy rates. Educational intervention programs designed to involve family members are significantly more effective than programs aimed exclusively at students. Parents who participate in family involvement programs generally feel better about themselves and are more likely to enroll in courses that advance their own education [Flaxman & Inger 1991].

Comer [1986] incorporated parental involvement in a low-performing school in a poor neighborhood and observed substantial achievement gains for several years. Similar results have been attained with other low-performing schools. Comer attributes these results to management teams involving parents, parent-developed workshops, parental involvement in tutoring programs for children, and parents assisting teachers in classroom activities.

Epstein [1987] developed a theory of family-school connections after recognizing four important "microsystems" that influence children—families, peer groups, schools, and neighborhoods. The degree of psychological overlap among these microsystems represents the extent to which they share values, goals, and understandings of the social and cultural processes governing everyday life. The greater the overlap among these systems, the more common their cultures. It appears that when the home, school, peers, and larger community are similar, their impact on children and youth is greater.

A wide range of family involvement programs are being implemented by schools nationwide. Some programs help parents become better home educators and stress behaviors such as monitoring children's homework, providing academic assistance or tutoring, and reducing television time. These programs train family members to help their children develop good study habits and high expectations. Empirical results suggest that parent involvement in specific learning strategies has a positive effect on children's academic performance [Lee et al. 1993]. Other programs involve families in school management and encourage parents' presence in the school. Still others provide a host of services to families and children, including home visits, job training, career counseling, health care, mental health, and social support services.

The School Context

Many studies have identified particular educational practices and policies that enhance the learning of children in stressful life circumstances. Few, however, address the roles of school, classroom, and teacher as protective mechanisms that promote resilience development in general and educational resilience in particular. Those studies of resilience that have focused on features of the school environment suggest that schools can augment facilitative home and individual factors or compensate for the lack of a supportive home environment [Rutter 1979]. In a review of resilience literature, Rutter provides evidence that schools can promote resilience within the child, in the family, and outside the home. Well-functioning schools belong to the group of factors outside the home that can foster resiliency. Rutter contends that children from disadvantaged and discordant homes were less likely to develop life problems as a result of attending well-functioning schools. The critical features of these effective schools included appropriately high expectations of students, good group management, effective feedback to children with ample use of praise, teachers who are good behavioral models, pleasant working conditions, and assignment of students to positions of trust and responsibility.

Features of effective schools that promote resilience were further examined in a longitudinal program of research at the National Center on

Education in the Inner Cities [Wang 1995]. This research program suggests a consistent pattern of organizational and behavioral characteristics among inner-city schools that promote educational resilience [Wang et al. 1994; Yancey & Saporito 1995]. Longitudinal studies of inner-city schools in Houston and Philadelphia [Wang et al. 1994] showed, for example, significant differences between those schools that were effective in promoting achievement and those that were ineffective. Students in the more effective schools generally spent more time working independently; teachers spent more time interacting with students; and students expressed more positive perceptions about their schools overall. They were more satisfied with their schoolwork and peer relationships, saw their teachers as having high expectations of them, and had higher aspirations and achievement motivation and better social and academic self-concepts. In addition, students in effective inner-city schools felt more involved in school, believed their teachers were more supportive, and felt classroom rules were made clear to them.

Similarly, in a study using the NELS:88 database, Peng, Weishew, and Wang [1991] found that inner-city schools with high achievement scores were more orderly and structured (despite their disadvantaged circumstances) than low-achieving inner-city schools. Anderson and Walberg [1994] found that higher achieving Chicago schools had greater involvement of stakeholder groups and greater staff capacity for continuous learning. While the corpus of studies is small, researchers have been successful in identifying significant features of schools that promote educational resilience.

Table 12-2 shows examples of risk and protective factors that occur within the school context. In the following sections, ways of altering educational contexts to promote resilience are discussed. Protective factors can be introduced in school contexts through teachers' actions and beliefs, curricula, instruction, and school organization and climate. These protective factors mitigate against the ill effects not only of school-related risks, but also against those occurring in other contexts.

Teachers

Several major studies document the role that teachers play in mitigating severe adversities in students' lives. Werner's [1989] 30-year longitudinal

Table 12-2. An Illustrative List of Risk and Protective Factors Within the School Context

Risk Factors That Contribute to Educational Failure	Protective Factors That Mitigate Against Educational Failure
Teacher	
• Burned-out teaching staff • Low expectations for learning	• Caring and committed relationships between students and teachers • Holding high expectations for all students • Helping students master new experiences • Promoting student self-concept and self-esteem • Role modeling of problemsolving and prosocial behavior
Curriculum	
• Watered-down curricula • Insensitive to differences in students' ethnic/cultural backgrounds • Lockstep curriculum with little accommodation to students' prior knowledge • Curriculum not integrated across subject areas	• Teacher sensitivity to students' cultural and intellectual diversity • Use of culturally relevant texts and materials • Use of universal themes to make content more accessible • Adaptation of curriculum content and instructional strategies to ensure student learning • Overcoming knowledge deficits by teaching prerequisite knowledge • Opportunity to learn advanced contact and higher order thinking skills • Provide a motivating context for learning that recognizes differences in students' backgrounds, interests, and prior knowledge. • Curriculum articulation and organization

Table 12-2 (continued)

Instruction	
• Little time devoted to instruction	• Maximized learning time
• Stigmatizing labels for children with special needs	• High level of student engagement
• Teachers not familiar with knowledge base on effective instruction	• Student participation in goal-setting
• Few opportunities for teacher and student interaction	• Metacognitive and self-regulated learning activities
• Infrequent use of assessment to guide instruction	• Frequent and high-quality teacher-student interactions
	• Use of frequent assessments aligned to content
	• Effective classroom management
School Organization and Culture	
• Lack of education reform vision	• Smaller educational units that create a sense of involvement and belonging
• Many educationally disadvantaged students	• Safe and orderly school atmosphere that rewards student achievement
• School and classroom violence	• Strong leadership from principal
• Inadequately prepared teachers	• Active parent/community involvement programs
• Ineffective school leaders	• Inclusive classrooms and school
• Limited professional development	• Availability of school-linked, coordinated services
• Low parent/community involvement	• Presence of a preschool program
• Noninclusive programs	
• Inadequate resources	

study of the long-term effects of prenatal and perinatal stress on children of Kauai, Hawaii, for example, showed that teachers help children adapt to difficult life circumstances. Of the 142 high-risk children identified in her study, Werner found those who became competent, successful adults triumphed over physical disadvantages and deprived childhoods. They received emotional support from their families and an informal network of individuals, including teachers, ministers, older friends, and peers who in times of crisis and transition provided counsel and support. Schools and teachers had special status among these resilient children. They regarded schools as a home away from home—an orderly refuge from a chaotic household. When interviewed at the end of secondary school, many resilient youth identified a favorite teacher who became a role model, friend, and confidant and had been particularly helpful when their own families experienced discord and were threatened with dissolution. These teachers also praised children's problem-solving abilities and competence in reading. Thus, teachers who served as role models for these youth were not simply providers of knowledge and skills, but confidants, counselors, and models of resiliency themselves.

Masten [1990] and her colleagues have also conducted numerous studies of resilient children. These studies suggest that schools can be environments that help children who experience high stress or high-risk situations and can assist them in dealing positively with adversities. Masten's research demonstrates that close bonds with capable adults, opportunities to feel valued and competent, and friendships with peers foster resiliency.

In their study of public and private high schools, Coleman and Hoffer [1987] pointed to the role of caring teachers in helping students develop the values and attitudes necessary for persevering in their schoolwork and achieving high grades. They stressed the importance of sustained teacher encouragement of students' academic and social endeavors. The importance of caring teachers who support students' academic and social pursuits is also corroborated by the relationship between teachers' and students' social interactions and student learning (see Figure 12-1). Teacher and student social interactions are the fifth most powerful influence on learning. The frequency and quality of these social interactions contribute to enhanced student learning, which can lead to improved self-esteem and a sense of membership in the class and school.

Effective teachers also foster educational resilience by promoting students' self-concept and responsibility for active learning. As noted by Bandura [1993], belief in one's efficacy is best promoted through mastery of new experiences. When students become convinced they are instrumental in their learning success, they work harder to overcome difficulties. Students gain information about their own efficacy from several sources, including memories of similar experiences, observations and comparisons of their performance to that of others, motivation for engaging in the task, and persuasion by others. By providing students with opportunities to set and achieve realistic goals, and encouraging them in their efforts, teachers play a key role in fostering resilience and helping students develop expectations for their own success.

Curriculum and Instruction

Curriculum and instruction are important resources for the learning success of students, particularly those with diverse needs that require greater-than-usual instructional support. Significant theoretical and research advances, particularly in cognitive science and effective teaching, contribute much to a better understanding of learning and development [Brown 1994], what makes learning more productive [Wang et al. 1994], and the learning of children with special needs [Wang & Reynolds 1995].

Children with good comprehension skills usually relate new information to their personal experiences. A major risk factor encountered by many students, however, is the disconnection between their schooling experiences and family life. Differences in prior knowledge, which may be the product of cultural and socioeconomic differences, may be important sources of variation in students' learning strategies and outcomes. Students from culturally diverse backgrounds may not only have difficulty accessing background knowledge, but may also have knowledge deficits. This lack of knowledge is sometimes remedied by using culturally relevant texts and materials or teaching prerequisite knowledge. Teachers who are familiar with the background experiences students bring to the classroom can select materials that are culturally relevant. These teachers can also design more appropriate instructional experiences that facilitate students being able to access their prior knowledge.

Constructivist and adaptive approaches. The constructivist approach to instruction may also help children to develop competencies and attitudes that enable them to adapt to adverse circumstances [American Psychological Association 1993; Brown 1994]. Central to such development are the following:

- **Social competence.** The ability to establish and sustain positive caring relationships with peers and adults, to maintain a sense of humor, and to communicate compassion and empathy.
- **Resourcefulness.** The ability to critically, creatively, and reflectively make decisions, to seek help from others, and to recognize alternative ways to solve problems and resolve conflict.
- **Autonomy.** The ability to act independently, to exert some control over one's environment, to have a sense of identity, and to detach oneself from others engaged in risky or dysfunctional behaviors.
- **A sense of purpose.** The ability to foresee a bright future for oneself, to be optimistic, and to aspire toward learning success.

Intervention programs. Educational intervention programs with a resilience-promoting focus [Brown & Campione 1994; McCombs & Whisler 1997; Schaps et al. 1995; Wang 1992] tend to:

- foster caring relationships among peers and teachers that promote positive expectations and participation;
- provide curriculum that is thematic, experiential, challenging, comprehensive, and inclusive of multiple perspectives;
- use instruction that addresses a broad range of learning styles, builds from perceptions of student strengths, interests, and experiences, and is participatory and facilitative;
- implement instructional groupings that promote cooperation, shared responsibility, and a sense of belonging; and
- include evaluation methods that distinguish multiple intelligences, utilize appropriate assessment, and foster self-reflection.

These program features may help students develop expectations for their own success.

Compensatory approaches. Although many schools make significant efforts to compensate for poor academic potential, many students who are at risk of school failure still experience serious difficulties in achieving learning success. They need better help than they are now receiving. The prototypical special education, remedial, or compensatory education program often contributes to children's learning problems [Baker et al. 1995]. Students at risk of school failure may actually receive inferior instruction when schools provide them with pullout programs to meet their learning needs. These special programs often neglect fundamental content and provide less instruction in higher order, advanced skills. Students with special needs, for example, are likely to be pulled out of the regular reading classroom to be drilled in vocabulary. Comprehension, problem solving, and higher order reasoning are less often emphasized in the instruction of these children. Furthermore, teachers tend to underestimate what students with special needs can do. They tend to withhold challenging work and not provide a motivating context for learning.

Curriculum and instruction practices that are inclusive, based on constructivist principles of learning, and responsive to the diverse needs of students impact student learning. As shown in Figure 12-1, of the 28 influences on learning, the three curricular influences were ranked 13th, 19th, and 24th. Instructional practices, in comparison, were among the most powerful influences in the school context. Figure 12-1 reveals that six of the seven classroom practices examined—including classroom management, quantity of instruction, classroom climate, classroom instruction, and teacher-student interactions—exert strong influences on learning.

Classroom practices can improve the academic and social competencies of students and their ability to adapt to new situations. The findings describing the impact of curriculum and instruction on school learning depicted in Figure 12-1 are in agreement with the current literature on effective instruction and schooling. Among the practices and policies most frequently identified in studies of effective learning environments are maximized learning time, high expectations for student achievement, ample opportunity for students to respond during instruction, a high level of student engagement, student participation in goal setting and learning decisions, use of cooperative learning techniques, emphasis of cognitive and metacognitive processes, effective classroom management techniques, frequent and positive teacher-student interactions that focus on instruction, and effective curriculum organization and articulation [Means & Knapp 1991]. These practices confer achievement advantages on students at risk of school failure and act as protective factors that promote the development of educational resilience.

School Organization and Culture

Increasing evidence suggests that "resilient" schools create a sense of student involvement and belonging leading to reduced feelings of student alienation and disengagement [Lee et al. 1993; Raywid 1995]. The intimate relations among students, their peers and families, and educators in private, especially parochial schools [Coleman & Hoffer 1987], smaller schools [Fowler & Walberg 1991], and schools of choice may explain their appeal and possible achievement advantages. Newmann and Wehlage [1995] present evidence that the level of professional community in a school enhances its organizational capacity and students' achievement. Professional community, they assert, involves teachers engaging in three practices: sharing a clear purpose for students' learning, collaborating with other teachers to increase their effectiveness and enhance student learning, and assuming responsibility for student learning. Figure 12-1 further corroborates the finding that schoolwide culture impacts student learning. School culture was the 10th largest influence, with a greater impact on students' day-to-day lives than schoolwide policies or school demographics. The culture of effective, high-performing schools is described as positive, academically oriented, safe and secure, cooperative, and creating a sense of belonging.

Research suggests that reducing excessively bureaucratic and impersonal relations in school increases students' and teachers' engagement and morale. According to Lee et al. [1993], results from case studies and surveys point to negative effects related to large school size, including socially stratified learning opportunities. Although large schools provide more specialized services for children at risk of school failure, they often isolate children with poor academic skills, learning disabilities, or limited English proficiency by placing them in pullout programs for special services. This arrangement, although well intentioned to provide "extra" or "supplementary" resources, tends to deny special needs students access to crucial academic and social resources [Wang & Reynolds 1995].

Peer Context

Peer cultures can facilitate learning or conflict with academic values [Ogbu 1988; Taylor et al. 1994; Roderick 1995]. Student achievement is a product not only of a child's cognitive ability, but also of classroom practices and school culture, family values and practices, and the social network of peers. Recent research shows that, as students progress from elementary through high school, they become more peer-oriented, peer values become academically nonconforming [Seidman et al. 1994], and social support from teachers and school staff diminishes from the already low levels present in most junior high schools [Seidman et al. 1996].

As children make the transition into adolescence, peers become a key source of support and influence. Clark [1991] found that peers, after the family, are the most important source of support; they provide children and adolescents with a sense of being valued, cared for, and loved. Peer networks can facilitate the development of an individual and protect against stress by providing a stable and supportive source of concern; conversely, they can inhibit positive educational outcomes by pressuring children and youth to engage in misconduct rather than productive educational tasks.

Table 12-3 presents examples of risk factors that occur in peer cultures. It also shows illustrative protective factors that can promote educational resilience including peer support and opportunities for engagement in healthy, appropriate activities.

Anderson's [1990] case studies revealed the impact of peers on African-American male youth who were moving between two communities—one of low socioeconomic status and the other becoming middle class during community gentrification. He showed that adolescents appropriated

Table 12-3. An Illustrative List of Risk and Protective Factors Within the Peer Context

Risk Factors That Contribute to Educational Failure	Protective Factors That Mitigate Against Educational Failure
Peer Relations	
• Presence of gangs • Peer group antagonistic toward school and learning • Lack of social support from teachers and school staff	• Presence of support and caring by peers for those facing stressful life circumstances • Positive attitudes of peers toward productive educational activities
Peer Activities	
• High rate of substance abuse • High rate of school dropout • High rate of teen pregnancy • Few community-based activities • Few school-sponsored extracurricular activities	• Engagement of peers in prosocial constructive behaviors that foster good health, academic achievement, and responsible citizenship • Use of cooperative learning programs, mentoring, cross-age tutoring, use of small learning groups, and extracurricular activities • Fostering communities of learners made up of peers in schools and outside of school

the language, attitudes, and behaviors of the prevalent youth culture in each community. In the economically disadvantaged community, students displayed the more defensive physical postures and speech patterns that were characteristic of the youth in the community. In the gentrified community, the same youth exhibited more helpful acts to dispel perceptions of them as uncivil or criminal. Anderson's studies illustrate the responsiveness of youth to the attitudes, aspirations, and behaviors of their peers.

Coleman and Hoffer [1987] described how students in boarding schools are supportive of their peers when their families are absent. The positive influence of peers is also demonstrated in alcohol and drug use programs where peer counselors can be effective in reducing and preventing substance abuse [Bangert-Downs 1988]. Similarly, Watt, Moorehead-Slaughter, Japzon, and Keller [1990] showed that children of divorced parents can find respite from home situations in social networks that distance them from stressed parents. Peer networks have a greater impact on the school performance of children of divorce than they do on children from intact homes. Children of divorce, in particular, look to school friends for care and companionship.

Peers can also have a significant impact on a student's self-perceived academic competence and attitude toward school. Cauce [1986] found that the peer group's attitude toward school was a significant predictor of grades, achievement test scores, value placed on being a good student, and perceived competence. Patchen [1982] found that students with peers who valued high achievement spent more time on homework, finished more of their homework assignments, attended school more regularly, and were less often tardy or absent without permission.

Creating small communities for learning that are made up of adults and peers is a key intervention strategy to forestall student disengagement from schooling [Carnegie Council for Adolescent Development 1989]. Such communities are most readily created in school organizations that have been restructured as mini-schools, schools-within-schools, houses, or other small educational units. These restructured schools provide stable, supportive, close relationships that are fundamental to healthy development, meaningful and lasting learning, and educational resilience. Brown and her colleagues have been developing instructional activities, based on cognitive principles of learning, that foster communities of learners [Brown 1994; Brown & Campione 1994]. In these interventions, peers collaborate in the teaching and learning of valuable content. Participating students differ in their levels of expertise, goals, interests, and engagement; these differences are recognized and valued. Learning communities built upon these principles establish a discourse structure, goals, values, and beliefs. Participating students learn that they are interdependent, which in turn fosters responsibility and respect for other participants and enhances students' personal and group identities. Peers acquire new knowledge through their interchanges, learn to interact in socially competent ways, and succeed at intellectually complex endeavors. Such experiences promote healthy development and learning; they engage the peer culture in socially constructive learning and confer desirable benefits on participants.

Figure 12-1 corroborates the effect of the peer context on student learning: Participation in the peer group itself influences learning, as does students' use of out-of-class time. The peer group was the 8th most powerful influence, while student use of out-of-class time was the 23rd most influential. Students' participation in extracurricular activities and social clubs, while not as powerful as some other contextual features, can also contribute to academic accomplishment if the activities are well-designed and well-executed. Opportunities to interact with students who have high achievement motivation, positive attitudes toward school, and a positive academic self-concept can be beneficial to students at risk of school failure. Communities of learners, mentoring programs, cooperative learning programs, cross-age tutoring, use of small learning groups, and extracurricular activities provide mechanisms for children and youth to develop positive peer relationships and stronger support networks.

Community Context

Common sense suggests that communities affect their residents' sense of well-being, safety, and worth. Table 12-4 shows community adversities that can be mitigated by protective factors, including the availability of resources and the community culture.

Figure 12-1 reveals that community influence was the 12th most powerful contextual influence on student learning. Specific features and actions of communities that foster educational resilience are described below. Health care organizations, child care services, job training opportunities, religious institutions, and recreational facilities are some of the social organizations that serve human needs [Garmezy 1991]. Communities with well-developed and integrated networks of such social organizations have fewer social problems [Yancey & Saporito 1995] and can support resiliency among residents.

Table 12-4. An Illustrative List of Risk and Protective Factors Within the Community Context

Risk Factors That Contribute to Educational Failure	Protective Factors That Mitigate Against Educational Failure
Availability of Resources	
• Few community services • Service barriers (language, cost, client eligibility, transportation) • Fragmented community services • Limited tax base	• Access to a variety of human services, including medical, psychological, legal, social, financial, and transportation • Prevention-oriented, school-linked services addressing multiple needs and co-occurring risks of students and families • Use of family-based interventions • Opportunities for children and youth to participate in meaningful community activities
Community Culture	
• High crime rate • Substance abuse • Racial discrimination • Little attention to learning and human development in community efforts • High unemployment rate • Number and density of impoverished families • Low educational attainment of residents	• Emphasis on public safety • Consistent, frequently expressed prosocial norms and values expressed by community members and media • Expectations for schooling success of children and youth • Demand for quality education offered by neighborhood schools • Presence of health-promotion activities

Benard [1991] emphasizes the role of community values as a protective factor that promotes resilience. The expression of consistent social and cultural norms by a variety of community institutions and groups helps children and youth understand what constitutes desirable behavior. Masten et al. [1990] identified abstract beliefs in religious protective figures and concrete relationships with members of the religious community as protective factors. Historically, religious beliefs have provided standards and expectations for good conduct for various ethnic groups and social classes.

Coleman and Hoffer [1987] described the importance of community values in achieving urban high school effectiveness. Based on results of their study, they suggested the idea of "social capital" in which the school and the broader community substitute for the absence of social capital in families. Government and the business community help to build human, social, and cultural capital. Partnering among individual agencies and parents, community resources, and national organizations will develop effective community programs that can produce positive outcomes for children and families in circumstances that place them at risk [Brookins et al. 1997]. Communities that link all their resources to promote healthy, prosocial values and develop their residents' human, social, and cultural capital support the development of resilience.

A similar conclusion has been reached by policymakers and educational reformers who argue that failing urban school systems can be revitalized only when the entire community unites in a decisive effort to improve. Communities with high expectations for good citizenship provide protective mechanisms for residents, as shown in studies that explore the importance of cultural norms on student alcohol and drug abuse. Analyzing the effectiveness of community-based substance abuse programs for African American youth, Nettles [1991] found that school-based clinics are only partially effective in reducing risk. The programs that fostered resilience provided more social support and adult aid, gave concrete help on tasks, and provided opportunities for students to develop new interests and skills.

Communities with a high concentration of economically disadvantaged families often lack a well-integrated network of social organizations for children and youth. The services provided to impoverished, deteriorating urban communities are often compartmentalized and fragmented [Boyd & Crowson 1993]. In their analysis of the impact of social policies on the quality of human resources available to African American youth, Swanson and Spencer [1991] emphasized the twofold importance of finding ways to reduce risk and making opportunities and resources available to break adverse chain reactions.

Because schools have the most sustained contact with children and their families, several authorities hold that educators should consider the potential benefits of coordinating and integrating children's services across school and community organizations when designing their school improvement programs [Flaxman & Passow 1995]. In a review of more than 100 programs designed to change adolescents' high-risk behaviors (e.g., delinquency, substance abuse, teen pregnancy, and school failure), Dryfoos [1990] reports that 60% of intervention programs were school-based, 30% were community-based and relied upon agency coalitions, and 10% were family-based. The linking of parent, school, and community resources through these programs may amplify children and youth's sense of nurturance and support.

Energetic parent and community involvement programs support children's academic efforts, assist families in the development of good parenting skills, and reinforce the values promoted at school. One such example is coordinating school-linked services to provide ready access to medical, psychological, legal, transportation, and social services for students and their families [Rigsby et al. 1995]. Although early evaluation results have demonstrated few beneficial outcomes from school-linked services, the early efforts at coordinated services often did not stress powerful instructional techniques in combination with access to the services [Center for the Study of Social Policy 1995]. School-linked programs, if designed with attention to the resources of families, schools, and communities, may improve the overall quality of life for these students and promote educational resilience [Oates et al. 1998].

Conclusions and Future Directions

Research on resilience and resilience promotion helps formulate new questions and provides a framework for effective intervention—first to prevent dysfunction and, when necessary, to correct and heal. Though the educational research base is limited, new ideas and investigations are gaining increased attention. The term "educational resilience" offers a provocative challenge to educational researchers and practitioners. In a single phrase, it can suggest several useful notions and priorities. For educators, the term suggests the potential benefits of early experience; the role of curriculum and instruction in mitigating adverse circumstances; and the importance of educationally facilitative and alterable protective factors in communities, homes, schools, and classrooms. The term offers the intriguing hypothesis that early alterable and possibly sustained conditions fortify students to persist successfully through difficulties.

Promising Research

The idea of educational resilience, moreover, shifts research from studies of risk, deficiency, disorder, and maladaptation to studies of interventions that foster learning and development [Wang & Gordon 1994b]. As noted by Masten [1994], "Now the pendulum has swung to resilience, and there is great enthusiasm for understanding good and poor outcomes in high-risk children" [p. 21]. As we advance toward the 21st century, the nation's attention has been captured by the severe problems that plague many children, youth, and their families. The lives of many children and youth are jeopardized by poverty, parents who are overwhelmed by life adversities, physical and mental health problems, and fragmented social and health services. Many live in neighborhoods that are plagued by crime, disorder, and despair that erode their opportunities and prospects. In responding to these challenges, researchers are focusing on factors that promote healthy development and learning among children and youth in adverse circumstances.

Following two decades of resilience studies by clinical and developmental psychologists, new research on educational resilience concerns features of the family, school, peer group, and community that foster competence among children placed in a variety of high-risk circumstances. This research points to the many factors—economic, political, psychological, and sociological—that influence educational and other life outcomes, and ways to coordinate school and community services to provide a more integrated network of resources and protective mechanisms for children and their families.

Still, several caveats and related priorities for future research are in order. Even though much of the initial research on resilience has yielded promising knowledge, some of the argument relies on analogy or hypothesis rather than empirical confirmation. It would seem imperative that researchers probe the validity of the construct in its several manifestations, in multiple contexts, and over extended periods of time.

Ideally, large-scale experiments that randomly assign students to hypothesized conditions would each provide definitive evidence on one or a few of these conditions. These, however, are admittedly difficult to conduct. Alternatively, comprehensive multivariate studies could be carried out to investigate sets of these potential influences simultaneously. Such studies would allow how estimates of the extent that one context such as the school or home can compensate for another such as the community or peer group. Finally, careful case studies of demonstrably resilient children would further elucidate the processes and mechanisms of resilience.

Educational resilience research has been carried out on a variety of small samples as well as large national data sets. Still, it remains to be ascertained whether the findings extend robustly across urban, rural, and suburban settings, grade levels, and socioeconomic and ethnic groups. What requires further testing is the extent to which the most powerful influences on learning are uniform across settings and student characteristics.

Resilience by definition implies development over time, which requires longitudinal studies. These studies would be best started with substantial numbers of children living in adverse circumstances and then followed over a period of years. Such prospective studies allow careful and direct measurement of contexts over time. They allow detection of "inoculation effects" of early experience and cumulative effects of sustained experience. Though retrospective and cross-sectional studies have a place, they provide less definitive causal evidence on such effects and their mechanisms.

Promising Policies and Practices

Educational resilience research and programs have gained considerable momentum, but much remains to be done by educators. In view of students in high-risk circumstances, such as economically disadvantaged, isolated, and especially rural communities and the nation's inner cities, resilience research provides an "enabling" framework to advance a vision of educational success for all children and youth. For researchers, such a vision offers an exciting challenge for new investigations and evaluations.

For educators, especially those working in inner cities and in other often adverse circumstances, this vision should be a call for action. Although new research is always needed, precedents and principles established in psychology and confirmations in education settings warrant careful expansion in programs for schools, homes, and communities. The research summarized above provides many useful starting points for designing and implementing such programs. They deserve trials and evaluation in a wide variety of circumstances, most urgently in our nation's cities.

References

American Psychological Association Task Force on Psychology in Education. (1993). *The learner-centered psychological principles: Guidelines for school redesign and reform.* Washington, DC: APA and Mid-Continent Regional Educational Laboratory.

Anderson, E. (1990). *Streetwise: Race, class, and change in an urban community.* Chicago: University of Chicago Press.

Anderson, L., & Walberg, H. J. (1994). The applicability of data envelopment analysis to education research. In T. Husen & T. N. Postlethwaite (Eds.), *International Encyclopedia of Education* (Vol. 3, pp. 1381-1387). Oxford, UK: Pergamon Press.

Baker, E. T., Wang, M. C., & Walberg, H. J. (1994/1995). The effects of inclusion on learning. *Educational Leadership, 52*(4), 33-35.

Bandura, A. (1993). Perceived self-efficacy in cognitive development and functioning. *Educational Psychologist, 28*(2), 117-148.

Bangert-Downs, R. (1988). The effects of school-based substance abuse education. *Journal of Drug Education, 18*(3), 1-9.

Benard, B. (1991, August). *Fostering resiliency in kids: Protective factors in the family, school and community.* Portland, OR: Northwest Regional Education Laboratory.

Bennett, L., Wolin, S., & Reiss, D. (1988). Cognitive, behavioral, and emotional problems among school-age children of alcoholic parents. *American Journal of Psychiatry, 145*(2), 185-190.

Blumenfeld, P.C. (1992). Classroom learning and motivation: Clarifying and expanding goal theory. *Journal of Educational Psychology, 84*, 272-281.

Brookins, G. K., Petersen, A. C., & Brooks, L. M. (1997). Youth and families in the inner city: Influencing positive outcomes. In H. J. Walberg, O. Reyes, & R. P. Weissberg (Eds.), *Children and youth: Interdisciplinary perspectives.* Issues in Children's and Families' Lives. Vol. 7. Thousand Oaks, CA: SAGE Publications, Inc.

Boyd, W., & Crowson, R. (1993). Coordinated services for children: Designing arks for storms and seas unknown. *American Journal of Education, 101*, 140-179.

Bronfenbrenner, U. (1986). Ecology of the family as a context for human development: Research perspectives. *Developmental Psychology, 22*, 723-742.

Brown, A. (1994). Advancement of learning. *Educational Researcher, 23*(8), 4-11.

Brown, A. L., & Campione, J. C. (1994). Guided discovery in a community of learners. In K. McGilly (Ed.), *Classroom lessons: Integrating cognitive theory and classroom practice* (pp. 229-270). Cambridge, MA: MIT Press/Bradford Books.

Carnegie Council on Adolescent Development. (1989). *Turning points: Preparing American youth for the 21st century.* New York: Carnegie Corporation.

Cauce, A. (1986). Social networks and social competence: Exploring the effects of early adolescent friendships. *American Journal of Community Psychology, 14*, 607-628.

Center for the Study of Social Policy. (1995). *Building new futures for at-risk youth: Finding of a five-year, multisite evaluation*. Washington, DC: Author.

Chess, S. (1989). Defying the voice of doom. In T. Dugan & R. Coles (Eds.), *The child in our times* (pp. 179-199). New York: Brunner/Mazel.

Clark, M. (1991). Social identity, peer relations, and academic competence of African-American adolescents. *Education and Urban Society, 24*(1), 41-52.

Coleman, J. S., & Hoffer, T. (1987). *Public and private high schools: The impact of communities*. New York: Basic Books.

Comer, J. P. (1986). Parent participation in the schools. *Phi Delta Kappan, 67*(6), 442-446.

Dryfoos, J. G. (1990). *Adolescents at risk: Prevalence and prevention*. New York: Oxford University Press.

Epstein, J. L. (1987). Toward a theory of family-school connections. In K. Hurrelmann, F. Kaufmann, & F. Losel (Eds.), *Social intervention: Potential and constraints*. New York: W. De Gruyter.

Flaxman, E., & Inger, M. (1991). Parents and schooling in the 1990's. *ERIC Review, 1* (3), 2-6.

Flaxman, E., & Passow, H. (Eds.). (1995). *Changing populations: Changing schools*. Yearbook of the National Society for the Study of Education, Vol. 95, Part 2. Chicago: National Society for the Study of Education.

Fowler, W. J., & Walberg, H. J. (1991). School size, characteristics, and outcomes. *Educational Evaluation and Policy Analysis, 13*(2), 189-202.

Garmezy, N. (1974). The study of children at risk: New perspectives for developmental psychopathology. Paper presented at the 82nd annual meeting of the American Psychological Association, New Orleans, LA.

Garmezy, N. (1991). Resiliency and vulnerability to adverse developmental outcomes associated with poverty. *American Behavioral Scientist, 34*(4), 416-430.

Garmezy, N., Masten, A. S., & Tellegen, A. (1984). The study of stress and competence in children: A building block for developmental psychopathology. *Child Development, 55*, 97-111.

Hogman, F. (1983). Displaced Jewish children during World War II: How they coped. *Journal of Humanistic Psychology, 23*(1), 54-66.

Lee, V. E., Bryk, A. S., & Smith, J. B. (1993). The organization of effective secondary schools. In L. Darling-Hammond (Ed.), *Review of research*, Vol. 19 (pp. 171-267). Washington, DC: American Educational Research Association.

Lee, V. E., Winfield, L. F., & Wilson, T. C. (1991). Academic behaviors among high-achieving African-American students. *Education and Urban Society, 24*(1), 65-86.

Masten, A. S. (1994). Resilience in individual development: Successful adaptation despite risk and adversity. In M. C. Wang & E. W. Gordon (Eds.), *Educational resilience in inner-city America: Challenges and prospects* (pp. 3-25). Hillsdale, NJ: Lawrence Erlbaum Associates.

Masten, A. S., Best, K. M., & Garmezy, N. (1991). Resilience and development: Contributions from the study of children who overcome adversity. *Development and Psychopathology,* 2, 425-444.

Masten, A. S., Morison, P., Pelligrini, D., & Tellegen, A. (1990). Competence under stress: Risk and protective factors. In J. Rolf, A. S. Masten, D. Cicchetti, K. H. Nuechterlein, & S. Weintraub (Eds.), *Risk and protective factors in the development of psychopathology* (pp. 236-256). New York: Cambridge University Press.

McCombs, B. L., & Whisler, J. S. (1997). *Creating learner-centered classrooms and schools*. San Francisco: Jossey-Bass.

Means, B., & Knapp, M. S. (Eds.). (1991). *Teaching advanced skills to educationally disadvantaged students* (Final Report, Contract No. LC89089001). Washington, DC: U.S. Department of Education.

Nettles, S. M. (1991). Community contributions to school outcomes of African-American students. *Education and Urban Society, 24*(1), 132-147.

Newmann, F. M. & Wehlage, G. C. (1995). *Successful school restructuring: A report to the public and* educators by the Center on Organization and Restructuring of Schools. Madison, WI: University of Wisconsin-Madison.

Oates, J., Flores, T., & Weishew, N. (1998). Achieving student success in inner cities is possible, provided... In M. C. Wang (Ed.), *Fostering resilience: Mobilizing school, family, and community resources* (pp. 87-100). Philadelphia, PA: Temple University Center for Research in Human Development and Education.

Ogbu, J. U. (1988). A cultural ecology of competence among inner-city blacks. In M. Spencer, G. Brookins, & W. Allen (Eds.), *Beginnings: The social and affective development of black children* (pp. 43-66). Hillsdale, NJ: Lawrence Erlbaum Associates.

Patchen, M. (1982). *Black-white contact in schools: Its social and academic effects.* West Lafayette, IN: Purdue University Press.

Peng, S. S., Lee, R. M., Wang, M. C., & Walberg, H. J. (1992, April). Resilient students in urban settings. Paper presented at the annual meeting of the American Educational Research Association, San Francisco, CA.

Peng, S. S., Weishew, N., & Wang, M. C. (1991). High-achieving schools in disadvantaged communities: What are their attributes? Unpublished manuscript, Temple University Center for Research in Human Development and Education, Philadelphia, PA.

Raywid, M. A. (1995). Alternatives and marginal students. In M. C. Wang & M. C. Reynolds (Eds.), *Making a difference for students at risk: Trends and alternatives* (pp. 119-155). Thousand Oaks, CA: Corwin Press.

Rigsby, L. C., Reynolds, M. C., & Wang, M. C. (Eds.). (1995). *School-community connections: Exploring issues for research and practice.* San Francisco: Jossey-Bass Publishers.

Roderick, M. (1995). School transitions and school dropout. In K. Wong (Ed.), *Advances in educational policy.* Greenwich, CT: JAI.

Rolf, J., Masten, A. S., Cicchetti, D., Nuechterlein, K. H., & Weintraub, S. (Eds.). (1990). *Risk and protective factors in the development of psychopathology.* New York: Cambridge University Press.

Rutter, M. (1979). Protective factors in children's responses to stress and disadvantage. In M. W. Kent & J. E. Rolf (Eds.), *Primary prevention of psychopathology. Vol 3: Social competence in children* (pp. 49-74). Hanover, NH: University Press of New England.

Rutter, M. (1990). Psychosocial resilience and protective mechanisms. In J. Rolf, A. S. Masten, D. Cicchetti, K. H. Nuechterlein, & S. Weintraub (Eds.), *Risk and protective factors in the development of psychopathology* (pp. 181-214). New York: Cambridge University Press.

Schaps, E., Lewis, C., & Watson, M. (1995). *Schools as caring communities: Resources for restructuring.* New York: Columbia University, National Center for Restructuring Education, Schools, and Teaching.

Seidman, E., Allen, L., Aber, J. L., Mitchell, C., & Feinman, J. (1994). The impact of school transitions in early adolescence on the self-system and social context of poor urban youth. *Child Development, 65*, 507-522.

Seidman, E., Aber, J. L., Allen, L., & French, S. (1996). The impact of the transition to high school on the self-system and perceived social context of poor urban youth. *American Journal of Community Psychology, 24*, 489-515.

Straits, B. C. (1987, January). Residence, migration, and school progress. *Sociology of Education, 60*, 34-43.

Swanson, D. P., & Spencer, M. B. (1991). Youth policy, poverty, and African-Americans: Implications for resilience. *Education and Urban Society, 24* (1), 148-161.

Taylor, R. D., Casten, R., & Flickinger, S. (1993). The influence of kinship social support on the parenting experiences and psychosocial adjustment of African-American adolescents. *Developmental Psychology, 29* (2), 382-388.

Taylor, R. D., & Wang, M. C. (Eds.). (in press). *Resilience across contexts: Family, work, culture, and community.* Philadelphia, PA: Temple University Center for Research in Human Development and Education.

Teddlie, C., & Stringfield, S. (1993). *Schools make a difference: Lessons learned from a 10-year study of school effects.* New York, NY: Teachers College Press.

Wang, M. C. (1992). *Adaptive education strategies: Building on diversity.* Baltimore: Paul H. Brookes.

Wang, M. C. (1995). *Next steps in inner-city education: Focusing on resilience development and learning success*. Philadelphia, PA: National Center on Education in the Inner Cities.

Wang, M. C., Freiberg, H. J., & Waxman, H. J. (1994). *Case studies of inner-city schools* [Interim report]. Philadelphia, PA: National Center on Education in the Inner Cities.

Wang, M. C., & Gordon, E. W. (Eds.). (1994a). *Educational resilience in inner-city America: Challenges and prospects*. Hillsdale, NJ: Lawrence Erlbaum Associates.

Wang, M. C., & Gordon, E. W. (1994b). Epilogue: Educational resilience—Challenges and prospects. In M. C. Wang & E. W. Gordon (Eds.), *Educational resilience in inner-city America: Challenges and prospects* (pp. 191-194). Hillsdale, NJ: Lawrence Erlbaum Associates.

Wang, M. C., Haertel, G. D., & Walberg, H. J. (1993, Fall). Toward a knowledge base for school learning. *Review of Educational Research, 63*(3).

Wang, M. C., Haertel, G. D., & Walberg, H. J. (1994). Educational resilience in inner cities. In M. C. Wang & E. W. Gordon (Eds.), *Educational resilience in inner-city America: Challenges and prospects* (pp. 45-72). Hillsdale, NJ: Lawrence Erlbaum Associates.

Wang, M. C., & Reynolds, M. C. (Eds.). (1995). *Making a difference for students at risk: Trends and alternatives.* Thousand Oaks, CA: Corwin Press.

Watt, N. F., Moorehead-Slaughter, O., Japzon, D. M., & Keller, G. G. (1990). Children's adjustment to parental divorce: Self-image, social relations, and school performance. In J. Rolf, A. S. Masten, D. Cicchetti, K. H. Nuechterlein, & S. Weintraub (Eds.), *Risk and protective factors in the development of psychopathology* (pp. 281-304). New York: Cambridge University Press.

Werner, E. (1989, April). Children of the garden island. *Scientific American, 260*(4), 107-111.

Werner, E., & Smith, R. (1982). *Vulnerable but invincible: A longitudinal study of resilient children and youth.* New York: Adams, Bannister, and Cox.

Yancey, W. L., & Saporito, S. J. (1995). Ecological embeddedness of educational processes and outcomes. In L. C. Rigsby, M. C. Reynolds, & M. C. Wang (Eds.), *School-community connections: Exploring issues for research and practice* (pp. 193-227). San Francisco: Jossey-Bass.

About the Editors

Arthur J. Reynolds is Associate Professor of Social Work, Educational Psychology, and Child & Family Studies at the University of Wisconsin-Madison. He also is affiliated with the Institute for Research on Poverty and the Waisman Center on Mental Retardation and Human Development. His major areas of interest are child development and social policy, prevention research, and program evaluation. As Director of the Chicago Longitudinal Study, a federally funded investigation of the effects of a large-scale early childhood intervention, he has published widely on the short- and long-term effects of participation for both child and family outcomes. In 2000, a volume will be published on the age 15 follow-up of graduates of the Child-Parent Center Program. He also has published in the fields of program evaluation and educational psychology, most recently as co-editor (with Herbert Walberg) of *Evaluation Research for Educational Productivity* with JAI Press.

Herbert J. Walberg, Research Professor of Education and Psychology at the University of Illinois at Chicago (UIC), was awarded a Ph.D. in Educational Psychology by the University of Chicago and was formerly Assistant Professor at Harvard University. He completed a term as Founding Member of the National Assessment Governing Board, sometimes referred to as "the national school board," because it has been given the mission to set subject matter standards for U.S. students. He has written and edited more than 50 books and contributed more than 380 articles to educational and psychological research journals on such topics as educational effectiveness and productivity, school reform, and exceptional human accomplishments. He frequently writes for widely circulated practitioner journals and national newspapers, serves as an advisor on educational research and improvement to public and private agencies in the United States and other countries, and testifies before state and federal courts and U.S. Congressional committees.

A fellow of four academic organizations, he has won several awards and prizes for his scholarship and is one of three U.S. members of the International Academy of Education. He holds appointments in the UIC Center for Urban Educational Research and Development and the Mid-Atlantic Laboratory for Student Success. He currently served on several not-for-profit boards and is chairman of the board of the Heartland Institute (web address: www.heartland.org), which provides policy analyses for federal and state legislators and news people and publishes the magazine “Intellectual Ammunition” and two newspapers, including “School Reform News.”

Roger P. Weissberg is Professor of Psychology and Education at The University of Illinois at Chicago. At UIC, he is the Director of Graduate Studies in Psychology and directs a NIMH-funded Pre-doctoral and Post-doctoral Prevention Research Training Program in Urban Children’s Mental Health and AIDS Prevention. Professor Weissberg is the Executive Director of the Collaborative for the Advancement of Social and Emotional Learning (CASEL). He also holds an appointment with the Mid-Atlantic Laboratory for Student Success funded by the Office of Educational Research and Improvement of the U.S. Department of Education. The author of more than 100 articles and chapters focusing on preventive interventions with children and adolescents, he has also co-authored nine curricula on school-based social-competence promotion programs to prevent drug use, high-risk sexual behaviors, and aggression. His research interests include school and community preventive interventions, urban children’s mental health, and parental involvement in children’s education. He received his Ph.D. in clinical psychology from the University of Rochester in 1980 and from 1980 to 1982 was Research Director for the Primary Mental Health Project, a program for the early detection and prevention of school maladjustment.

Dr. Weissberg was a Professor in Yale University's Psychology Department between 1982 and 1992 and also directed its NIMH-funded Prevention Research Training Program. A Past President of the American Psychological Association's Society for Community Research and Action, he is a recipient of the William T. Grant Foundation's five-year Faculty Scholars Award in Children's Mental Health, the Connecticut Psychological Association's 1992 Award for Distinguished Psychological Contribution in the Public Interest, and the National Mental Health Association's 1992 Lela Rowland Prevention Award. Most recently, he was named a 1997 University Scholar at the University of Illinois.

About the Contributors

Gilbert J. Botvin is a Professor in both the Department of Public Health and the Department of Psychiatry at Cornell University Medical College, and is the Director of Cornell's Institute for Prevention Research. Dr. Botvin is widely recognized as an expert in the field of tobacco, alcohol, and drug abuse prevention. He has published more than 140 peer-reviewed articles and book chapters, and has presented more than 160 papers and invited addresses at national and international scientific meetings.

Dr. Botvin has been a principal investigator on 20 federally funded school-based prevention projects involving more than 300 schools and 40,000 students. He is currently the Principal Investigator on several NIDA-funded grants, including a ten-year drug abuse prevention follow-up study, a drug abuse and violence prevention trial with inner-city youth, and a center grant with collaborators at Columbia University focusing on drug abuse prevention with multi-ethnic youth. In 1997, Dr. Botvin was the first prevention researcher to received a prestigious MERIT award from the National Institute on Drug Abuse—an award given to the most outstanding senior scientists funded by NIH. He is also the recipient of the Society of Prevention Research's Disque Dean Presidential Award for Prevention Excellence. Finally, Dr. Botvin has been appointed by SPR to be the inaugural Editor of the Society's new journal, *Prevention Science.*

Dr. Botvin holds a Ph.D. from Columbia University (1977) with training and experience in both developmental and clinical psychology. He also holds an M.A. in psychology from Columbia University (1994) and a B.A. in philosophy from Colgate University (1969).

Wanda Brooks is a doctoral candidate in the Reading/Writing/Literacy Program of the University of Pennsylvania Graduate School of Education. Her research interests focus on middle school and African American children's reading practices.

Toni Falbo is Professor of Educational Psychology and Sociology at The University of Texas at Austin. Dr. Falbo is a social psychologist whose research interests include social influence, socialization, family size, motivation, and achievement. During her 25-year career, she has become an internationally recognized expert on only children. Dr. Falbo has studied only children and their families in the United States and in China. In particular, Dr. Falbo studied contemporary Chinese school children to determine the impact of the one-child policy on the quality of children and youth in the People's Republic of China. Dr. Falbo is a research associate of the Population Research Center at the University of Texas where she has served as Acting Director. Dr. Falbo began her research on high school dropouts in 1989, following a sample of "at risk" Latino youth through four years of high school. On the basis of what she found, she wrote *Latino High School Graduation: Defying the Odds*, with Harriett D. Romo. Currently, Falbo is completing research about the transition to high school to determine how family, school, and community resources are used to facilitate this transition.

Vivian L. Gadsden is Director of the National Center on Fathers and Families (NCOFF) and Associate Professor in the Graduate School of Education at the University of Pennsylvania. From 1990 to 1995, Dr. Gadsden also served as Associate Director of the National Center on Adult Literacy at the University of Pennsylvania. She received her doctorate in developmental psychology and education with a specialty in policy from The University of Michigan.

Dr. Gadsden's research focuses on family development and learning across the life-span and within multiple cultures—primarily African American, Latino, and American Indian families, and families living in poverty. Her work examines the nature of persistence and consequences of intergenerational learning within families and explores the issues of race, class, and gender within home, school, and social contexts. Dr. Gadsden's current research projects include a multigenerational study of 25 African American families, a parent-child Head Start project with African American and Puerto Rican families, a project with adolescent and young adult mothers and fathers, and a project on cooperative parenting. Dr. Gadsden has published more than 30 journal articles and book chapters on issues related to families, learning, race, and culture; recently completed a booklength volume from her multigenerational study. She is currently completing a co-edited volume, entitled *In Our Father's Image, In Our Mother's Heart: Life Notes on Families, Race, and Gender.* A third volume, co-edited with Daniel Wagner, *Literacy Among African American Youth: Issues in Learning, Teaching, and Schooling*, was published in 1995. She serves on several review boards and professional committees in organizations such as the Society for Research in Child Development and the American Education Research Association, foundations, and federal agencies.

Robert W. Glover is a Research Scientist at the Center for the Study of Human Resources, Lyndon B. Johnson School of Public Affairs, The University of Texas at Austin, where he has studied various aspects of work and learning for nearly three decades. Dr. Glover is a labor economist and his research interests include human resource development, apprenticeship and training, school-to-career programs, and industry training practices. He has taken a special interest in education and training that combines learning in workplaces with classroom instruction, such as apprenticeships, internships in school-to-career programs for youth, and project-based learning developed through industry-school partnerships. He served as chair of the Federal Committee on Apprenticeship from 1978 to 1982. He also helped to staff the Commission on Skills of the American Workforce in preparation of the report, *America's Choice: High Skills or Low Wages!* and the Carnegie Quality of Education for Minorities that produced the report, *Education That Works*. Currently, he works with the Texas State Systemic Initiative for the Improvement of Mathematics and Science administered by the Charles A. Dana Center at the University of Texas at Austin under funding from the National Science Foundation.

Kenneth W. Griffin is an Assistant Professor in the Department of Public Health at Cornell University Medical College, and also serves as Senior Data Analyst at Cornell's Institute for Prevention Research. In the latter capacity, Dr. Griffin evaluates the effectiveness of the Institute's intervention programs using a variety of statistical methodologies. In addition, Dr. Griffin conducts epidemiological and etiological studies of adolescent risk behaviors, including tobacco, alcohol and marijuana use, illicit drug use, and violent and aggressive behaviors. His research examines how demographic factors, social influence variables, and individual-level characteristics are associated with the initiation and escalation of substance use and aggression among youth, particularly urban, minority adolescent populations. Dr. Griffin has also published in the area of quality of life in those with chronic illness, and has conducted several studies examining factors associated with psychological adjustment in patients with HIV/AIDS, rheumatoid arthritis, and end-stage renal disease. His research has examined how psychological and disease-related factors may mediate the psychosocial impact of chronic disease, including factors such as social support, individual coping styles, and level of physical disability. Prior to joining Cornell, Dr. Griffin spent two years as a postdoctoral fellow at Columbia University, in the Department of Psychiatry and the HIV Center for Clinical and Behavioral Studies. Dr. Griffin holds an M.P.H. in Epidemiology from Columbia (1997) and a Ph.D. in Social and Health Psychology from the State University of New York at Stony Brook (1995). He also holds an B.A. in psychology from the University of Chicago (1986).

Geneva D. Haertel is a senior research associate at the Temple University Center for Research in Human Development and Education, where she conducts research syntheses on the achievement of children at risk of school failure. In 1990 she co-edited, with Herbert J. Walberg, *The International Encyclopedia of Educational Evaluation.*

Stephen F. Hamilton is Professor of Human Development at Cornell University. After graduating from Swarthmore College, he received a Master of Arts in Teaching degree from Harvard and taught for three years in a Washington, DC vocational high school before returning to Harvard for a doctorate in education. Professor Hamilton's primary concerns are adolescent development and education. A major portion of his responsibility at Cornell involves developing youth programs as part of Cooperative Extension. His research investigates the interaction of school, community, and work during the transition from adolescence to adulthood. As a Fulbright Senior Research Fellow, Professor Hamilton spent a year studying Germany's apprenticeship system. The major product of that study is a book, *Apprenticeship for Adulthood: Preparing Youth for the Future* (Free Press, 1990), which contrasts the transition from school to career of noncollege youth in the United States and West Germany and recommends adaptation of elements of apprenticeship in the United States. As Co-Director of the Cornell Youth and Work Program, he helped develop and direct a youth apprenticeship demonstration project in Broome County, New York. Research on this project addresses informal teaching and learning in workplaces. He has also investigated school-to-career transition systems in Sweden, Denmark, Austria, and Switzerland.

Jacqueline K. Jackson is a doctoral candidate in the Reading/Writing/Literacy Program of the University of Pennsylvania Graduate School of Education. Her research interests focus on literacy meanings and experiences of low-income women and their families.

David W. Johnson is Professor of Educational Psychology at the University of Minnesota. He is Co-Director of the Cooperative Learning Center. He held the Emma M. Birkmaier Professorship in Educational Leadership at the University of Minnesota from 1994 to 1997. Dr. Johnson received his doctoral degree from Columbia University and has published more than 300 research articles and book chapters. He is the author of more than 40 books and is a past editor of the American Educational Research Journal. Dr. Johnson is also the recipient of awards for outstanding research and teaching from the American Personnel and Guidance Association (1972), the American Psychological Association (1981), the American Society for Engineering Education (1984), the National Council for Social Studies (1986), the American Association for Counseling and Development (1988), Ball State University (1990), the Minnesota Association for Supervision and Curriculum Development (1990), the Southwest Ohio Planning Council for Inservice Education (1990), and the Department of Defense Schools, Panama, (1994). He is currently listed in Marquis' Who's Who in the World. For the past 30 years Dr. Johnson has served as an organizational consultant to schools and businesses in North America, Central America, Europe, Africa, Asia, the Middle East, and the Pacific Region.

Roger T. Johnson is Professor of Curriculum and Instruction with an emphasis in Science Education at the University of Minnesota. He holds an M.A. degree from Ball State University and Ed.D. from the University of California in Berkeley. He has taught in the public schools in several innovative schools and has done training on cooperative learning throughout the United States, Canada, and in several other countries. He is the author of numerous articles and book chapters and co-author with his brother David on several books including *Learning Together and Alone, Circles of Learning*, and *Active Learning: Cooperation in the College Classroom*. He has received several awards, including an outstanding teaching award (Jefferson County Schools, Colorado), and the Gordon Allport Intergroup Relations Award (American Psychological Association).

Martin L. Maehr is Professor of Education and Psychology at the University of Michigan, Ann Arbor, where he is affiliated with the Combined Program in Education and Psychology. He was formerly Professor of Educational Psychology and Director of the Institute of Human Development at the University of Illinois, Urbana-Champaign. He is a fellow of the American Psychological Association and the American Psychological Society and the author of approximately 100 articles and research reports. His most recent book (with Carol Midgley) is entitled *Transforming School Cultures*. Together with Paul Pintrich he edits a series of scholarly books entitled "Advances in Motivation and Achievement."

Carol Midgley is a Research Scientist with the Combined Program in Education and Psychology at the University of Michigan. She currently is overseeing two large-scale longitudinal studies examining the relation between the learning environment and adolescent academic and emotional well-being. In the first study, funded by the William T. Grant Foundation, data have been gathered from more than 600 students from four ethnically and economically diverse school districts as they moved from the last year of elementary school, through the middle school years, and into high school. In the second study, funded by the Spencer Foundation, survey and observation data are being combined to examine students' avoidance beliefs and behaviors in mathematics before and after the transition to middle level schools. She is the author of a number of journal articles and book chapters dealing especially with the effect of the transition to middle school on early adolescent development. With Martin Maehr, she co-authored *Transforming School Cultures* (1996) which is part of the "Lives in Context Series," published by Westview Press. This chapter is based in part on work described in detail in that book.

Eva Patrikakou received her Ph.D. from the University of Illinois-Chicago (UIC) in 1995. She is currently Research Assistant Professor at the Psychology Department of UIC and director of the School-Family Partnership Project. She is also a Senior Program Associate with the Mid-Atlantic Laboratory for Student Success at Temple University, working on the dissemination of school-family partnership efforts. She has done extensive research in parent involvement and its effects on children's academic and emotional development, and currently she has been directing the development of a school-family partnership program to enhance home-school relations. Her clinical work focuses on psychoeducational assessment and her teaching areas are behavioral measurement, human exceptionality, and learning disabilities. She has presented her work on parent involvement, school-family partnerships, academic achievement, and individuals with disabilities in numerous national and international conferences. Her publications include articles in *Diagnostique*, the *Journal of Educational Psychology*, the *Journal of Research and Development in Education*, and the *Journal of Special Education.*

Douglas R. Powell is Professor and Head, Department of Child Development and Family Studies, Purdue University, West Lafayette, Indiana. His areas of interest are early childhood education and intervention and parenting education and support programs. He is former editor of the *Early Childhood Research Quarterly* and past chair of the Early Education/Child

Development Special Interest Group of the American Educational Research Association. Dr. Powell is author of numerous scholarly articles and chapters and author or editor of six books and monographs. He is a member of many national advisory boards and commissions, including advisory appointments with the federal Even Start Family Literacy Program and the National Education Goals Panel.

Michelle I. Rubenstein is a doctoral candidate in the Clinical Psychology program at the University of Illinois-Chicago (UIC). She is interested in establishing effective strategies to promote urban children's mental health and academic performance. In recent years, she has collaborated on the development and evaluation of the School-Family Partnership project at UIC and in conjunction with the Mid-Atlantic Laboratory for Student Success.

Dorothy Rich called the "Dr. Spock of Education," is founder and president of the nonprofit Home and School Institute (HSI) based in Washington, DC. An acclaimed expert in family educational involvement, she is the author of the original MegaSkills publications and is the developer of the MegaSkills training programs, which is used by more than 2,000 schools across the United States and abroad. In her lifetime of work in the field she has focused on helping families and educators team together to build achievement for school and beyond. Her most recent honors include selection by the National Association of Elementary School Principals as Distinguished Lecturer 1998.

Dr. Rich's work has received the A+ for Breaking the Mold Award from the U.S. Department of Education and recognition from the MacArthur Foundation and other distinguished foundations. Her work has been tested, researched and found to be effective in raising student achievement, decreasing discipline problems, increasing homework time, and decreasing TV time. Her work has been featured in the *Washington Post, The New York Times, The Los Angeles Times, NBC Today, Education Weekly, Good Morning America and Reader's Digest.* Among Dr. Rich's newest materials are *MegaSkills: Building Children's Achievement for the Information Age* (Houghton Mifflin, 1997) and *What Do We Say? What Do We Do?* (Tor, 1997).

Olivia N. Saracho is Professor of Education in the Department of Curriculum and Instruction at the University of Maryland. She was also been a classroom teacher in the public schools and Director of the Child Development Associate Program at Pan American University. For several decades, she has conducted research related to cognitive style, academic learning, teacher education. She is the author of numerous articles and books on the areas of play and cognitive style, including *Multiple Perspectives on Play in Early Childhood Education* (co-editor), *Teachers' and Students' Cognitive Styles in Early Childhood Education*, and *Cognitive Style in Early Education*. Professor Saracho is also the author of *Right from the State: Teaching Children Ages Three to Eight*, and *Dealing with Individual Differences in the Early Childhood Classroom*. Since 1990, she has been the co-editor of the *Yearbook of Early Childhood Education*. Currently she has added family literacy to her research and writing.

Margaret C. Wang is Professor of Educational Psychology at Temple University and the founder and current director of the Temple University Center for Research in Human Development and Education (CRHDE). Dr. Wang also serves as Director of the Laboratory for Student Success, the mid-Atlantic Regional Educational Laboratory, and the National Center on Education in the Inner Cities, both funded by the Office of Educational Research and Improvement of the U.S. Department of Education.

Dr. Wang has published 15 books and more than 100 articles. She is the senior editor of the four-volume Handbook or Special Education: Research and Practice. Other publications include Adaptive Education Strategies: Building on Diversity, Rethinking Policy for At-Risk Students, and Social and Emotional Adjustment and Family Relations in Ethnic Minority Families. In addition to her research, Dr. Wang has developed an extensive network of collaborating schools across the country, including schools in such urban centers as Houston, Los Angeles, Washington, DC, and Philadelphia.

Author Index

C

D

E

R

S

T

U

V

W

Y

Z

Subject Index

D

Q

R

S

T